Gender in Eighteenth-Century England

1·

Gender in Eighteenth-Century England

Roles, Representations and Responsibilities

Edited by Hannah Barker and Elaine Chalus

Longman
London and New York

Addison Wesley Longman Limited
Edinburgh Gate,
Harlow, Essex CM20 2JE,
United Kingdom
and Associated Companies throughout the world

*Published in the United States of America
by Addison Wesley Longman Inc., New York*

First published 1997

ISBN 0 582 27826 0 PPR
0 582 27827 9 CSD

British Library Cataloguing in Publication Data
A catalogue record for this book is available from the British Library

Library of Congress Cataloging-in-Publication Data
Gender in eighteenth-century England : roles, representations, and
responsibilities / edited by Hannah Barker and Elaine Chalus.
p. cm.
Includes bibliographical references (p.) and index.
ISBN 0–582–27826–0
1. Sex role—England—History—18th century. 2. Women—England—
History—18th century. I. Barker, Hannah. II. Chalus, Elaine.
HQ1075.5.E5G46   1997
305.3′0942′09033—dc21   96–49487
CIP

Transferred to digital print on demand 2001

Printed and bound by Antony Rowe Ltd, Eastbourne

Contents

Acknowledgements

This book has benefited from the help of numerous individuals. We owe a particular debt to Philip Carter, Leonore Davidoff, Ann Hughes, Joanna Innes, Diana Leonard, Eve Setch and Roey Sweet for reading the introduction and providing astute criticism. Others who attended an informal colloquium where many of the essays were presented as papers, in particular Patricia Crawford, Faramerz Diabhowala, Janet Howarth, Kim Reynolds, Jane Shaw and Stephen Taylor, also gave valuable advice and asked many thought-provoking questions. Wolfson College, Oxford, was extremely generous in sponsoring the colloquium. Finally, we would like to thank both Paul Langford and John Stevenson for their help and encouragement.

The publishers are grateful to the Bodleian Library, Oxford, for permission to reproduce Plate 1 (shelfmark Hope Adds. 468–447) and Plates 2 and 3 (shelfmark Per.2705e.674).

List of plates

List of abbreviations

The place of publication of all works cited in the footnotes and 'Further reading' section is London unless otherwise stated. For brevity, some frequently used sources have been abbreviated, as follows:

Locations

Bodl.	Bodleian Library, Oxford
BL	British Library
ERO	Essex County Record Office
HMC	Historical Manuscripts Commission
PRO	Public Record Office
SRRU	Shropshire Records and Research Unit
WSRO	West Sussex Record Office
Wwk RO	Warwick County Record Office
YCA	York City Archives

Manuscript sources

BP	Bray Papers, Exeter College, Oxford
CH MSS	Castle Howard manuscripts
Chats. MSS	Chatsworth manuscripts
GP	Granville Papers
PP	Portland Papers, University of Nottingham
SNRA	Scottish National Register of Archives
WP	Wrest Park (Lucas Papers)

Printed sources

EM	The *European Magazine*
GM	The *Gentleman's Magazine*
JOJ	*Jackson's Oxford Journal*
LC	The *London Chronicle*
LM	The *London Magazine*
MP	The *Morning Post*

Journals

AHR	*American Historical Review*
CC	*Continuity and Change*
EcHR	*Economic History Review*
ECS	*Eighteenth-Century Studies*
FS	*Feminist Studies*
GH	*Gender and History*
HJ	*Historical Journal*
HT	*History Today*
HWJ	*History Workshop Journal*
JAH	*Journal of American History*
JBS	*Journal of British Studies*
JFH	*Journal of Family History*
JSH	*Journal of Social History*
PP	*Past and Present*

Notes on contributors

Hannah Barker is Lecturer in History at Keele University.

Philip Carter is Junior Research Fellow at Wolfson College, Oxford, and Research Editor for the new *Dictionary of National Biography*.

Elaine Chalus is Junior Research Fellow at Wolfson College, Oxford, and edits *Past & Present*.

Richard Connors is Assistant Professor at the University of Alberta, Edmonton, Canada.

Kimberly Crouch lectures at Northwestern University, Chicago, Illinois.

Amanda Foreman is a researcher at Lady Margaret Hall, Oxford.

Stephen Howard is a researcher at Lincoln College, Oxford.

Cindy M'Creery is Junior Research Fellow at Wolfson College, Oxford, and the Senior Caird Research Fellow at the National Maritime Museum in Greenwich.

Susan Skedd is a researcher at Merton College, Oxford, and Research Editor for the new *Dictionary of National Biography*.

CHAPTER ONE

Introduction

HANNAH BARKER AND ELAINE CHALUS

The Sexes have now little other apparent Distinction, beyond that of ·
Person and Dress: Their peculiar and characteristic Manners are
confounded and lost: The one Sex having advanced into *Boldness*, as
the other have sunk into *Effeminacy*.[1]

(John Brown, 1757)

Women must be understood . . . in terms of relationship – with other
women, and with men. . . .[2]

(Michelle Zimbalist Rosaldo, 1980)

For John Brown, England's dismal performance at the beginning
of the Seven Years' War was the result of a deterioration in national
character that he attributed, at least in part, to changes in manner
and behaviour that blurred and diminished the differences between
the sexes. Like other eighteenth-century moralists and conduct-book
writers who attempted to coax, cajole or chastise their readers into
complying with idealized notions of masculinity and femininity, he
believed that clearly defined gender roles were central to the stabil-
ity of English society, and by extension, to England's status as a
world power.

In general, eighteenth-century prescriptive texts argued that men
and women were 'naturally' different, and that these differences
not only shaped their characters but suited each sex to specific activities and roles in society. Authors mustered powerful religious,
philosophical and scientific arguments to explain, rationalize and
legitimize implicit and explicit inequalities between the sexes. While
men and masculinity were occasionally the subjects of such texts,
the overwhelming majority of this literature was aimed at women,
who were, by nature, considered to be in need of closer supervision.

1 John Brown, *An Estimate on the Manners and Principles of the Times* (1757), p. 51.
2 Michelle Zimbalist Rosaldo, 'The use and abuse of anthropology: reflections on feminism and cross-cultural understanding' *Signs* 5, 3 (1980), p. 409.

1

With untiring regularity and varying degrees of polemic, authors reminded women of their subordinate status and attempted to mould them into a static image of an idealized femininity – modest, chaste, pious, and passively domestic.

In assuming that these ideals were not merely prescriptive, but actually descriptive, historians have often confused rhetoric with reality. Most research has accepted as a fundamental and self-evident truth that eighteenth-century men's and women's lives were defined by starkly contrasting and increasingly rigid gender roles, most specifically exemplified by an increasing confinement of women to a private, separate, domestic sphere. These beliefs have been reinforced by women's historians' early tendency to rely heavily on a straightforward reading of didactic literature and a relatively narrow range of printed primary sources. As a result, not enough attention has yet been paid to the underlying implications of ostensibly prescriptive arguments like John Brown's, or to those presented in the other extensive and varied sources that survive for the period. These suggest that contemporaries saw gender in a more complex, pluralistic and even idiosyncratic way than has been assumed previously.

Until recently, the history of gender in eighteenth-century England had fared worse than the history of the period as a whole. Sandwiched between the seventeenth and nineteenth centuries, both of which have been extensively researched, the eighteenth century has often been considered either as an afterthought or a precursor – a period of consolidation that followed sixteenth- and seventeenth-century developments, or one of transition between the pre-industrial world and the triumphs of nineteenth-century industrialization and modernization. The eighteenth century has lately experienced something of a renaissance, however, as the wide-ranging works of historians such as John Brewer, J.C.D. Clark, Linda Colley and Paul Langford have revitalized interest in the period.[3] These new and more sophisticated interpretations are varied and sometimes contradictory; yet, what is lost in universality is more than gained in detail. Arguments for a monolithic Anglican and aristocratic *ancien régime* co-exist uneasily with others that celebrate

3 See, for instance, John Brewer, *Party Ideology and Popular Politics at the Accession of George III* (Cambridge, 1981); idem, *The Sinews of Power: War, Money and the English State, 1688–1783* (1989); J.C.D. Clark, *English Society: Ideology, Social Structure and Political Practice During the Ancien Regime* (Cambridge, 1985); Linda Colley, *Britons: Forging the Nation, 1707–1837* (New Haven, CT, and London, 1992); Paul Langford, *A Polite and Commercial People: England, 1727–1783* (Oxford, 1989); idem, *Public Life and the Propertied Englishman, 1689–1798* (Oxford, 1991).

pluralism, the growth of an influential and commercial middle class, widespread politicization, the development of an increasingly powerful centralized state, and an incipient and increasingly unified national culture.

It is in the light of such reassessments, and with the needs of students and scholars in mind, that this collection was envisaged. By examining the relationships between and among eighteenth-century men and women through a wide assortment of subjects and sources, these essays are intended to introduce specialists and non-specialists alike to new research in what is still an under-researched field; moreover, by exploring gender through contemporaries' understandings of themselves – specifically in regard to roles, representations and responsibilities – the essays reveal the complexity and multiplicity of gender roles in a society where the boundaries between 'public' and 'private', or 'social' and 'political', were blurred and permeable. As such, they not only argue against any simplistic application of the notion of separate spheres to the period, but also add further weight to the claims of feminist revisionist historians who question the utility of the model as an over-arching explanatory concept.[4] Finally, the collection as a whole continues the process of historical retrieval that was begun under the aegis of women's history. It points towards a more integrated understanding of the eighteenth century by placing gender into the wider historical context.

Gender history

Gender history is an offshoot of women's history, but both are relatively new fields of study. Women's history has grown swiftly since its re-emergence in conjunction with the feminist movement of the 1960s and 1970s. In the struggle for women's liberation, 'second wave' feminists appropriated history as a political tool, a means of explaining women's oppression and tracing their path towards liberation and equality. In writing 'herstory',[5] they posed a radical challenge to the discipline of history itself. While it would

4 See, for example, Linda Kerber, 'Separate spheres, female worlds, woman's place: the rhetoric of women's history' *JAH* 75, 1 (1988); Amanda Vickery, 'Golden age to separate spheres? A review of the categories and chronology of English women's history' *HJ* 36, 2 (1993). For an incisive critique of the separate spheres model and poststructuralist feminist theory, see Ann-Louise Shapiro, ed., *Feminists Revision History* (New Brunswick, NJ, 1994).

5 See, for example, June Sochen, *Herstory* (New York, 1974).

be a vast over-simplification to assume that feminist historians approached the past with a common agenda, they did, however, share some concerns. Most specifically, they questioned the validity of interpretations which denied women historical agency or dismissed women's activities and experiences as ahistorical. Too much history failed to take women into account and consequently presented a one-sided, 'male' view of the past. In order to redress this imbalance, they argued that women's experiences had to be given equal weight, and that the challenge of accommodating women's different historical experience – beginning with the application of standard periodization – needed to be carefully reconsidered.

As women's history developed, powerful conceptual arguments emerged to explain women's (shared) historical experiences.[6] Central to these was a belief that differences between the sexes – whether these differences were biologically determined or socially constructed – resulted in men and women inhabiting mutually exclusive and asymmetrical worlds. Modern women's subordinate status was deemed the consequence of continuous historical oppression that stemmed from, and was replicated by, the personalized and institutionalized domination of men over women in patriarchal society.[7] Thus, women's historians often emphasized the commonalty rather than the diversity of women's historical experiences. For Marxist and socialist historians, however, this shared experience was sometimes subordinated to class. In spite of these differences, women's history was considered 'indispensable and essential to the emancipation of women'.[8] A whiggish paradigm evolved that viewed the modern struggle for women's liberation in terms of a long but steadily progressive campaign for rights lost after the collapse of a pre-patriarchal Eden of sexual equality. Sally Alexander's justification of the existence of feminist history in 1976 is representative of the way that these beliefs were amalgamated:

> Men and women *do* inhabit different worlds, with boundaries which
> have been defined (and from time to time re-arranged) for them by

6 Although some interpretations have gained wider acceptance than others, women's history remains very diverse. It reflects a wide and conflicting variety of feminist standpoints, and therefore it is not, and should not be expected to be, politically consistent. Jean Bethke Elshtain provides a detailed and accessible examination of the similarities and differences among radical, liberal, Marxist and psychoanalytic feminisms. See her chapter, 'Feminism's Search for Politics', in *Public Man, Private Woman: Women in Social and Political Thought* (Princeton, NJ, and Oxford, 1981), pp. 202–97.

7 See Gerda Lerner, *The Creation of Patriarchy* (Oxford, 1986); and, for an overview of the thinking about patriarchy, see Judith M. Bennett, 'Feminism and history' *GH* 1 (1989).

8 Ibid., p. 3.

the capitalist mode of production as it has made use of and strengthened the sexual division of labour and patriarchal authority.[9]

While debates over the relative importance of these initial presuppositions are still continuing,[10] their acceptance as universally applicable explanations for women's historical experiences has become increasingly challenged by the publication of more sophisticated and academically rigorous research.[11] The discipline's link with a modern political agenda has also come under scrutiny. Concerns have been raised repeatedly, by gender historians among others, about the tendency to read the past anachronistically, as a result of projecting current women's issues backwards.[12]

The appearance of concerns like these marks the higher standards and increasing professionalism of women's history, but it also reflects the impact of postmodernism and the associated development of gender history. At its best, the adoption of poststructuralist thought has resulted in more sensitivity to context, plurality, nuance and contradiction, and less willingness to see the past linearly or to accept grand, sweeping generalizations. Increased recognition and acceptance of discontinuity, divergence and difference have given women's history more complexity and depth; however, they have simultaneously undermined many basic premises, including the supposed universality of women's experiences and oppression, and the fundamental belief in progress.

It is in fostering the use of gender as a primary category of analysis and the subsequent development of gender history, as distinct from women's history, that postmodernism has made the most significant contribution to scholarship. The study of gender in its own right developed in the 1980s, as women's historians began to appropriate ideas about the construction of meanings and identities put forward by French poststructuralists, especially Michel

9 Sally Alexander, 'Feminist History', in *Becoming a Woman: and other Essays in Nineteenth and Twentieth Century Feminist History* (1994) (first published in *HWJ* 1 (1976)), p. 276.

10 See, for instance, the debate between Bridget Hill and Judith Bennett over the relative merits of economic factors and patriarchy in explaining the historical experience of women and work. Hill stresses the importance of economic change in bringing about women's economic marginalization and subordination; Bennett, on the other hand, argues for continuity, by asserting that the unchanging nature of patriarchal oppression had a more significant impact on women than economic variation. Judith M. Bennett, ' "History that stands still": women's work in the European past' *FS* 14, 2 (1988), and 'Women's history: a study in continuity and change' *WHR* 2, 2 (1993); Bridget Hill, 'Women's history: a study in change, continuity or standing still?' *WHR* 2, 1 (1993).

11 Gisela Bock, *History, Women's History, Gender History*, European University Institute Working Paper No. 87/291 (Florence, 1987), p. 6.

12 Ibid.

Foucault, Jacques Derrida and Jacques Lacan.[13] As women's historians began to incorporate these ideas, they focused attention on gender as an alternative explanation for historical inequalities. Instead
of seeing sexual differences between men and women as a reflection
of purely natural, biological differences, they accepted the notion
that these distinctions were socially constructed and, therefore, varied
with time, place, culture, class and ethnicity. Thus, the concepts of
masculinity and femininity are not fixed, but are rather continuously
redefined.[14] Although women's historians had already been using
gender as a less overtly political synonym for woman, and as a concept that facilitated the study of things pertaining to women, it was
reformulated under the influence of postmodernist thought to serve
as a comprehensive category of analysis that examined both 'the
social organization of sexual difference' and the deep structure of
relationships of power.[15]

Since constructions of femininity and masculinity take place in
relation to one another, gender widened the historical focus to
include examinations of the male as well as the female experience.
By integrating the sexes, gender history has encouraged a more
organic understanding of past societies and shed new light on intra-
as well as inter-sexual relationships.[16] Its interest in, and toleration
of, difference – in experiences, interests and beliefs – has revealed
that neither women nor men can be assumed to constitute uni-
formly homogenous groups. Not only has this enriched the study of

13 See, for example, Michel Foucault, *The History of Sexuality* (1979); Jacques Derrida,
Writing and Difference, trans. Alan Bass (1978; reprinted 1990); and Jacques Lacan, *Ecrits:
a selection*, trans. Alan Sheridan (1977).

14 Some writers, like Thomas Laqueur, have gone even further and claimed that sex
itself is a social construct and not a natural category. See Thomas Laqueur, *Making Sex:
Body and Gender From the Greeks to Freud* (Cambridge, MA, 1990); J. Butler, *Gender Trouble:
Feminism and the Subversion of Identity* (New York, 1990), and *Bodies that Matter: on the
Discursive Limits of Sex* (1993); D. Leonard and L. Adkins, eds, *Sex in Question: French
Materialist Feminism* (1996).

15 Joan Wallach Scott, 'Introduction', in *Gender and the Politics of History* (New York,
1988), p. 2; and 'Gender: a useful category of historical analysis', ibid., p. 42. Other
important early works on gender include Michelle Zimbalist Rosaldo and Louise Lamphere,
eds, *Woman, Culture and Society* (Stanford, CA, 1974). Rosaldo refines the argument in
'The use and abuse of Anthropology'. See also Ruth Bloch, 'Untangling the roots of
modern sex roles: a survey of four centuries of change' *Signs* 4, 2 (1978), and Joan Kelly,
Women, History, and Theory (Chicago, IL, 1984).

16 See, for instance, S.B. Ortner and H. Whitehead, eds, *Sexual Meanings: The Cultural
Construction of Gender and Sexuality* (Cambridge, 1981); Denise Riley, '*Am I That Name*'?
Feminism and the Category of 'Women' in History (Basingstoke, 1988); Ludmilla Jordanova,
*Sexual Visions: Images of Gender in Science and Medicine Between the Eighteenth and Twentieth
Centuries* (Hemel Hempstead, 1989); and Anthony Fletcher, *Gender, Sex & Subordination in
England, 1500–1800* (New Haven, CT, 1995).

women in relation to men and each other, but it has also led to the development of an entirely new field of study: a gendered history of men. In the last few years, a small number of gender historians have begun to challenge the traditional association between women and gender and to address the question of men's history. Although relatively little has been published thus far, interest in the field is growing rapidly, as men's historians begin to analyse the historical construction of 'hegemonic masculinity' and its variants.[17]

Unsurprisingly, these developments have met with mixed reactions. Historians like Gisela Bock have welcomed gender history as a way to end the marginalization of women's history; others are disconcerted by the change. Joan Hoff, for instance, argues that a shift to gender history can only 'sever' women's history from its political roots and 'reduce the experiences of women, struggling to define themselves and better their lives in particular historical contexts, to mere subjective stories'.[18] While this rift is partially generational, it also reflects ideological and methodological differences. Much of gender history challenges the connection between women's history and feminist activism; it also revives much earlier arguments over the merits of theory versus empiricism. Hoff's current fears awake echoes of Sally Alexander and Barbara Taylor's debate with Sheila Rowbotham in 1979. Their defence of patriarchy, against Rowbotham's call for more wide-ranging research into women's lives, rests on the same argument that Hoff levels against the use of gender: without the structure provided by a unifying theoretical model such as patriarchy, women's history would 'founder in a welter of dissociated and contradictory "facts"'.[19]

Despite these differences, the gaps between women's history, men's history and gender history should not be overestimated.[20] As

---

17 See, for instance, Ava Baron, 'On looking at men: masculinity and the making of a gendered working-class history', in Shapiro, ed., *Feminists Re Vision History*, pp. 146–71; John Tosh, 'What should historians do with masculinity? Reflections on nineteenth-century Britain' *HWJ* 38 (1994); and Michael Roper and John Tosh, eds, *Manful Assertions: Masculinities in Britain Since 1800* (1991). For masculinity in the context of a wider study, see also Leonore Davidoff and Catherine Hall, *Family Fortunes: Men and Women of the English Middle Class, 1780–1850* (1987); and G.J. Barker-Benfield, *The Culture of Sensibility: Sex and Society in Eighteenth-Century Britain* (Chicago, IL, 1992).

18 Joan Hoff, 'Gender as a postmodern category of paralysis' *WHR* 3, 2 (1994), here pp. 149–50.

19 See Sheila Rowbotham, 'The trouble with patriarchy' *New Statesman* 21 (Dec. 1979); Sally Alexander and Barbara Taylor, 'In defence of patriarchy' *New Statesman* 21 (Dec. 1979), reprinted in Alexander, *Becoming a Woman*, here p. 272.

20 See Gisela Bock, 'Women's history and gender history: aspects of an international debate' *GH* 1, 1 (Spring 1989).

this volume demonstrates, history that is ostensibly about women can have important things to say about women's relationships with men; conversely, men's history, in deconstructing masculinity, not only provides an insight into men's relationships with each other, but also with women. Any lens that historians use to look at the ways that men and women interacted with each other and with society – be it women, men or gender – increases our understanding of the past considerably.

Models of change and continuity

To date, the majority of 'gendered' historical research into eighteenth-century England has followed the patterns established by historians of other periods, and has centred primarily on women and femininity.[21] Similarly, the study of eighteenth-century men and masculinity is still very much at a formative stage.[22] Research on eighteenth-century women, however, has become established enough to have fallen into some well-worn grooves.[23] Two areas of concentration have been particularly influential in shaping the way that historians think about the period: one has centred on the way

21 The same can largely be said for both early modern England and Europe. For England, see Susan Amussen, *An Ordered Society: Gender and Class in Early Modern England* (Oxford, 1988); Martin Ingram, '"Scolding Women Cucked or Washed": A crisis of gender relations in early modern England', in J. Kermode and G. Walker, eds, *Women, Crime and the Courts in Early Modern England* (1994); Linda A. Pollock, '"Teach her to live under obedience": the making of women in the upper ranks of early modern England' *CC* 4 (1989). Recent European examinations include Merry E. Weisner, *Women and Gender in Early Modern Europe* (Cambridge, 1993); and Olwen Hufton, *The Prospect Before Her: The History of Women in Western Europe, Volume One: 1500–1800* (1995). This gender imbalance is somewhat less noticeable in literary studies, where developments in literary criticism have resulted in widespread attention being paid to the construction of meanings and gendered identities.

22 The groundwork for eighteenth-century men's history is only beginning to be established. See, for instance, Fletcher, *Gender, Sex & Subordination*; Randolph Trumbach, 'London's sodomites: homosexual behaviour and western culture in the early eighteenth century' *JSH* xi (1977–8); idem, 'Sex, gender and sexual identity in modern culture: male sodomy and female prostitution in enlightenment England', in John C. Fout, ed., *Forbidden History: The State, Society and the Regulation of Sexuality in Modern Europe* (1992); Carolyn D. Williams, *Pope, Homer & Manliness: Some Aspects of Eighteenth-Century Classical Learning* (1993); Anthony Simpson, 'Masculinity and control: the prosecution of sex offences in eighteenth-century London' (unpub. Ph.D. thesis, New York, 1984); and Philip Carter, 'Mollies, fops and men of feeling: aspects of male effeminacy and masculinity in Britain, c.1700–1780' (unpub. D.Phil. thesis, Oxford, 1995).

23 Anthony Fletcher has suggested that women's history has two 'modes': one deals with the 'universals', while the other deals with the 'varieties' of the female experience. Both are represented in research on eighteenth-century women. See Fletcher, *Gender, Sex & Subordination*, p. xix.

that changing economic circumstances have affected women, specifically those of the lower orders; the second has been concerned with women's domestic and specifically female experiences, and has focused more frequently on women of the middling and upper ranks. In addition, there has also been relatively consistent attention paid to the contributions of exceptional women, especially those such as Mary Astell, Mary Wollstonecraft or Catherine Macaulay, whose writings or lives have been interpreted as feminist or proto-feminist.[24] Other topics have been more unevenly researched.[25] Forays are made increasingly into other areas – religion, criminality, consumer society, material culture, the arts – but more extensive and wide-ranging research is still necessary if a comprehensive understanding of the period is to be achieved.[26]

24 For Mary Astell, see Bridget Hill, *The First English Feminist: Reflections on Marriage and Other Writings by Mary Astell* (Chicago, IL, and London, 1986); J.K. Kinnaird, 'Mary Astell and the conservative contribution to English feminism' *Journal of British Studies* 19 (1979); and Ruth Perry, *The Celebrated Mary Astell: An Early English Feminist* (Chicago, IL, and London, 1986); for Catharine Macaulay, see Bridget Hill, *That Republican Virago: The Life and Times of Catharine Macaulay, Historian* (Oxford, 1992). Mary Wollstonecraft's life and works have become a specialized field of study in their own right. For recent publications see Gary Kelly, *Revolutionary Feminism: The Mind and Career of Mary Wollstonecraft* (Basingstoke, 1991); Jennifer Lorch, *Mary Wollstonecraft: The Making of a Radical Feminist* (New York and Oxford, 1990); and Claire Tomalin, *The Life and Death of Mary Wollstonecraft* rev. edn (1992).

25 For instance, early interest was shown in eighteenth-century women's concept of self and in the construction of femininity. While the topic has continued to attract research and has developed to include the construction of masculinity, recent publications still tend to rely on similar prescriptive and didactic sources. What remains to be done is to go below this surface and examine the wide range of personal manuscript sources left by eighteenth-century women and men in order to determine how they saw themselves. See, for example, Miriam J. Benkowitz, 'Some observations on woman's concept of self in the 18th century', in Paul Fritz and Richard Morton, eds, *Woman in the 18th Century and Other Essays. Publications of the McMaster University Association for 18th-Century Studies* 4 (Toronto and Sarasota, 1976), pp. 37–54; Marlene LeGates, 'The cult of womanhood in eighteenth-century thought' *ECS* 10, 1 (Fall 1976); Jean E. Hunter, 'The 18th-century Englishwoman: according to the *Gentleman's Magazine*', in Fritz and Morton, eds, *Woman in the 18th Century*, pp. 73–88; Barbara Schnorrenberg with Jean E. Hunter, 'The eighteenth-century Englishwoman', in Barbara Kanner, ed., *The Women of England from Anglo-Saxon Times to the Present. Interpretive Bibliographical Essays* (Hamden, CT, 1979); Susan Moller Okin, 'Women and the making of the sentimental family' *Philosophy and Public Affairs* 11, 1 (1981); and Katharine M. Rogers, *Feminism in Eighteenth-Century England* (Urbana, IL, 1982). Anthologies also address this issue: see Bridget Hill, ed., *Eighteenth Century Women: An Anthology* (1984), and Vivien Jones, ed., *Women in the Eighteenth Century. Constructions of Femininity* (London and New York, 1990). More recent examinations of the construction of femininity include Alice Browne, *The Eighteenth-Century Feminist Mind* (Brighton, 1987), and Barker-Benfield, *The Culture of Sensibility*.

26 For religion, see David Hempton, 'Women and evangelical religion in Ireland, 1750–1900', in idem, *The Religion of the People: Methodism and Popular Religion, c.1750–1900* (1996); and Jeremy Gregory, 'Gender and the clerical profession in England, 1660–1850', in R.N. Swan, ed., *Gender and the Christian Religion* (forthcoming). See also J.M. Beattie,

This is starting to take place. As women's historians and gender historians ask new questions and consult new sources, they are beginning to revise some of the basic assumptions on which previous interpretations were based; moreover, this process will only be accelerated if the contributions of mainstream historians, who are becoming increasingly sensitive to gender, are integrated.[27] There is some discomfort that old models are being broken down without being replaced, and with the contradictions, complexities and idiosyncrasies revealed by new research; however, these new perspectives demonstrate that women's and men's lives were both less rigidly defined and more widely affected by gender than was previously assumed.[28]

Many historians see a transformation in the relative economic and social position of men and women taking place between the seventeenth and nineteenth centuries. Although accounts differ as to timing, most interpretations centre on the impact of capitalism. According to this influential model, as the pre-industrial family economy gave way to an exploitative wage economy with the development of capitalism, women were increasingly marginalized, confined, and made subject to men. In the 'golden age' of the family economy, historians have been inclined to suppose that all family members shared the work that secured their livelihood, and, by implication, the status that was attached to it. In agriculture, the move away from the family economy was linked to the commercialization of farming and the enclosure of common land, developments which were understood to have introduced an increasingly rigid sexual division of labour. Men benefited most from this

---

'The criminality of women in eighteenth-century England' *JSH* 8 (Summer 1975); Londa Schiebinger, *The Mind Has No Sex? Women in the Origins of Modern Science* (Cambridge, MA, 1989); N. McKendrick, J. Brewer and J.H. Plumb, eds, *The Birth of a Consumer Society. The Commercialization of Eighteenth-century England* (1982); Joyce Ellis, ' "On the Town": women in Augustan England' *HT* (Dec. 1995); Amanda Vickery, 'Women and the world of goods; a Lancashire consumer and her possessions, 1751–81', in John Brewer and Roy Porter, eds, *Consumption and the World of Goods* (1993), pp. 274–301; Trevor Lummis and Jan Marsh, *The Woman's Domain: Women and the English Country House* (1993); and Cheryl Turner, *Living By the Pen. Women Writers in the Eighteenth Century* (1992).

27 Amanda Vickery, 'The neglected century: writing the history of eighteenth-century women' *GH* 3, 2 (Summer 1991), p. 211. David Cannadine has expressed similar concerns about the discipline as a whole. He has pointed out that the social and economic frameworks upon which women's history is based have been so extensively revised in the past twenty years that many women's historians are now basing their research on assumptions that are a generation out of date. He believes that this has increased the marginalization of women's history and that there is now an 'urgent need' to reintegrate women's history, both with other areas of enquiry and with more recent historiographical developments. David Cannadine, 'Through the keyhole' *New York Review of Books* (21 Nov. 1991).

28 Vickery, 'Golden age to separate spheres?'

gendering of tasks and work locations. As the notion of the male breadwinner emerged, women were gradually pushed into jobs with the lowest pay and status; as their economic contributions declined and were devalued, their earlier parity with men disintegrated; as their subordination increased, they were also confined more and more to the home. A similar tale has been told about manufacturing, where the introduction of new technology and modern methods of production is depicted as leading to the separation of home and workplace. With industrialization, manufacturing moved away from the domestic environment, with its sexual equality, to the male-dominated institution of the factory. Where women were allowed to leave the home to work in manufacturing, they were once again relegated to the lowest-paid and least prestigious jobs, in contrast to their male counterparts who assumed an ever-greater degree of economic power and status.

This model of emerging capitalism has had profound implications for historians' understanding of gender relations in all sections of society, but in particular among the middle classes who had the most to gain. As middle-class men embraced and came to dominate a new aggressive economic world and their womenfolk became increasingly dissociated from the workplace, they were assumed to have retreated into 'graceful indolence' in a strictly domestic setting.[29] These economic changes were presumed to have coincided with an emerging social ideology of female domesticity that was encapsulated in the notion of 'separate spheres'. Such thinking dictated that women and men were naturally suited to different spheres: for women, the 'private sphere' of the home and the family; for men, the 'public sphere' of work and politics.

Historians locate these broad developments within different periods. For Alice Clark, it was the late seventeenth century that witnessed the decline of the family economy, the gradual economic marginalization of women and the withdrawal of middle-class women from the workplace. In *Working Life of Women in the Seventeenth Century*, Clark describes how the introduction of capitalist industry consigned women to exploitation or a domestic prison.[30] In another early classic, *Women Workers and the Industrial Revolution*, Ivy Pinchbeck attributed the transformation in women's work to the Industrial Revolution, which she located between 1780 and 1850. She acknowledged that the move from shared agricultural labour or

29 Amanda Vickery, 'Shaking the Separate Spheres', TLS (12 March 1993), p. 6–7.
30 Alice Clark, *Working Life of Women in the Seventeenth Century* (1919).

domestic industry to factory work or other forms of wage labour outside the home was not an easy one for women; however, she believed that the changes had to be viewed more positively, for while they caused a short-term decline in female economic activity, in the long term they benefited women greatly. For Pinchbeck, industrialization not only brought women more economic and social independence, but also led ultimately to better education and training, thus allowing them to take their 'proper' place in the world.[31]

Subsequent historians have chosen to adapt rather than revise these two approaches. For Bridget Hill, like Pinchbeck, the changes in women's economic role and social status are located in the eighteenth century, but her outlook is much more pessimistic. Hill mourns the disintegration of the family economy, which she believes resulted in a permanent loss of status for women and their continued marginalization within the economy as a whole. In *Women, Work and Sexual Politics in Eighteenth-Century England*,[32] Hill has argued that the intrusion of capitalism in both agriculture and rural manufacture sounded the death knell of the family economy, and from around the mid-century, caused a significant shift in the patterns of women's work. As the sexual division of labour became more pronounced, the rough-and-ready sexual equality of the earlier period was lost, and by the late eighteenth century had been replaced by a new system of male dominance and diminished status, earning power and independence for women. Moreover, the disintegration of the family economy had negative repercussions for women well beyond the lower orders. As the household ceased to be the focus of work within the family, housework was similarly feminized and devalued, and women who were not forced to seek waged labour from economic necessity were left stranded in their homes. This state of affairs was justified by a belief system that made it 'the moral duty of wives and mothers to devote themselves exclusively to home and family'.[33]

Historians who are concerned with women of the lower orders, such as Hill, have come to regard this connection between industrialization and women's declining status as a self-evident truth: the onset of capitalism with its subsequent transformation of society

31 Ivy Pinchbeck, *Women Workers and the Industrial Revolution, 1750–1850* 2nd edn (1969; first publ. 1930).

32 Bridget Hill, *Women, Work and Sexual Politics in Eighteenth-Century England* 2nd edn (1994).

33 Ibid., p. 123.

is used to explain women's oppression.[34] Nevertheless, it is also common for historians of the middle classes, like Leonore Davidoff and Catherine Hall, to set their examination of gender in the nineteenth century against a background of eighteenth-century industrialization.[35] Accounts that presume that changes in the economic organization of English society during the eighteenth century led to fundamental shifts in the social structure, which in turn helped to produce a new system of gender relations, are at variance with much recent economic and social research. At the most basic level, the model of the Industrial Revolution itself has become problematic.[36] Not only has the assumption that industrialization happened suddenly and dramatically been shown to be unfounded, but the accompanying belief that it had a broadly uniform impact on all areas of the economy, and that it caused an inevitable shift away from the family economy (with the resultant emergence of the male breadwinner), has also been radically revised.

Many economic historians now question the very use of the term 'revolution'. Instead, they propose a gradual and uneven industrializing process which took place over a much longer period and was marked more by continuity than by profound and rapid change.[37] Rather than presenting the economy prior to 1780 as backwards and stagnant, the revisionists see both the seventeenth- and eighteenth-century economies as dynamic, based upon Britain's growing status as a powerful trading nation and its burgeoning domestic manufacturing industry. In addition, they extend the argument of continuity into the nineteenth century, suggesting that the rapidity with which industrialization and urbanization were presumed to have caused societal change has been overstated. An important exception to this trend can be found in the work of Maxine Berg, who argues that the concept of industrial revolution is not redundant. She maintains that a better understanding of the level of women's and children's labour, and the role of organizational and technological

---

34 This trend in modern society is attacked by sociologists Christine Delphy and Diana Leonard, *Familiar Exploitation: A New Analysis of Marriage in Contemporary Western Societies* (1992), pp. 31–5. For a more subtle historical interpretation, see Jane Rendall, *Women in an Industrializing Society: England 1750–1880* (Oxford, 1990); Deborah Valenze, *The First Industrial Woman* (Oxford, 1995); and Pamela Sharpe, *Adapting to Capitalism: Working Women in the English Economy, 1700–1850* (Basingstoke, 1996).

35 Davidoff and Hall, *Family Fortunes.*

36 Vickery, 'Golden age to separate spheres?'

37 See N.F.R. Crafts, *British Industrial Growth During the Industrial Revolution* (Oxford, 1985); E.A. Wrigley, *Continuity, Chance and Change: the Character of the Industrial Revolution in England* (Cambridge, 1989); Pat Hudson, *The Industrial Revolution* (1992); Patrick O'Brien and Roland Quinault, eds, *The Industrial Revolution and British Society* (Cambridge, 1993).

innovation in the period traditionally equated with the Industrial
Revolution, might reveal more significant productivity gains than
recent research has allowed.[38]

This idea of gradual economic change has begun to gain in
popularity with historians of women's work. The 'golden age' of
women's work has proved remarkably elusive to empirical research,
whether it was supposed to be located in the medieval period or in
the seventeenth and eighteenth centuries. As early as 1983, Olwen
Hufton attacked the notion of an earlier, egalitarian Eden succeeded by a decline in the status of female employment and the
economic marginalization of women.[39] Her most recent work on
women in Europe between the sixteenth and eighteenth centuries
describes women's experience as broadly unchanging. What is more,
while stressing the important part that class and geographical differences could play in shaping individual experience, she has suggested that 'secularization, increasing social sophistication, and a
vocabulary paying homage to the sensibility and moral fibre of
women' all contributed to an overall improvement in the conditions of women's lives.[40]

Louise Tilly and Joan Scott have also stressed continuity. They
have argued that industrialization in England and France did little
to alter the working lives of women: in the nineteenth century,
women were still involved in the same type of low-status, low-paid
and low-skilled work that they had been for centuries.[41] Their interpretation is echoed by Judith Bennett, who contends that women
faced 'profound and enduring disadvantages in their relations with
men' long before the arrival of capitalism and industrialization.[42]
Even medieval women, she argues convincingly, were never offered
anything like equality with men within the family economy.[43] In
lieu of an explanatory model based upon economic change, she
substitutes one of long-term continuity, arguing that women's work

---

38 Maxine Berg, *The Age of Manufactures, 1700–1820: industry, innovation, and work in
Britain* 2nd edn (1994). See also her 'What difference did women's work make to the
industrial revolution?' *HWJ* 35 (1993).

39 Olwen Hufton, 'Women in history' *PP* 101 (1983).

40 Hufton, *The Prospect Before Her*, pp. 501–4.

41 Louise A. Tilly and Joan W. Scott, *Women, Work and Family* 2nd edn (New York,
1987), p. 77.

42 Bennett, ' "History that stands still" '. See also Janet Thomas, 'Women and capitalism: oppression or emancipation?' *Comparative Studies in Society and History* 30 (1988); J.
Rendall, 'Women's history beyond the cage' *History* 75 (1990); and Katrina Honeyman
and Jordan Goodman, 'Women's work, gender conflict, and labour markets in Europe,
1500–1900' *EcHR* 2nd ser., 44, 4 (1991).

43 Judith M. Bennett, 'Medieval women, modern women: across the great divide', in
David Aers, ed., *Culture and History, 1350–1600* (Hemel Hempstead, 1992), pp. 151ff.

was always 'low-skilled, low-status and low-paying'. While acknowledging that economic factors may have shifted over time, she suggests that they did so within the framework of patriarchy. According to Bennett, it is patriarchy that must be examined in order to explain women's historical subordination and marginalization.[44]

As one of the earliest concepts of women's history, patriarchy has been important in affecting the way that both women's and gender historians have approached the past.[45] In its most traditional aspect, the system of patriarchy refers to the absolute legal and economic control that the male head of a household had over his dependants, male and female. According to this interpretation, patriarchy was institutionalized in antiquity but ended in the nineteenth century, when women were freed from absolute male control by changes in the law that gave them civil and, particularly in the case of married women, property rights. Historians who subscribe to patriarchy usually employ a wider definition, however. As the personal and societal 'institutionalization of male dominance',[46] they assume that patriarchy not only marginalized women and limited or denied them access to power in the past, but that it continues to do so in the present through men's overwhelming control of positions of economic, social, political and legal power. Under pressure from research that has thrown up questions about the universality of female powerlessness and oppression, patriarchy, as a conceptual model, has lost much of its earlier monolithic character.[47] Instead, historians have reinterpreted it as both insidious and

44 See Bennett, ' "History that stands still" ', here p. 278; and idem 'Women's history: a study in continuity and change' *WHR* 2 (1993).

45 The following is perhaps best expressed by Gerda Lerner in *The Creation of Patriarchy*, especially pp. 228–9, 238–9.

46 Ibid., p. 239.

47 For instance, the matriarch may have been as powerful a figure as the patriarch. See Margaret Ezell, *The Patriarch's Wife: Literary Evidence and the History of the Family* (Chapel Hill, NC, and London, 1987). Demographic research has revealed that widows and spinsters formed a 'significant minority' of the population in early modern Britain – for example, Peter Laslett has suggested that one-fifth of the households in any community in early modern England were run by widows; moreover, 'spinster clustering' led to the creation of all-female households. Furthermore, recent research on women and property has revealed that ordinary women not only had more access to property than had been assumed, but that they were inclined to distribute it differently to men; furthermore, examinations of wills and settlements have demonstrated that the needs of daughters and sons tended to be carefully considered and balanced by parents, with the settlements for younger sons and daughters often created specifically to suit individual circumstances. See, for example, Peter Laslett, 'Mean household size in England since the sixteenth century', in Peter Laslett and Richard Wall, eds, *Household and Family in Past Times* (Cambridge, 1972), pp. 77–8; Olwen Hufton, 'Women without men: widows and spinsters in Britain and France in the eighteenth century' *JFH* 9, 4 (Winter 1984); Amy Louise Erickson, *Women and Property in Early Modern England* (1993); Susan Staves, 'Resentment or resignation? Dividing the spoils among daughters and younger sons', in John Brewer and Susan Staves, eds, *Early*

enduring, appearing in different guises at various times and places. Anthony Fletcher's recent publication, *Gender, Sex & Subordination in England, 1500–1800*, is illustrative. In exploring the survival of patriarchy over a period that 'seems to exhibit features of crisis in men's control over women', he argues that patriarchy remained intact because of its inherent adaptability: 'in the end the simple fact is that men revised a scheme of gender relations that served their interests as men so effectively during the three centuries from 1500 to 1800 that it has survived'.[48]

Considering the importance that is ascribed to the family as an economic unit and as the primary institution of patriarchy, it is not surprising that it has been described as 'the Atlas upon whose giant shoulders the world of women's history has reposed'.[49] In spite of this, and although marriage and parenthood have been assumed to have been the norm for the vast majority of women and men in the past, the 'fit' between family history and women's and gender history remains uneasy. As Louise Tilly's comparison of publications in family and women's history has demonstrated, this is primarily due to differing concerns. Family history, in concentrating on the household as a unit or on marriage as an institution, has tended to search for quantifiable data rather than individual experience; thus, little attention has been paid to the meaning that the family or marriage had for contemporaries.[50]

Women's history, on the other hand, has traditionally taken a negative view of the family. By assuming that the subordinate position of women in the ideal family of prescriptive literature was the reality, or equally, by accepting at face value the negative picture of the family that emerged from suffrage propaganda, early women's historians cast the family in the role of 'a central institution of women's oppression'.[51] According to Rosemary O'Day, this has led women's historians to lock themselves into 'a self-fulfilling investigation' of familial power relations. Women's historians need to

---

Modern Concepts of Property (London and New York, 1995), pp. 194–218; and, for a similar re-evaluation of bourgeois women's relationship to property (and familial power) in *ancien régime* France, see Barbara B. Diefendorf, 'Women and property in *ancien régime* France: theory and practice in Dauphiné and Paris', also in Brewer and Staves, eds, *Early Modern Concepts of Property*, pp. 170–93.

48 Fletcher, *Gender, Sex & Subordination*, pp. xvi, 411.

49 Hufton, 'Women without men', p. 355.

50 Louise A. Tilly, 'Women's history and family history: fruitful collaboration or missed connection?' *JFH* 12, 1–3 (1987). It should, however, be noted that Davidoff and Hall succeed in integrating these fields to a significant extent in *Family Fortunes*.

51 Ellen DuBois, 'The radicalization of the woman suffrage movement: notes toward the reconstruction of nineteenth-century feminism' *FS* 3 (1975), p. 63.

break out of this cycle, she argues, as only more detailed examinations of the 'lived' family experience will reveal its full variety and complexity. They need to appreciate that the family was a flexible institution, made up of individuals who adopted, adapted or refuted current behavioural ideals, and that the relationships among these individuals were not fixed, but changed according to time and circumstance.[52]

O'Day's advice is particularly relevant to women's and gender historians studying the eighteenth century, as it lies at the heart of a long standing debate among family historians over the timing of the emergence of the modern nuclear family; moreover, and unusually for family history, the argument is formulated around the meaning of the family and the institution of marriage for contemporaries. Proponents of this 'sentiments' approach to family history identify a new emphasis on love and affection between family members as central to the formation of the modern family.[53] Lawrence Stone elucidated this most powerfully for English history in 1977, with the publication of *The Family, Sex and Marriage in England 1500–1800*.[54] This text has been criticized severely and repeatedly, yet it remains highly influential.

According to Stone, a series of changes occurred in England between 1500 and 1800 that resulted in the replacement of the traditional 'open lineage family' with the modern 'closed domesticated nuclear family'. This transition was attributed to a remarkable change in family relationships that occurred as a result of the growth

52 Rosemary O'Day, *The Family and Family Relationships, 1500–1900: England, France and the United States of America* (Basingstoke and London, 1994), pp. 266–74. While O'Day is right to call for more studies, some important work on the early modern family has appeared. See Pollock, '"Teach her to live under obedience"'; A. Wall, 'Elizabethan precept and feminine practice: the Thynne family of Longleat' *History* 75 (1990); V. Larminie, 'Marriage and the family: an example of the seventeenth century Newdigates' *Midland History* 9 (1984); and Naomi Tadmor, 'The concept of the household-family in eighteenth-century England' *PP* 151 (1996).

53 Michael Anderson, *Approaches to the History of the Western Family, 1500–1914* (Cambridge, 1995), p. 25. For Anderson, this approach is encapsulated in four main texts: Philippe Ariès, *Centuries of Childhood* (Eng. trans., 1962); J.-L. Flandrin, *Families in Former Times: Kinship, Household and Sexuality* (Cambridge, 1979); Edward Shorter, *Making of the Modern Family* (1976); and Lawrence Stone, *The Family, Sex and Marriage in England, 1500–1800* (1977).

54 Stone's work has been discussed and dissected by a wide variety of historians. See, for instance, Alan Macfarlane's review of Stone in *History and Theory* 18 (1979) and his *Marriage and Love in England 1300–1840* (Oxford, 1986); Anderson, *Approaches to the History of the Western Family*; Ralph A. Houlbrooke, *The English Family, 1450–1700* (London and New York, 1984); Eileen Spring, 'Law and the theory of the affective family' *Albion* 16, 1 (Spring 1984); and Lloyd Bonfield, 'Marriage, property and the "affective family"' *Law and History* 1, 2 (Fall 1983).

of what Stone termed 'affective individualism'. For Stone, pre-industrial society was bleak and unappealing. Life was nasty, uncertain and short. Privacy was almost non-existent; little value was placed on the individual; and people were inherently suspicious and prone to violence. Unsurprisingly, therefore, the traditional family was correspondingly unemotional, distant, deferential and patriarchal. Since the uncertainty of life made emotional investment in others, including children, risky, emotional bonds between family members remained weak, and parents' relations with children were distinctly authoritarian. By the beginning of the eighteenth century, however, Stone believes that family relationships had been transformed by the growth of individualism, which was associated with increasing concerns about privacy, personal autonomy and individual rights, but most importantly, by a new emphasis on affection. The resulting family was modern: nuclear, close, emotional, child-centred and, with regard to husbands and wives, increasingly egalitarian.

This model sits uncomfortably with discussions of eighteenth-century English society that interpret gender relations in terms of economic change or through the continuum of patriarchy. Stone's work has attracted serious academic criticism on grounds ranging from his use of evidence, through his exaggeration of the degree, timing and uniformity of change, to his tendency to present official doctrine as personal practice; moreover, it tends to subsume the personal experiences of both men and women in its pursuit of 'the family'. Despite these caveats, the emphasis that it places on affection and on egalitarian relationships between men and women, at least at élite levels, is important and requires further examination by women's and gender historians alike.

As an interpretation that incorporates economic arguments, notions of patriarchy, questions of family relationships and concerns about gender, the separate spheres model has had an enormous impact on historians' understanding of the past. In *Family Fortunes: Men and Women of the English Middle Class, 1780–1850*, one of the most influential publications in recent years, Leonore Davidoff and Catherine Hall melded these arguments into a model that explained changes in nineteenth-century English society, including the creation of middle-class femininity. It was their elaboration of separate spheres ideology, in conjunction with gender as a motor for class formation, that made the study so significant. Drawing on standard assumptions that developments within late eighteenth-century capitalism led to the formation of a class society, they extended this argument to explain the self-identification of the middle class. As a group that was heavily influenced by the turmoil of the French Revolution and the conservative response it spawned, and by the ideas of sharply defined male and female roles that were simultaneously being promulgated by the evangelical revival, the middle class not only adopted a domestic ideology that promoted the clear separation of spheres according to gender, but made it central to their class identity. This new, moral world-view reflected their overwhelming desire for order: 'middle-class gentlemen and middle-class ladies each had their appointed place in this newly mapped social world'.[55] Masculinity became decisively equated with the public sphere of 'work, politics and power', femininity with that of the private sphere of the 'home, family and emotion'.[56]

Family Fortunes was based on a carefully delimited examination of predominantly evangelical commercial families in Birmingham, Essex and Suffolk, and its conclusions must be interpreted in that light. While adopting (and refining) the model of separate spheres, Davidoff and Hall presented a complicated argument, which reveals that in practice the actual separation between the spheres was often indistinct and subject to personal interpretation. The importance of their contribution should not be underestimated. By making the connection between the formation of the English middle class and gender, and by examining the male as well as the female experience, they succeeded in bringing gender to the forefront of mainstream social history.

Indeed, the separate spheres model has enjoyed remarkable popularity, especially among women's historians. Created by interweaving pre-existing ideas about public and private with the notion of separate spheres, the model has been described as 'one of the most powerful concepts within women's history since its recrudescence in the 1960s'.[57] It emerged from early, often uncritical, readings of nineteenth-century prescriptive and political literature, and attained widespread acceptance, often without being validated by manuscript sources.[58] Like Whig, Marxist or Namierite interpretations in their heydays, it has been projected backwards indiscriminately into other

55 Davidoff and Hall, *Family Fortunes*, p. 30.

56 Vickery, 'Shaking the separate spheres', p. 6.

57 Leonore Davidoff, 'Regarding some "Old Husbands' Tales": public and private in feminist history', in *Worlds Between: Historical Perspectives on Gender and Class* (Cambridge, 1995), p. 227. The separation between public and private, man and woman, is also central to feminist political thought, as it is used to define the political. For an overview of the various strands of feminist political thought, see Elshtain, *Public Man, Private Woman*.

58 Vickery, 'Golden age to separate spheres?', p. 387; P. Branca, 'Image and reality: the myth of the idle Victorian woman', in Mary S. Hartman and Lois W. Banner, eds, *Clio's*

centuries. As summarized and applied to the eighteenth century by Kathryn Shevelow,[59] the model posits that middle- and upper-class women were steadily enclosed within the private sphere of the home in response to the growth of a 'narrow and restrictive model of femininity':

> Increasingly throughout the eighteenth century, the interrelated categories of masculine and feminine, public and private, home and 'world', assumed the shape of binary oppositions in which the meaning of each category was produced in terms of its opposite. Gender was constructed through the naturalizing of this system of oppositions; women were represented as naturally possessing qualities that rendered them unfit for the masculine public realm, but endowed them with considerable authority within the private context of the home.[60]

In general, separate spheres ideology appears to be almost as unquestioningly established for the eighteenth century as it has been for the nineteenth. Just as patriarchy, at its most extreme, was simplified to the point of caricature, so too has this model occasionally been reduced to depicting eighteenth-century society as one in which women and men lived in completely different worlds, where women had no autonomy and were little more than the passive victims, and where men dominated personal relations, society and institutional life.[61] While most interpretations are somewhat more subtle, the routine acceptance of a simplistic separation of spheres

Consciousness Raised (New York, 1974), pp. 179–91; M.J. Peterson, 'No angels in the house: the Victorian myth and the Paget women' *AHR* 89 (1984); Kerber, 'Separate spheres, female worlds, woman's place; J. Lewis, 'Separate spheres: threat or promise?' *JBS* 30, 1 (1991).

59 Kathryn Shevelow, *Women and Print Culture: the Construction of Femininity in the Early Periodical* (1989), p. 1.

60 Ibid., p. 10.

61 For instance, Richard Leppert's study of eighteenth-century domesticity rests upon the assumption that eighteenth-century women were already firmly fixed in the private sphere: 'Females, young and old alike, lived out their lives within the metaphorical or literal confines of domestic walls.' The separation of the spheres is assumed to have been so great that it even affected men's and women's relation to time: men controlling it, through their activity in the public world; women being controlled by it, through their need to find ways to cope with enforced leisure. In this patriarchal society, women's activities were passive and confined, 'expressive of stationary time'; their musical accomplishments encouraged by men in order to create an 'ideologically correct species of woman'. In the war between the sexes, men had not only succeeded in the 'desensualization of upper-class women', but in 'the establishment of an ideology of domesticity and the social structures designed to institutionalize it. Men had in effect "won"....' Richard Leppert, *Music and Image: Domesticity, Ideology and Socio-cultural Formation in Eighteenth-century England* (Cambridge, 1988), pp. 29–31. Another recent publication that is based unquestioningly on the separate spheres model – this time mixed with psychology – is Betty Rizzo, *Companions Without Vows: Relationships Among Eighteenth-Century Women* (Athens, GA, and London, 1994).

still plays an important structural role in the majority of arguments about women and gender.[62]

As more extensive research has begun to dismantle interpretations that have been based on the premise of a rapid Industrial Revolution, so too has it become apparent that there are serious discrepancies between the hard-and-fast oppositions upon which the separate spheres model is based and the realities of life for men and women in the past.[63] In the introduction to an impressively varied collection of revisionist essays, Ann-Louise Shapiro has pointed out that it is particularly difficult to divide the histories of men and women into meaningful public and private spheres, because of the extremely 'slippery' nature of the concepts of 'public' and 'private' themselves.[64] Historians must

> distinguish among the possible meanings and effects of 'separate spheres' as used in the past – the way in which it invented a past – and to clarify the distinctions between past usages and the language of current historical analysis.[65]

While acknowledging that the research that has been carried out under the aegis of this model has yielded a significant amount of information, especially with regard to middle-class women in western cultures, she declares that it has also called into question the very notion of 'separation' upon which the model is based. In its stead, she offers 'permeability' or 'overlap'.[66]

Lawrence Klein has raised similar questions about what he calls the 'domestic thesis', and particularly about the use of binary oppositions to describe gender relations for the eighteenth century. Like Shapiro, he advises historians not to accept 'public' and 'private' at face value, or to approach them through modern definitions. He points out that these terms held a multiplicity of meanings for

62 See, for example, Browne, *The Eighteenth-Century Feminist Mind*; Barker-Benfield, *Culture of Sensibility*; Anne Laurence, *Women in England 1500–1760: A Social History* (1994); Shevelow, *Women and Print Culture*; and Jones, ed., *Women in the Eighteenth Century*.

63 See, for example, Nancy Armstrong, *Desire and Domestic Fiction: A Political History of the Novel* (Oxford, 1987); and Margaret Hunt, 'Wife beating, domesticity and women's independence in eighteenth-century London' *GH* 4 (1992).

64 It is a mark of the distance that eighteenth-century feminist and gender history have to travel, that in a collection of essays that extend from the ancient world to the twentieth century, the eighteenth century receives no direct attention. Ann-Louise Shapiro, 'Introduction', in Shapiro, ed., *Feminists Revision History*, p. 6; Leonore Davidoff acknowledges the difficulty with the terms and uses the same vocabulary. See 'Regarding some "Old Husbands' Tales"', here p. 227.

65 Davidoff, 'Regarding some "Old Husbands' Tales"'.

66 Ibid.

individuals at the time and suggests that gendering these terms may well be anachronistic.[67] Stella Tillyard's examination of the lives of the Lennox sisters supports his arguments, for it reveals that at least these eighteenth-century women did not see notions of public and private as fixed, but fluid. Indeed, they were defined idiosyncratically, according to individual and situation, and varied even among members of the same family.[68]

Historians currently researching eighteenth-century English political and social history have raised additional doubts, both as to the change in social structure that led to the establishment of the middle class, and about the validity of separate spheres ideology and the existence of a 'domestic thesis' of gender relations. A substantial body of research now exists that demonstrates that the eighteenth-century middling sort was already taking shape well before the traditional periodization of industrialization and capitalism. Peter Earle has located its emergence in the seventeenth century, at least a century before the presumed industrial take-off. This group grew in numbers, wealth and prominence as the country experienced more, and more rapid, urban development.[69] An identifiable and

67 Lawrence E. Klein, 'Gender and the public/private distinction in the eighteenth century: some questions about evidence and analytic procedure' *ECS* 29, 1 (1995); and 'Gender, conversation and the public sphere in early eighteenth-century England', in Judith Still and Michael Worton, eds, *Textuality and Sexuality: Reading Theories and Practices* (Manchester and New York, 1993), pp. 100–15. This problem of definition, either by eighteenth-century contemporaries or by modern historians, is complicated and sometimes obfuscating. Much recent historical work draws heavily on the concept of the public sphere formulated by Jürgen Habermas, and that of the private sphere construed by Philippe Ariès and Roger Chartier. See especially Habermas, *The Structural Transformation of the Public Sphere: an Inquiry into a Category of Bourgeois Society*, trans. Thomas Burger with Frederick Lawrence (Cambridge, MA, 1989); Philippe Ariès and Georges Duby, eds, *A History of Private Life* 5 vols (Cambridge, MA, 1987–91); and, within that series, Roger Chartier, ed., *A History of Private Life III: Passions of the Renaissance* (1989). For discussions of these ideas, see Geoff Eley, 'Re-thinking the political: social history and political culture in 18th and 19th century Britain' *Archiv für Sozialgeschichte* 21 (1981); and Dario Castiglione and Lesley Sharpe, eds, *Shifting the Boundaries: Transformations of the Language of Public and Private in the Eighteenth Century* (Exeter, 1995). John Brewer's contribution to the last-named work is particularly relevant: see 'This, that and the other: public, social and private in the seventeenth and eighteenth centuries', pp. 1–21.

68 Stella Tillyard, *Aristocrats: Caroline, Emily, Louisa and Sarah Lennox 1740–1832* (1994).

69 See, among others, McKendrick, Brewer and Plumb, *The Birth of a Consumer Society*; Nicholas Rogers, *Whigs and Cities: Popular Politics in the Age of Walpole and Pitt* (Oxford, 1989); Peter Earle, *The Making of the English Middle Class* (1989); Langford, *A Polite and Commercial People*; idem, *Public Life and the Propertied Englishman*; Peter Borsay, ed., *The Eighteenth-Century English Town: A Reader in English Urban History, 1688–1820* (1990); J. Barry and C. Brooks, eds, *The Middling Sort of People: Culture, Society and Politics in England 1550–1800* (Basingstoke, 1994); P.J. Corfield, *Power and the Professions in Britain, 1700–1850* (1995); idem, 'The making of the English middle class, c.1700–1850' *JBS* Special Issue, 2, 4 (1993).

increasingly important social phenomenon, the eighteenth-century middling sort did not display the same type of class-consciousness which has been assumed for the nineteenth-century middle class;[70] nevertheless, it did share a culture of 'politeness' and commercial enterprise which ensured that a sense of identity was not altogether absent. Associated with this culture of politeness was a two-edged, but nonetheless expanded, role for women.[71] As Paul Langford has demonstrated, polite society provided women with more status; it also created more opportunities for them to mix with men, both inside and outside the home. In addition, they were also able to turn increased literacy, the commercialization of leisure and the expansion of consumer society to their benefit and carve out larger roles for themselves.[72] Similarly, Linda Colley's examination of women's increasing involvement in socio-political and patriotic activities at the end of the century has led her to conclude that while there was an increasing concern among moralists that women should remain within the domestic sphere, it arose precisely because so many women appeared to be active outside it.[73] Kathleen Wilson's examination of gender and eighteenth-century imperialism presents a more complex picture, as it demonstrates the involvement of women – actresses, in this case – in disseminating an imperialist vision that defined, and was defined by, constructions of masculinity.[74]

In a review article examining the 'categories and chronology' of English women's history, Amanda Vickery has argued powerfully that the orthodox categories of women's history – and thus of gender history as well – need to be 'jettisoned'.[75] Well-established though these conceptual models are, she suggests that they have been so undermined by inconsistencies of chronology, historical revisionism and the implications of new research, that they are no longer useful. For her, the future lies in going beyond the safety of these boundaries and conducting the detailed research needed to write the micro- and macro-histories necessary to create a new chronology. While

70 Recent scholarship has re-emphasized the political and economic strength of landed power in the nineteenth century, as well as the divisions within the middle classes and the resilience of 'cross-class' vertical alliances within society as a whole: see F.M.L. Thompson, *The Rise of Respectable Society: A Social History of Britain, 1830–1900* (1988).

71 See, for instance, Klein, 'Gender, conversation and the public sphere'.

72 Langford, *A Polite and Commercial People*, pp. 109ff; see also McKendrick, Brewer and Plumb, eds, *The Birth of a Consumer Society*.

73 Colley, *Britons*, pp. 241ff.

74 Kathleen Wilson, 'Empire of virtue: the imperial project and Hanoverian culture, c.1720–1785', in Lawrence Stone, ed., *An Imperial State at War: Britain, 1689–1815* (1994), pp. 128–64.

75 Vickery, 'Golden age to separate spheres?', esp. pp. 412–13.

Vickery is certainly correct in stressing the need for stepping over the traces and conducting more extensive, manuscript-based research, the concerns at the heart of older models remain important and require further investigation. What is even more important, however, is that new research breaks down the barriers that still divide women's history and gender history from 'mainstream' history. By moving beyond the boundaries of established models, it becomes easier to ask new questions, which in turn reveals new sources, or at least new ways of using old sources.

The quest for this new conceptual framework should take a lower priority for historians studying eighteenth-century English society than the desire to gain a better understanding of the complexity of that society and of the operation of gender within it. While it is axiomatic that more detailed research is essential, historians must also become more aware and accepting of the sharp contradictions and infinite variations of women's and men's experiences in pre-industrial societies. Eighteenth-century English society was earthy, robust and dynamic, yet it remained decidedly diverse. The great, sweeping tides of change that have attracted so much historical attention could, and did, often leave areas and individuals almost entirely untouched. Differences imposed by region, custom, social status, occupation, religion or ethnicity, and by irregularities in the rates of technological change, urbanization and commercialization, all complicate attempts to create meaningful generalizations.[76]

Blurring the boundaries

The essays in this text reflect these preoccupations. They engage with and go beyond conventional models, particularly those of economic change and separate spheres. As discrete studies, each draws upon a wide assortment of sources in order to shed new light on gender in eighteenth-century England. The diversity and ambiguity that they reveal reflect a society that was both complicated and contradictory. Eighteenth-century men and women had a multiplicity of roles and responsibilities, and represented themselves and each

76 In her examination of late nineteenth-century Britain, Jose Harris has called attention to British society's lack of uniformity and limited modernity, describing it as 'a large, ramshackle and profoundly custom-based society'. She has also highlighted the striking differences in gender relations that resulted from localism and the sheer variety of differences in attitudes, interests, beliefs, customs and behaviours throughout the country. Jose Harris, *Private Lives, Public Spirit. A Social History of Britain 1870–1914* (Oxford, 1993), here p. 95.

other in many ways, depending upon situations and circumstances. Most importantly, the essays draw attention to the fluidity and flexibility of gender relations. Through the disparities and idiosyncrasies that they reveal, they remind historians of the important part that individuals played in fashioning their personas and their society.

Acknowledging the limitations of a simple model of gender relations does not, however, negate the impact of gender on the lives of eighteenth-century men and women. They were subject to a vast array of social rules and obligations, many of which were gendered. For example, it is clear that participation in public life was conditioned by such codes of behaviour. The culture of refined sensibility which many perceived as increasingly typifying middle-class and élite social relations did not, however, conform to simple rules of gender relations. The public sphere was neither solely male, nor openly accessible to females. Some arenas of public interaction, such as coffee-houses and clubs, were male preserves, while debating societies, assemblies and libraries were often mixed. The writing and reading of literature offered opportunities for female, as well as male, involvement. Indeed, certain forms of print culture, especially novels and some forms of conduct literature, appeared specifically feminine in their production or their appeal.

Not only were the rules governing gender relations complex, but they were further complicated and altered by other factors: class, age, location, occupation and religion, as well as more idiosyncratic considerations such as personality. Without taking account of these factors, existing historical models are too simplistic at best, and positively unhelpful at worst. For instance, though it is undeniable that urbanization and industrialization did have an important impact on gender relations in the eighteenth century, historians should be wary of assuming that their effects were universal. The growth of a gendered division of labour, which has been correctly identified as occurring in some parts of the textile industry, cannot be seen as representative of changes in the country as a whole. Even in textile production, such developments were not always uniform. Any account of gender and work that does not take into account other complicating factors fails to capture the diversity of men's and women's experiences.

Such complexities remind historians that gender is a useful, if perplexing, category of analysis. To some extent, the historian's choice of sources determines his or her understanding of gender. The decision to examine prescriptive or satirical literature, for example, provides insights into a particular aspect of the subject: namely, information about the way that contemporaries conceptualized and talked about gender, as well as depictions of desirable or deviant behaviours. Looking at the experiences of real individuals, either through statistical analyses or biographical accounts, may provide a somewhat different insight, as the ways that gender was played out in daily life differed from the ways that it was discussed in the pages of guides or periodicals. Both approaches are valid, and both are followed in these essays. The picture of eighteenth-century English society that emerges is inevitably complex and pluralistic, at least in part because it begins to capture the multiplicity of ways that gender was conceptualized and actually employed.

The essays have been grouped into four general categories: social reputations; work and poverty; politics and the political élite; and periodicals and the printed image. While women are ostensibly the subjects of most of the essays, each contributes to our understanding of gender in eighteenth-century England by exhibiting the variety of ways in which women and men interacted with each other or were integrated into society as a whole. Detail, rather than comprehensive coverage, has been a primary objective; moreover, subjects that have received little historical attention to date have been preferred to ones that are frequently studied.

Philip Carter and Kimberly Crouch discuss the construction of masculinity and femininity, in conjunction with aspects of social reputation and sexuality, through studies of two eighteenth-century experts in self-presentation, the fop and the actress respectively. Carter demonstrates that earlier equations of effeminacy with homosexuality should not be accepted unquestioningly, as the fop type was an extreme example of a public and social – but heterosexual – masculinity that arose in response to changing societal conditions. In exploring the way that notions of public and private were mixed in the lives and reputations of eighteenth-century actresses, Kimberly Crouch reveals the perspicacity with which these women drew on positive and negative aspects of contemporary femininity to construct a range of personas – some of them purposefully sexual – which they then exploited for their own purposes.

In three essays that focus on women, work and poverty, Hannah Barker, Susan Skedd and Richard Connors question the degree to which eighteenth-century women were economically and socially marginalized. Barker's examination of the work experience of women from printing families reveals overall continuity, not marginalization, during the period of the 'industrial revolution', and while she points out that women's experiences were individually varied, she emphasizes their economic integration. Skedd contends that preconceptions about the quality and availability of female education, as well as ideas about middle-class women's increasing alienation from productive labour, need to be revised in light of the expansion of girls' schooling in eighteenth-century England. More fee-paying female institutions meant that teaching became a viable option, even a career, for more women; furthermore, girls' schools were commercial ventures that depended upon publicity, performance and popularity for success – and that success, when it came, could be lucrative. Connors moves the focus away from work and the middling sort to the little-known world of eighteenth-century pauper women. In a series of case studies, he argues that accepted notions of separate spheres are of limited explanatory power when examining the way that the parish and the Hanoverian state became involved in the lives of poor women through the operation of the Poor Laws and Settlement Laws. Disadvantaged though these women were, he reveals that they were by no means passive victims. They not only demanded their rights – often successfully – before male authorities who ranged from parish overseers up to the Justices of the Peace at Quarter Sessions, but also occasionally became part of the local system itself, through their employment in the parishes.

Women's involvement in politics and the political élite forms the third section of the book. Since this area has been largely ignored by women's and political historians alike, Elaine Chalus breaks the electoral process down into its constituent parts and examines women's contributions at each stage. She reveals a vigorous familial political world, where the social and political arenas, and the public and private spheres, were inextricably intertwined, and where women as well as men had well-established political roles and responsibilities. Amanda Foreman sharpens the focus by concentrating on the political career of Georgiana, Duchess of Devonshire, who is often assumed to have been shamed into political silence and private life after the much-publicized kisses-for-votes incident of the 1784 Westminster election. Instead, Foreman demonstrates that the Duchess reconciled gender with politics, and that over the course of the next twenty years she carved out a role for herself as a leading Whig politician in her own right.

In the last section of the book, contributions by Cindy McCreery and Stephen Howard explore gendered roles and representations in image and text. McCreery's analysis of text and image in the accounts of adulterous, or at least illicit, affairs in the *tête-à-tête* series of the *Town and Country Magazine*, reveals that women's images could act as a hook upon which to attach discussions of male morality, rather than female chastity. While arguing that visual representations remained relatively static throughout the series, she points out that gendered differences did exist in the construction of men's and women's public personas in print, thus echoing concerns raised in the first section of the book. Her argument reminds readers that prescriptive notions of reputation cannot be accepted at face value, by demonstrating that factors in addition to gender played a part in the way that eighteenth-century individuals were presented. Howard's examination of eighteenth-century obituaries and biographies exposes the way these reflect the ambiguities of contemporary beliefs about womanhood. Most importantly, he demonstrates that women's lives were gaining public visibility through the periodical at a time when historians have generally believed that they were increasingly being denied a public presence in person.

PART ONE

Social reputations

CHAPTER TWO

Men about town: representations of foppery and masculinity in early eighteenth-century urban society

PHILIP CARTER

In 1702, the essayist, historian and editor, Abel Boyer, published his *English Theophrastus*, a survey of the 'Manners of the Age: Being the Modern Characters of the Court, the Town and the City'.[1] Boyer's text comprised a miscellaneous collection of sayings and sketches from classical and contemporary writers designed both to entertain and instruct readers in conduct suitable for life in modern urban society. Amongst a series of his own character sketches, Boyer provided a portrait of 'A Beau', one Sir John Foppington, a well-travelled man now resident in London. The study offers an account of Foppington's daily routine, which begins with his waking and running to 'the Oracle' (his mirror) in front of which he 'pays his first Devotions to the dear figure of himself [and] plays the Narcissus with his own Shadow'. For the next two hours, Sir John is occupied with dressing, paying particularly close attention to 'tying his Garters, Careening his Wig, tiffling the Curls, [and] tying and untying the Cravat'. Finally satisfied with his appearance, it is time to leave for a day about the town. Resembling 'a Vessel with all her Rigging without Balast', Foppington is launched from the door 'and down he comes, scented like a Perfumer's Shop' on his way to his first appointment with a seamstress. After shopping, Sir John spends the rest of the morning at White's chocolate house in St James's Street

---

1 Abel Boyer, *The English Theophrastus* (1702). The following references are taken from pp. 52–6.

where he offers an Hour's Compliment to himself in the great Glass,
he faces about and salutes the Company. When he has made his
Cringes round, and play'd over all his Tricks, out comes his fine
Snuff-Box, and his Nose is regal'd a while. After this, he . . . starts
some learned Argument about the newest fashion, and hence
takes occasion to commend Sir Awkward Spruce's Fancy in his
Cloaths.

Lunch is taken at the Blue-Post where, after a glass or two of wine,
'he begins to talk of his Intrigues, and pretends at least a particular
acquaintance with all the ladies'. From there, Sir John journeys to
Will's coffee-house, 'to gather some fragments of Wit, and to hear
the Sentiments of the Criticks about the last new Play, that he may
give an account of it to my Lady Tattle'. With the afternoon taken
up by such diversions, Foppington leaves Will's at six o'clock and
heads for the playhouse. From a side box, he passes 'several enjoyable hours' during which, rather than watch the play, he 'makes his
Court to all the Ladies in general with his Eyes' before 'he takes to
pieces every face, examines every Feature, passes his censure upon
every one, and so on to his Dress [and] . . . in conclusion, sees no
Body Compleat but himself, in the whole House'. Finally, he engages
in a loud conversation with the 'lady in the Mask' who he insists
must provide him with the 'Scandal of the Town . . . at which he
laughs aloud and often, not to shew his satisfaction, but his Teeth'.
After the performance, Foppington visits Locket's for dinner where
he consumes too much wine – more than his usual two glasses – as
a result of which he falls ill and, fearful of the effects of alcohol on
his complexion, confines himself to bed to be tended by his three
physicians.

Boyer's sketch of the trivial, delicate and exhibitionist Sir John
Foppington provides a particularly good example of the characteristics and conduct which early eighteenth-century readers would
have expected to find in an account of the popular figure of the
fop. However, while notable for the comprehensiveness of its char-
acterization, Boyer's study was far from original in its subject matter, or in the themes considered in its execution. The fop proved
a conspicuous figure across a series of literary categories, including
satirical, social documentary and conduct studies, in a range of
text-based genres such as verse, novels, pamphlets and periodical
essays. Representations of fops were also a standard feature of late
seventeenth- and eighteenth-century comedy theatre. Few playwrights
could resist the comic potential and theatrical spectacle of a fop
character, the best known of which include Sir Fopling Flutter from

George Etherege's *The Man of Mode* (1676) and Lord Foppington in Sir John Vanbrugh's *The Relapse* (1696).[2]

It is perhaps surprising, given the conspicuousness of the fop in eighteenth-century literature, that historians have, as yet, paid little attention to describing the type, and to speculating on its place within a wider debate on notions of deviant and acceptable male conduct. The omission is symptomatic of the absence of scholarly accounts of masculinity for the early modern period. This chapter seeks to examine the construction of aspects of masculinity as depicted in early eighteenth-century representations of the stereotypical fop. It needs to be stressed that the sources used in this chapter referred to fops as a social type, rather than as real people who might have been identified and labelled as fops. References to the fop type appeared in sketches carried in periodicals, and freestanding pamphlets and verse taking the form, as in Abel Boyer's study, of essays on 'The Character of the Fop'. Discussions of the fop type also appeared in satirical accounts of other subjects, such as town life, in which fops were depicted as an important manifestation of the fashionable excesses of urban culture. This chapter therefore looks at the construction and function of certain stereotypes of 'desirable' and 'deviant' masculinity, not at discussions of actual behaviour. This decision to focus on representations derives, in part, from the undeveloped state of historical research into eighteenth-century masculinity. Understanding how eighteenth-century social commentators debated masculinity, and how these debates were played out in depictions of widely recognized stereotypes, allows us to discover those qualities that contemporaries viewed as determining acceptable or unacceptable male conduct. Having established the nature of the debate over masculinity, it will in future be possible to build up a more complex picture of early modern masculinity through a study of the interrelationship of advice and action, representation and reality.

The decision to concentrate on the early eighteenth century – here taken as c.1690–1740 – stems from a desire for this chapter to be read alongside an existing, if piecemeal, historiography which has argued that this period saw the emergence of 'modern' standards of male and female gender identity in a rapidly developing urban culture. Central to this thesis is the claim that sexual beha-

---

2 Pictorial images of the fop type were uncommon in the first half of the eighteenth century. Images, when found, took the form of illustrations on pamphlet frontispieces. Visual representations became more common from the 1760s with the increasing popularity of the caricature print.

viour proved the key determinant of acceptable and unacceptable masculinity in the early eighteenth-century town.[3] In contrast, it is argued here that early eighteenth-century debates on masculinity defined their subject by reference to social rather than sexual criteria. Attention is given to representations of the fop, a character which historians have mistakenly identified as a sexual deviant whose conduct was determined by a 'homosexual' orientation. It is argued that a historiography that stresses the importance of sexuality in delineating the boundaries between acceptable and unacceptable forms of masculinity exaggerates the importance of sexual deviancy and the figure of the male sodomite, at the expense of what, to contemporaries, would have been the more familiar fop type, ridiculed less for sexual activity than for a range of social misdeeds.

The power of the fop stereotype in eighteenth-century literature derived from its ability to combine a series of traditionally undesirable features, such as male displays of vanity, ignorance and irresponsibility, found in earlier images of the Jacobean 'gull' or 'gallant', with new characteristics relevant to an eighteenth-century audience. Early eighteenth-century representations of the fop underwent elaboration, notably in their identification of fops as extrovert and overly refined social actors, located within an emerging urban network of public arenas, three of which – coffee-houses, public parks and theatres – are considered here. The popular depiction of fops as overly refined socialites provided early eighteenth-century satirists and conduct writers with a means of commenting on more general debates concerning changing notions of acceptable and unacceptable male conduct in an urban environment given over to socializing facilitated by displays of politeness.

For its early eighteenth-century advocates, politeness was understood as behaviour that promoted easy and sincere social interaction. Polite theorists encouraged men to adopt such behaviour as a suitably enlightened code of conduct that distanced its proponents from the incivility of earlier societies. However, authors also realized that the dissemination of politeness was not without its potential pitfalls. It was recognized that many would-be gentlemen interpreted politeness less as refined and relaxed social intercourse than as a strict adherence to established codes of civility or ceremony.

3 Anthony Simpson, 'Masculinity and control: the prosecution of sex offences in eighteenth-century London' (unpub. Ph.D. thesis, New York University, 1984); Randolph Trumbach, 'Sex, gender and sexual identity in modern culture: male sodomy and female prostitution in enlightenment England', in John C. Fout, ed., *Forbidden History: The State, Society and the Regulation of Sexuality in Modern Europe* (1992). These and other studies receive an uncritical review in Tim Hitchcock, 'Redefining sex in eighteenth-century England' *HWJ* 41 (1996), pp. 73–90.

The result produced artificial conduct by which 'men of ceremony', as they were often termed, reduced social encounters to a laborious display of formal, and essentially anti-social, manners. Conduct writers were similarly critical of men whose behaviour was thought to be too refined. Excessive politeness stemmed from an overexposure to trivial or fashionable sources of refinement. Commentators drew particular attention to the detrimental effects of an overly 'polite' education and to the dangers of men spending too much time in female society. Individuals who failed to heed warnings would, it was argued, be in danger of adopting feminine characteristics, equating politeness with a renunciation of masculine identity. Such qualities were regularly found in descriptions of the early eighteenth-century fop.

The remainder of this chapter is divided into four parts. Part one provides a brief discussion and critique of existing studies that consider the nature of masculine identity in eighteenth-century England. This is followed by an examination of early eighteenth-century representations of fops, revealing the foppish personality to be a combination of traditional and more modern aspects of social deviance, with particular emphasis being given to the image of fops as exhibitionistic and affected social actors. Part three places discussions of fops in the context of a general eighteenth-century debate concerning the merits and potential ill-effects of the diffusion of politeness and its impact on contemporary notions of deviant and acceptable male conduct. The concluding section explains the popularity of the fop type in the early eighteenth century in terms of its usefulness to conduct writers of different political persuasions confronting the relationship between masculinity and polite society.

Historiography

A growing interest in images of masculinity in the past owes much to an understanding of sexuality and gender roles as socially constructed. This thesis, in developing the theoretical standpoint adopted in feminist, women's and gay histories, has stimulated attempts to understand masculinity as a subject worthy of historical investigation, creating what John Tosh has termed a 'gendered history of men'. Such studies seek to highlight the importance of discussions of masculinity to historical communities, and so to question the traditional identification of women alone as ' "carriers" of gender, because their reproductive role was held to define their place in society and their characters'. In so doing, men's histories

challenge prevailing notions of 'hegemonic masculinity' and seek
to develop a more nuanced understanding of masculinity as a complex series of shifting social and cultural constructions.[4] Providing
an understanding of male conduct as gendered is intended to open
up new fields of historical enquiry, as well as to supplement existing
areas of research into the relations of gender, race and class with
information and insight into the structure and mechanisms of patriarchal authority.

Much of the research that has been undertaken so far in this
field has focused on writing a history of nineteenth- and twentieth-
century masculinities. This emphasis owes a great debt to the attention that feminist and women's historians have given to tracing the
origins of contemporary concepts of gender identity. Historians
of masculinity have since identified the emergence of a notion of
male conduct proposed by bourgeois educators and social commentators during the period 1840–1930.[5] Studies produced during
the 1980s by scholars such as Norman Vance, James Mangan and
James Walvin describe a shift from early Victorian codes of ideal
male conduct, which associated masculinity with a concept of 'muscular Christianity', displayed through moral courage, earnestness
and responsible piety, to a later emphasis on neo-stoical hardiness,
athleticism and discipline enshrined in public school culture.[6]

The attention given to the modern period is in contrast to relatively few studies examining the eighteenth century. This shortfall is
notable given the considerable interest shown in the proliferation
of eighteenth-century discussions of deviant sexuality – those phe-
nomena, such as sexual hybridization, prostitution and pornography,
that were judged as being outside the boundaries of legal or social
acceptability.[7] An issue given particular consideration in such works
is eighteenth-century representations of male homosexuality. Interest in this subject has contributed to an already well-developed tradition of gay studies greatly inspired during the late 1970s and 1980s
by Michel Foucault. In the introduction to his proposed six-volume

4 John Tosh, 'What should historians do with masculinity? Reflections on nineteenth-
century Britain' *HWJ* 38 (1994), p. 180.

5 Michael Roper and John Tosh, eds, *Manful Assertions: Masculinities in Britain since
1800* (1991), esp. pp. 4–8.

6 On 'muscular Christianity' see Norman Vance, *The Sinews of the Spirit: The Ideal of
Christian Manliness in Victorian Literature and Religious Thought* (Cambridge, 1985). The
theme of neo-stoicism is discussed in James Mangan and James Walvin, eds, *Manliness and
Morality: Middle-Class Masculinity in Britain and America, 1800–1940* (Manchester, 1987).

7 These subjects are considered in, amongst others, Robert P. Maccubbin, ed., '*Tis
Nature's Fault. Unauthorized Sexuality in the Enlightenment* (Cambridge, 1987); George S.
Rousseau and Roy Porter, eds, *Sexual Underworlds of the Enlightenment* (Manchester, 1987).

History of Sexuality (1976), Foucault stressed the need to understand modern notions of sexuality, including homosexuality, not as expressions of biological truth but as inventions or social constructions specific to the late nineteenth century.[8]

Foucault's dating of the invention of the modern homosexual type, understood as an individual whose exclusive sexual orientation denoted an effeminate and passive personality, has provoked debate amongst historians. In contrast to scholars such as Jeffrey Weeks who validate Foucault's findings, others have suggested that the emergence of the modern homosexual can be traced to the appearance of homosexual subcultures in late seventeenth and early eighteenth-century western Europe.[9] This thesis has been most eloquently expressed by scholars such as the American gender historian, Randolph Trumbach, who identifies the early eighteenth century as a crucial period for both the invention of a definition of the modern homosexual male, and the emergence of modern concepts of male and female gender identity.

Trumbach bases the first of these claims on his identification of the appearance of an early eighteenth-century urban subculture of meeting places and semi-clandestine homosexual brothels where an increasingly coherent and self-conscious group of exclusively 'homosexual' men met for sex. Participants in this culture, labelled 'mollies' by contemporaries, were popularly characterized as misogynist and effeminate individuals whose effeminate identity entailed transvestism, adoption of female names, and imitation of female speech and conduct.[10] The emergence of the molly is explained as a response to changing relations between men and women. Traditional distinctions between the sexes were, Trumbach argues, eroded with the rise of companionate marriage. Within this new role, male and female social habits became increasingly interdependent. As a result, men were required to distinguish themselves from women through the creation of a distinct male identity defined in terms of sexual behaviour. For Trumbach, the molly was an individual who

8 Michel Foucault, *The History of Sexuality. An Introduction* (Engl. trans., 1978).

9 Jeffrey Weeks, *Sex, Politics and Society. The Regulation of Sexuality Since 1800* (1982).

10 Trumbach's discussion of an emerging 'homosexual' subculture first appeared in 'London's sodomites: homosexual behaviour and western culture in the early eighteenth century' *JSH* 11 (1977–8), pp. 1–33. The function of this subculture for the development of modern notions of masculinity and femininity is proposed in Trumbach, 'The birth of the queen: sodomy and the emergence of gender equality in modern culture, 1660–1750', in Martin B. Duberman *et al.*, eds, *Hidden from History: Reclaiming the Gay and Lesbian Past* (1991). Trumbach's thesis is worth detailed analysis given that it is widely cited in studies of eighteenth-century sexuality and gender construction. See, for example, Kristina Straub, *Sexual Suspects: Eighteenth-Century Players and Sexual Ideology* (Princeton, NJ, 1992).

compromised masculine identity through participation in same-sex sexual activity and served as a 'wall of separation between the genders'; thus, the molly made possible 'an unprecedented development of equality between the other two genders' while serving to demonstrate 'what awaited a man who tried to cross the boundary between sexual desire in the two legitimated genders'.[11]

Trumbach's notion of effeminacy as the product of same-sex sexuality leads him to argue that eighteenth-century commentators also equated other examples of effeminate male conduct with the sexual deviation of the sodomite, and hence with the emerging molly stereotype. This is most clearly seen in his consideration of the representation of the fop, which Trumbach believes to have become subsumed within the prevailing definition of effeminacy established in the molly connection between effeminacy and sodomy. He argues for an eighteenth-century redefinition of the fop from the seventeenth-century image of a vain and elaborately dressed fool, to one in which fops' identification as effeminate denoted and derived from participation in homosexual acts. Redefinitions of effeminacy thus prompted what Trumbach terms the 'transformation of the fop into the molly', so that, 'after 1720 the fop's effeminacy ... came to be identified with the effeminacy of the then emerging role of the exclusive adult sodomite – known in the ordinary language of his day as a *molly*'.[12]

Trumbach's thesis can be questioned at two points. Firstly, it posits the existence of a specific eighteenth-century use of the term 'effeminacy', based on the act of sodomy and the culture of a specific homosexual type. This fails to acknowledge the alternative definitions and applications of the concept of effeminacy – a complex eighteenth-century idea – that appeared in satirical, political, behavioural and sexual discourses. Secondly, Trumbach's belief in an eighteenth-century equation between the molly and fop types reduces the latter to a representation of sexual deviancy based on participation in sodomitical acts. As is clear from the brief account of Sir John Foppington's character and activities cited above, such a reductionist interpretation of masculinity can be accused not only of failing to recognize the complexities of eighteenth-century representations of the fop stereotype but also of attempting to conflate two quite distinct representations of deviant masculinity: one, the molly, being sexual in origin, and misogynist, transvestite and

11 Trumbach, 'Birth of the queen', p. 140.
12 Ibid., p. 134.

clandestine in practice; the other, the fop, being social, flamboyant, vigorously heterosocial and, above all, conspicuous.[13]

Recently, attempts to equate the histories of male identity and male sexuality have come in for criticism with the emergence of a more sophisticated understanding of masculinity in past societies. Susan Amussen has argued that sixteenth- and seventeenth-century definitions of manhood were 'not based on sexual activity' but on social qualities, including independence and honour, that were increasingly cultivated and defended through recourse to the Church and the law courts rather than to personal violence.[14] However, despite her identification of a more complex notion of 'early modern' masculinity, Amussen accepts Trumbach's claim that 'modern' gender relations originated in the early eighteenth century when definitions of acceptable and deviant masculinity came to be grounded in terms of male sexual behaviour. At present, it is left to scholars such as Anthony Fletcher to revise Trumbach's reading of the eighteenth century; something which he does more by ignoring than by criticizing the thesis.[15] Fletcher rightly points to the eighteenth century's cultivation of a new notion of polite or refined masculinity, although his interpretation is not without its shortcomings. Fletcher's equation of male refinement with élite gentlemanliness underestimates the cross-class influence that theories of politeness had amongst eighteenth-century writers who promoted and warned of the dangers of male refinement. To ignore the discussions that accompanied the promotion of new standards of masculinity is to overlook the nature, function and significance of the fop stereotype, one of the most popular figures in the debate concerning aspects of acceptable and deviant masculinity.

This tendency to overlook the significance of the fop derives from historians' readiness to accept Trumbach's attempts to collapse the fop into the molly type. Trumbach's attempt to trace the origin and subsequent vilification of the homosexual type has led him to

13 The attention paid to delineating and condemning social misconduct should not obscure the fact that discussions of the type did make a number of references to fops' sexual identity and activity. Sketches identified the fop with a range of sexual behaviour, including homosexuality, as well as asexuality, and fulfilled and unfulfilled heterosexuality. Philip Carter, 'Mollies, fops and men of feeling: aspects of male effeminacy and masculinity in Britain, c.1700–1780' (unpub. D.Phil. thesis, Oxford University, 1995), pp. 56–9, 114–26.

14 Susan Dwyer Amussen, ' "The part of a Christian man": the cultural politics of manhood in early modern England', in Susan Dwyer Amussen and Mark A. Kishlansky, eds, *Political Culture and Cultural Politics in Early Modern England* (Manchester, 1995), p. 227.

15 Anthony Fletcher, *Gender, Sex & Subordination in England, 1500–1800* (New Haven, CT, 1995), esp. ch. 16.

overemphasize the importance of the molly in early eighteenth-century discussions of gender identity. Thus, while Trumbach and others are correct in identifying the emergence of a new type of male sodomite, it remains that the predominant eighteenth-century image of unmanliness was that of the fop, not the relatively obscure molly. Descriptions of the molly appeared in what might be termed 'less respectable' publications, including prose or verse pamphlets specifically discussing sexuality, commentaries on the urban underworld or more risqué social satires; in contrast, discussions of fops regularly featured in the more 'respectable' format of essay periodicals, serious or satirical social commentaries, courtesy books and conduct guides. Eighteenth-century readers of periodical, social documentary and behavioural literature would have seen the debate over notions of masculinity as focusing predominantly on men's social conduct, and would have encountered the fop type in this context. It was the figure of the socially deviant fop that commentators invariably presented, and readers acknowledged, as the key figure in their attempts to define the boundaries between acceptable and deviant male conduct.

The fop

Discussions of the fop type were not new to the eighteenth century. Jacobean critiques of male vanity or irresponsibility had illustrated unacceptable forms of conduct with reference to the stereotypical 'gallant' or 'gull'. The dramatist, Thomas Dekker, provided a good example of such figures in his mock conduct guide, *The Gull's Hornbook* (1608), which informed men on the behaviour becoming a gallant. Under Dekker's instruction, the gallant emerged as a vain, idle, insolent 'show off' who spent his days dressing in elaborate clothes, lazing around, insulting the watch and whoring. The term 'fop' also predated the eighteenth century, though its usage was not yet associated with these qualities. Dating from the mid-fifteenth century, 'fop' appears to have been employed as an alternative label for a fool, which according to the *Oxford English Dictionary* derived from the Latin *fatuus* via the French term *fat*. Towards the end of the seventeenth century, 'fop' developed a more specific meaning as dramatists began to equate instances of folly with a specifically 'gallant' display of vain and superficial conduct. By the late seventeenth century, references to gallants were becoming increasingly rare. Men who displayed characteristics such as vanity, pride and foolishness during the 1700s were usually described as 'fops'. Eighteenth-century fops were commonly depicted as young men who, like Boyer's Sir John, were characterized as narcissistic, idle, superficial and exhibitionist. This shift from an understanding of fop as fool to foolish man of fashion was clearly evident in eighteenth-century dictionary definitions, though traditional associations also persisted. Nathan Bailey's *Universal Etymological English Dictionary* (1721) defined the fop as 'a fantastick fellow, one who is over nice and affected in his Dress, Speech and Behaviour'. According to Thomas Dyche's *New General English Dictionary* (1735), the fop was 'a whimsical empty fellow, one whose mind is totally taken up with modes and fashions', while Samuel Johnson's *Dictionary of the English Language* (1755) defined the fop as a 'man of small understanding and much ostentation'.

The prominence of references to dress and appearance in these definitions provides a good example of one foppish trait which continued to feature in references to the type – whether identified as gull, gallant or fop – throughout the early modern period. The typical eighteenth-century fop, like his predecessors, was renowned for spending a large amount of time decorating his unimpressive physique with colourful and fashionable dress, an elaborate and meticulously groomed wig, cosmetics and perfumes. Costume historians have shown that the style of acceptable male dress, a three-piece suit consisting of waistcoat, breeches and coat, finished with tricorn hat, changed little during the first three-quarters of the eighteenth century, with developments in fashion being variations on this theme. Fops' dress tended to follow the prevailing styles of the day. Distinctions between smart, acceptable male appearance and foppish dress were found in fops' love of excessively colourful fabrics and impractical accessories, which men of fashion spent hours discussing, buying and arranging.

The durability of the image of fops as vain individuals preoccupied with fashion indicates that satirists considered some forms of appearance and social behaviour incompatible with early modern notions of acceptable masculinity. Fops' fine appearance, far from denoting social status or professional authority, was deemed symptomatic of a superficial and trivial character. Critics censured fops for time-consuming and emulative dressing that left irresponsible men incapable of fulfilling public duties. Fops' irresponsibility was explained in terms of an innate foolishness that distanced 'men of fashion' from the more disciplined, rational and learned 'men of sense', as worthy males were often referred to in the period.

A number of discussions of foppish vanity also commented on the impact of fine dress on more sober individuals with whom fops came into contact. The image of heavily decorated fops exuding wig powder, powder and perfumes, and carrying all manner of accessories including canes, swords and ribbons, proved a stock figure in accounts detailing the hazards of the modern world. John Gay's poem, 'Trivia; or, the Art of Walking the Streets of London' (1716), offered sound advice when warning readers of the pleasures and perils of metropolitan street life: encountering the bewigged fop 'pass with Caution by/from his Shoulder Clouds of Powder fly'.[16] Fops on the street, if seen early enough, could be avoided; however, escape was less easy if, like the essayist Joseph Addison, one encountered a man of fashion as a passenger in a carriage. Addison, writing in his essay periodical *The Spectator* under the pseudonym Mr Spectator, described the discomfort caused by his sitting too close to a 'dirty fop' whose fine clothes and wig had become soiled. Forced into confinement with this individual, Mr Spectator complained both of the foppish character that sought to dress in this fashion and of the discomfort that the fop caused to his fellow passengers by exposing them to the smell of an excess of stale perfumes and hair powder. This collection of rank odours and powders rendered the wearer intrusive to a neighbour's privacy and thus was anti-social. As Mr Spectator claimed, cleanliness and a smart but moderate appearance served as 'a Mark of Politeness'; 'no one unadorned of this Virtue' was able to 'go into Company without giving a manifest Offence'.[17]

Few fops were described as being this unconscious of the impression their clothes had on others. With little to recommend them other than their dress, fops were characterized as dependent on displaying their appearance, rather than their personalities, to gain public recognition. Reliance on appearance made eighteenth-century fops notably sociable creatures, though fops' lack of integrity meant that their love of social gatherings was motivated less by genuine fellow-feeling than by a desire to 'show off' to their contemporaries. This image of the fop as a social nuisance proved a central feature of eighteenth-century representations of the type. Discussions placed new emphasis on alternative aspects of deviant male conduct that confirmed fops as products of their age – the successful fop stereotype proving sufficiently adaptable to provide satirists with opportunities

16 John Gay, 'Trivia; or, the Art of Walking the Streets of London' (1716), in Vinton A. Dearing, ed., *John Gay: Poetry and Prose* 2 vols (Oxford, 1974), I, p. 145.
17 *Spectator*, no. 631 (10 Dec. 1714), in *The Spectator* (1711–12, 1714), ed. Donald F. Bond, 5 vols (Oxford, 1965), V, pp. 156–7.

to comment on new aspects of urban geography and the activities that took place in these locations. Accounts drew particular attention to the attempts of characters like Sir John Foppington to create a reputation for refined living through their energetic participation in the town's most fashionable arenas of public assembly.

Of course, the image of the fop putting himself on public show was not new to the period. Dekker's gallant was an *habitué* of St Paul's Cathedral where he joined other members of London's fashionable society in promenading and socializing in the nave between services.[18] Where references to early eighteenth-century fops differed was in the increasing range of available social spaces in which such figures were able to exhibit themselves to onlookers. This development mirrored the growing interest paid to the personal and societal benefits, and to the potential problems, of polite sociability in public places of assembly. Satirists and conduct writers used the fop type as a means of commenting on the nature of this phenomenon as it pertained to emerging notions of correct and incorrect forms of sociable masculinity.

Fops' attempts to exhibit themselves in front of an audience were certainly made easier by an expansion in the range of places for association and recreation.[19] The late seventeenth century saw the emergence of urban locations that facilitated public contact in an environment less influenced by court and clerical interests. These institutions developed in response to new forms of commercial prosperity and to the – albeit still limited – interaction of an increasingly diverse urban population composed of aristocrats, gentry, pseudo-gentry, professionals and traders. New modes of sociability were increasingly defined as conduct required for participation in an expanding network of commercially run meeting places that offered opportunities for civilized contact between private individuals of different social groups. Points of assembly such as coffee-houses, promenades, parks and pleasure gardens, which became popular during the late seventeenth and early eighteenth centuries, provided new arenas for socializing and recreation; moreover, these

18 'How a Gallant should behave himself in Paul's Walks', in Thomas Dekker, *The Gull's Hornbook* (1608), ed. R.B. McKerrow (New York, 1971), ch. 4.

19 These developments comprise what Jürgen Habermas has termed the emergence of the 'bourgeois public sphere'. Habermas sees the public sphere as a physical and ideological phenomenon by which private individuals (not exclusively bourgeois) came together via the interaction of print media and purpose-built social spaces to create an anonymous 'public' distinct from, and often critical of, public authority. See his *The Transformation of the Public Sphere* (1962; Engl. trans. Cambridge, MA, 1989), esp. pp. 29–43. Empirical evidence of the emerging network of social spaces is provided in Mark Girouard, *The English Town* (New Haven, CT, 1990), chs 7–9.

developments occurred alongside an increase in the number and an improvement of the facilities of existing arenas such as theatres.

Coffee-houses had first appeared in the mid-seventeenth century when they had been viewed suspiciously as centres that promoted radical political association, idleness and the consumption of enervating beverages. However, the attractions of an institution providing facilities for debate and recreation proved considerable amongst members of a growing professional class. By the early eighteenth century, coffee-houses were seen to have a more positive role in the development of a sociable, yet virtuous, urban culture, as new social arenas in which men from diverse backgrounds could participate equally in critical discussion and civilized recreation.[20]

Not surprisingly, coffee-houses also proved a popular setting for descriptions of attention-seeking fops who paraded and flaunted themselves in front of more respectable patrons. By using the coffee-house as a forum for displays of fashionable dress, fops were depicted as ignoring its function as a venue for the more serious business of political, philosophical or professional debate. Fops were further censured for disturbing those predominantly male patrons who engaged in worthy activities such as reading or serious discussion. Sir John Foppington, as we have seen, was typical of many men of fashion, viewing conversation at the coffee-house not as an opportunity to exchange opinions on business or current affairs, but as a chance to impose on others a display of his modishness and refinement by complimenting Sir Awkward Spruce's dress, or by using 'a few modish lewd words' to 'shew he has convers'd with the French *Petit Maîtres*'.[21]

While undoubtedly keen to impress both a sober coffee-house clientele and rival men of fashion who also gathered there, fops were thought to be principally concerned with the effect that their exhibitionism had on women. Naturally, this pursuit of female compliments led fops to patronize mixed arenas. Two of the most popular eighteenth-century locations for such contact were the promenade and the park. In good weather, London's polite society did much of its socializing along the public walks located at the Inns of Court and the Mall, or in parks, notably St James's and the 'Ring' at Hyde Park. London's example was also followed in a number of provincial towns, where new walks and gardens were established in

20 By 1700 there were an estimated 2,000 establishments in London. Aytoun Ellis, *The Penny Universities: A History of the Coffee Houses* (1956), p. xiv. On the emergence of coffee-houses see Steve Pincus, ' "Coffee politicians does create": coffeehouses and Restoration political culture' *Journal of Modern History* 67 (1995), pp. 807–34.

21 Boyer, *English Theophrastus*, pp. 52–3.

the period 1690–1740.[22] By the early eighteenth century, demand for more sophisticated public entertainments led to the creation of commercial pleasure gardens at Vauxhall (formerly the New Spring Gardens, established 1732), Marylebone (1738) and Ranelagh (1742). Garden owners sought to attract custom by depicting their respective institutions as locations of unrivalled civility, a reputation that quickly caught on amongst members of polite society eager for new opportunities to display modish refinements.[23]

Venues intended to serve as arenas for displays of dress and manners were naturally popular among vain men of fashion eager to exhibit their sophistications to polite promenaders. As in the coffee-house, fops employed a range of strategies to maximize their profile in the company of other modish individuals. Some, like Sir John Foppington, drew attention to themselves by dressing in conspicuous clothes: on a typical day, the beau might be dressed in a 'milk white Suit, designing to shew himself in it that Evening in the Park'.[24] Aside from providing an ideal location to be seen, the relative civility and cleanliness of a paved promenade was also more conducive to the wearing of such fine dress. John Gay noted the difficulties experienced by a fop in the street who 'At ev'ry Step he dreads the Wall to lose/And risques, to save a Coach, his red-heel'd Shoes'. Such hazards were less likely to be found on 'the Paths of fair Pell-Mell/Safe are thy Pavements, grateful is thy Smell!'[25]

Fops could also attract attention in the park by positioning themselves in conspicuous situations or locations. A discussion of a group of 'fawning Fools' from an anonymous verse essay of 1709 noted the practice for fops 'Like Talbot at Pell Mell' to 'ride in his Chair/ When other Folks are walking in the Air'.[26] Again, riding in a chair or coach served to protect fops' elegant appearance from the rigours of the weather and the crowd. Gay commented on the beau's habit of touring London in a 'gilded Carriage' and 'with Disdain/Views

22 The development and character of metropolitan park culture is discussed in David H. Solkin, *Painting for Money. The Visual Arts and the Public Sphere in Eighteenth-Century England* (New Haven, CT, 1991), ch. 4. For provincial venues see Peter Borsay, *The English Urban Renaissance: Culture and Society in the Provincial Town, 1660–1770* (Oxford, 1989), pp. 162–72.

23 The author of the anonymous *Description of Ranelagh Rotundo and Gardens* (1762) deemed this particular venue ideally suited for 'genteel and polite company' (p. 5). Satirists offered a different image of a garden culture in which fops' excesses featured prominently. 'The Temple of Luxury, the Theatre of Madness [and] the Habitation of Folly' was how one commentator characterized the recently opened Ranelagh: *Ranelagh House: A Satire* (1742), p. 5.

24 Boyer, *English Theophrastus*, p. 56.

25 Gay, 'Trivia', pp. 145, 150.

26 *St James's Park. A Satyr* (1709), p. 13.

spatter'd Passengers, all drench'd with Rain'.[27] Later in the century, patrons of commercial pleasure gardens made use of the spaces provided for dining, listening to music, or resting, to make themselves more visible by securing a prominent vantage point from which they could survey, and be surveyed by, other promenaders. Two devotees of the garden circuit, the foppish Mr and Mrs Beau Tibbs, described in Oliver Goldsmith's *The Citizen of the World* (1762), spent much of their visit to Vauxhall securing 'a genteel box, a box where they might see and be seen, one, as they expressed it, in the very focus of public view'.[28] Fops who failed to attract attention through their dress or position could always resort to more intrusive behaviour. The 'fickle Fop' described in a 1709 account of the Ring at Hyde Park created a spectacle through a 'Puppy-Show', which consisted of his laughing 'immoderately, vain, and loud/To raise the Wonder of th' attentive Crowd'.[29] The 'Peacock-Fops' described in *A Satyr on the Mall* (1733) provided onlookers with an 'empty Show' that saw them 'Chant, adjust the Ruffle, or twirl the Cane about'.[30] Fops like Beau Tibbs applied more direct tactics, displaying a degree of overfamiliarity that frequently characterized foppish behaviour in public arenas. Recalling an earlier visit to Vauxhall gardens, the fictional author of *The Citizen of the World* described how Tibbs had first sought their acquaintance by chasing him and his companion before saluting them with 'all the familiarity of an old friend', although they had clearly never met before.[31]

The time before the evening promenade was often spent in a visit to the playhouse. Satirical accounts of fops' daily routine usually included some reference to their regular attendance of the theatre, which arguably provided them with their most important arena for exhibitionism. Here, the fop was likely to come into contact with a captive audience made up of members of fashionable and leisured society who could be subjected to displays of foppish vanity. Few fops considered the theatre a source of entertainment in itself. As before, those wishing to create a spectacle had a number of techniques at their disposal. The time between arrival at the theatre and the beginning of the performance provided fops with an ideal opportunity to display themselves from a variety of locations within

27 Gay, 'Trivia', p. 158.
28 Oliver Goldsmith, *The Citizen of the World* (1762), in Arthur Friedman, ed., *The Collected Works of Oliver Goldsmith* 5 vols (Oxford, 1965), II, p. 295.
29 *The Circus. A Satyr on the RING in Hide Park* (1709), p. 7.
30 *A Satyr on the Mall in Great Britain* (1733), p. 8.
31 Goldsmith, *Citizen*, in *Works*, II, p. 229.

the auditorium. Sir John Foppington, for example, was typical in his use of this time to judge and criticize the appearance of his rivals while treating the audience to a display of his teeth. Others were more energetic in displaying their fashionable dress and refined manners at different places in the auditorium. One late seventeenth-century account described how the 'Nice, Affected Beau . . . soberly enters the House; first in one side Box, then in t'other; next in the Pit, and sometimes in the Galleries, that the Vulgar sort may as well behold and admire the Magnificence of his Apparel, as those of Quality'.[32] The interval was likewise spent standing on the benches, 'to show his Shape, his Leg, his Scarlet Stockings, his Meen and his Airs'. At the start of the next act, he 'descends bowing this way, that way, and the other way, that the Ladies in the Boxes may take notice of him'.[33]

The most suitable location for such displays was, of course, the stage. Patrons were able to gain access to this prime location due to the provision of stage seating in most early eighteenth-century theatres. Though the worst position to view plays, stage seats were naturally popular with fops, proving the most effective location to display clothes or manners. In 1711, *The Spectator*'s discussion of a production of Francis Beaumont and John Fletcher's *Philaster; or, Love Lies a Bleeding* (1687) also included reference to the antics of a 'sort of beau'. The beau had entered from a side box, and had made his way to the stage where:

> [he] . . . display'd his fine Cloaths, made two or three feint Passes at the Curtain with his Cane, then faced about and appear'd at t'other Door: Here he affected to survey the whole House, bow'd and smil'd at Random, and then show'd his Teeth which were some of them indeed very white. After this he retir'd behind the Curtain, and obliged us with several Views of his Person from every Opening.

Nor did these intrusions end with the play's commencement. This particular fop even appeared on the set being 'frequently in the Prince's Apartment . . . and the Hunting Match' in Act 4, and 'very Forward at the Rebellion' in Act 5.[34]

---

32 *The Character of the Beaux* (1699), p. 13.
33 Ibid., p. 15.
34 No. 240 (5 Dec. 1711), in *The Spectator*, II, p. 434. This account offers an interesting intersection between discussions of the fop as a stereotype and as a real person who may have attended the performance. Given that *The Spectator*'s accounts of town life were often allegoric, it is difficult to say whether this reference is an account of actual behaviour. It is more likely that the description served to ridicule a range of irritating habits performed by young men at the theatre.

Other fops drew attention to themselves by holding conversations during the performance or by directing comments at the play itself. It was not necessary for such judgements to be based on critical acumen, merely that they be delivered with sufficient bravura to impress an audience with the speaker's dress, wit or refined speaking voice. The fop described in *Hell Upon Earth* (1729), a miscellaneous collection of anecdotes concerning urban living, was typical of many who spent their time at the theatre in the guise of a 'true Critick' who 'to prove himself one of penetrating Judgement he'll curse the Actors ... though all the time his Eyes are upon the Ladies, and his Thoughts lifted up that some of them *per* Chance, may be smitten with his fine Appearance'.[35] Fops' lack of interest in the production was further revealed by their habit of leaving the theatre while the play was in progress – providing them with further opportunity to create a disturbance, and hence a spectacle, and to perform a similar routine in other playhouses during the same night.

Masculinity and polite society

The conspicuousness of fops' exhibitionism proved particularly acute in a society where more and more people sought, and could afford to seek, a reputation for refinement cultivated by involvement in polite social spaces. The importance of the eighteenth century as a period of social refinement has long been realized by historians. Norbert Elias's 1939 study, *The Civilizing Process*, identified the century as the one that saw a significant dissemination of courtly manners to members of an aspiring, city-based, commercially minded bourgeoisie. More recent studies have further emphasized the importance attached to social refinement as a goal obtainable through individual participation in a developing consumer society. Lawrence E. Klein has drawn attention to the efforts of early eighteenth-century writers, such as Anthony Ashley Cooper, 3rd Earl of Shaftesbury, and Whig essayists Joseph Addison and Richard Steele, to provide moral validation for modern forms of commercial wealth-formation through new theories of politeness.[36]

The attention that such writers attached to the value of refined

35 *Hell Upon Earth; or, Town in an Uproar* (1729), p. 35.
36 Norbert Elias, *The Civilizing Process* (1939), trans. Edmund Jephcott, 2 vols (Oxford, 1978); Lawrence E. Klein, *Shaftesbury and the Culture of Politeness. Moral Discourse and Cultural Politics in Early Eighteenth-Century England* (Cambridge, 1994).

conduct in urban commercial society had clear resonances for men. The emerging attractions of refined sociability stimulated a need for conduct writers to develop existing notions of acceptable masculinity – to create, in effect, a model of refined masculine conduct – that would allow urban males to display a capacity for refinement while maintaining their masculine identity. This was all the more necessary given the importance attached to contact with what writers identified as 'virtuous' female company in localities such as the promenade or the public garden.[37] Commentators who called for closer integration between the sexes were at pains to emphasize that refinement was not to be promoted at the expense of existing masculine virtues, such as integrity, independence and self-command, qualities typically associated with the 'man of sense'. Ideally, commentators sought to modernize existing requirements with a refinement befitting the inhabitants of enlightened society.

Writers seeking to educate their readership in the characteristics of refined masculinity emphasized a notion of polite male conduct that enabled men to act with a form of politeness that distinguished them both from women and from other boorish or superficial men. Two basic requirements had to be met: genuine sociability was to be motivated by natural goodwill; and care had to be taken not to offend one's companions. Goodwill, understood to be an altruistic impulse, was frequently described as 'complaisance', an important quality implying a display of genuine fellow-feeling and a desire to please, rather than the mere art of pleasing. Emphasis on goodwill as the motive for virtuous social interaction formed an important and much-discussed theme in the papers discussing male conversation that appeared in *The Tatler* and *The Spectator*, two of the most popular and influential eighteenth-century guides to the improvement of male manners. For Richard Steele, writing in *The Tatler*, conversation served as the foundation of sociable conduct and, thus, as a crucial component of an idealized model of refined masculinity. In order to fulfil this role, speakers were urged to treat one another as equals. Such an attitude could only be derived from expressions of relaxed and natural social affection. Thus, in his description of 'a Gentleman perfectly qualified for Conversation', Steele considered the talents of erudition, wit and good breeding to be inferior to benevolence. In a later paper, Steele deemed

37 On the benefits of men's involvement in female society and the ambiguous status this afforded women see Sylvana Tomaselli, 'The enlightenment debate on women' *HWJ* 20 (1985), pp. 101–24.

equality 'the Life of Conversation'. As a result, 'Benevolence must become the Rule of Society, and he that is most obliging must be most diverting'.[38] Complaisance proved an equally important theme in *The Spectator*'s discussions of acceptable social conduct. Addison, writing in no. 169, described compassion, benevolence and humanity as essential qualities for easing the difficulties that men experienced in their personal and public lives. A capacity for complaisance was again upheld over wit and good breeding, as a natural force 'generally born within us', without which 'there is no Society or Conversation to be kept up in the World'.[39]

Thus, genuine fellow-feeling produced a brand of sociability that was characterized by integrity and ease. At the same time, easiness was not expected to degenerate into an unregulated display of social affection. Such displays would indicate a lack of self-control and prove embarrassing to one's companions, and anti-social to observers. In order to avoid such situations, commentators characterized polite masculinity in terms of a second important characteristic, that of a regulated display of manners, as much concerned with avoiding offence as with promoting goodwill. Discussions emphasized the importance of men controlling their conversation so as to avoid comments or actions that could be deemed indelicate or intrusive. Avoiding such anti-social conduct required that men maintained a dignified, stoical detachment or independence, even from their closest friends. In a later section of *The English Theophrastus*, entitled 'On Conversation, Society, Civility, and Politeness', Abel Boyer stressed that it remained 'highly necessary for a man to avoid too much familiarity in Conversation', reminding readers of the risks involved in all close friendships since 'communication discovers Imperfections that reservedness concealed'.[40]

Again, essays carried in *The Tatler* and *The Spectator* proved influential in this understanding of politeness, developing and promoting it to a wider audience, with contributors providing lessons on acceptable conversational structures for strangers meeting in the busy public arenas. Details of these rules were clearly set out in Richard Steele's account of the 'Man of Conversation'. Steele claimed that, above all other accomplishments, sociable men needed to maintain 'good Judgement' and to avoid 'giving Offence'.[41] Self-control, which

38 No. 45 (23 July 1709), in *The Tatler* (1709–10), ed. Donald F. Bond, 3 vols (Oxford, 1987), I, pp. 325–6.
39 No. 169 (13 Sept. 1711), in *The Spectator*, II, pp. 165–6.
40 Boyer, *English Theophrastus*, p. 104.
41 No. 21 (28 May 1709), in *The Tatler*, I, p. 165.

Steele considered 'the greatest of human Perfections', provided the means for both personal and, more importantly, communal happiness, proving 'the most amiable Quality in the Sight of others'. By regulating their natural inclinations, virtuous men displayed 'a winning Deference to mankind' that facilitated genuine and edifying conversation.[42]

While asserting the attractions of politeness, however, advocates of refined masculinity were not unaware of the potentially problematic nature of a new definition of manliness based on a capacity to participate in civilized public conduct. Polite theorists were conscious that the desire to appear sociable brought with it pressures for the would-be fashionable individual to assume a polite persona at the expense of other important personality traits. It was evident to such commentators that some men understood politeness less as a display of easy, yet respectfully formal, conduct than as an ability to follow and perform codes of manners with meticulous accuracy. Strict observance of these codes left individuals characterized by a stiffness and formality that obstructed pleasant social interaction. Those noted for an over-observance of formal civilities were frequently described, not as polite, but as 'ceremonious'. As important themes in eighteenth-century discussions of social refinement, ceremony and ceremoniousness implied executing accepted rules of civilized behaviour for the purposes of presenting a display of polite conduct. As Johnson put it, 'ceremony' was an 'outside rite' or 'form of civility', and 'ceremonious' conduct was that which was 'observant to the rules of civility; civil and formal to a fault'.[43]

Such formalities proved unacceptable to those who equated sociability with genuine, relaxed and measured displays of social affection. Abel Boyer, for example, believed 'formal Civilities and Ceremonies' to be a 'kind of Tyranny, which render Men antisocial, even in Society itself'.[44] Conduct authors were equally aware that the fashion for gaining a polite reputation was forcing many men to over-expose themselves to refining influences and to adopt conduct incompatible with masculine responsibilities. While a degree of refinement was deemed an essential requirement of eighteenth-century masculinity, conduct guides warned of the debilitating effects of an over-enthusiastic participation in a polite education that consisted of nothing but dancing and French lessons and equipped an

42 No. 176 (25 May 1710), in *The Tatler*, II, p. 459.
43 Samuel Johnson, *Dictionary of the English Language* (1755, repr. 1979).
44 Boyer, *English Theophrastus*, p. 106.

individual for little more than a decorative and leisured drawing-room society.[45]

Pessimistic commentators frequently interpreted men's excessive refinement as an inevitable consequence of living in a society obsessed with fashion and self-image. The author Jonathan Swift, a staunch defender of traditional schooling in the classics, highlighted the damaging impact that the fashion for social education was having on young men. In an edition of *The Intelligencer* periodical in 1728, Swift lamented the decline of traditional education practices, in which upper-class youths were instructed in physically robust and intellectually sobering pursuits, in favour of an education dedicated to instruction in manners, fencing and modern languages provided by entertaining, rather than learned, tutors.

It was a measure of the perceived degree of societal decline that commentators like Swift identified superficiality and ceremoniousness as characteristics associated not just with civilian but also with military life. It was inevitable that soldiers stationed abroad acquired vices commonly associated with continental men. Indeed, Swift believed that by acting as 'the Dictators of Behaviour, Dress, Politeness to all Drawing-Rooms, Operas, Levees, and Assemblies', and 'as the Standard-Patterns of whatever was refined in Dress, Equipage, Conversation or Diversions', soldiers returning from the War of Spanish Succession (1701–13) had served as a conduit by which modern, excessive refinements were transported from Europe to London.[46] Samuel Johnson provided a similarly bleak picture in his slightly later poem, *London* (1737). He lamented the decline of a British character once characterized by 'rustic Grandeur' and 'surly Grace' to one where 'Sense, Freedom, Piety [were] refined away/ Of FRANCE the Mimic, and of SPAIN the Prey'. Johnson identified

---

45 Authors of guides on education considered the dancing master's contribution to upbringing with ambivalence. In order to be deemed polite, men were expected to acquire a capacity for controlled, yet easy, movement through dancing lessons. According to the conduct writer, William Darrell, tuition facilitated the adoption of a poise to 'give a pretty turn to Breeding': *The Gentleman Instructed* 5th edn (1713), p. 20. However, commentators stressed the need for parents to regulate sons' involvement in what was an essentially decorative discipline of use in polite, mixed company. Faced with a choice between incivility and enervating refinement, commentators naturally chose the former. John Locke preferred the natural, if clumsy, manners of the country gentleman to the 'apish, affected Postures' of one taught by 'an ill-fashion'd Dancing-Master': *Some Thoughts Concerning Education* (1693), in *The Educational Writings of John Locke*, ed. James L. Axtell (Cambridge, 1968), p. 310.

46 No. 9 (6–9 July 1728), *The Intelligencer* (1728), ed. James Woolley (Oxford, 1992), pp. 120–1.

this decline in microcosm in the figure of the once heroic 'Warriour dwindled to a Beau'.[47]

Commentators seeking to illustrate the ridiculous consequences of false or excessive politeness frequently did so with reference to the fop type. Fops, as we have seen, were commonly represented as proponents of contrived or artificial behaviour deriving less from a willingness to promote genuine and virtuous sociability than from a desire to appear more refined than, and socially superior to, their peers. For many, fops' misguided competitiveness epitomised an urban culture which, caught up in the frenzy to appear fashionably polite, had lost sight of classically 'manly' values such as heroism, sense and hardiness.

However, discussions of the fop character were not restricted to conservative satirists such as Johnson. References to fops as exponents of overly stiff manners also featured in more progressive discussions of male conduct, which used descriptions of their behaviour to highlight the unacceptable formality of conduct based on ceremoniousness and, through negative example, to educate men in more acceptable forms of polite sociability – that is, a model of refined masculinity balancing sociability with integrity and self-command. Contemporary discussions of fops' involvement in social spaces located three key ways by which their behaviour differed from, and in so doing helped to fashion, emerging notions of acceptable male conduct.

Firstly, fops' interest in attending social arenas was shown to be motivated less by their willingness to engage in genuine and virtuous sociability than by their desire to inhabit arenas ideal for gaining the attention so energetically sought by vain men of fashion. This selfish, rather than sociable, motive often resulted in fops intruding into private parties, either by accosting unfortunate individuals or by the loudness of their conversations, which were generally aimed towards anyone in earshot. Often these conversations caused greater offence on account of their being either inappropriate to the tone of a particular social gathering – ill-timed witticisms in the sober coffee-house environment, for example – or because of their overly personal nature – discussions of intrigues, dalliances, patronage ties and so on that were deemed unsuitable for public conversation in general.

Secondly, having entered into a group, fops' conduct was often revealed to be excessively ceremonious in its adherence to mannered

---

47 Samuel Johnson, 'London. A Poem' (1737), in David Nichol Smith and Edward L. McAdam, eds, *The Poems of Samuel Johnson* (Oxford, 1974), p. 73.

formalities, making not for entertaining social interaction, but for a laborious display of social rituals. In his guide to 'Conversation, Society, Civility and Politeness', Abel Boyer claimed it to be 'one of the most nauseous, mawkish Mortifications under the Sun, for a Man of Sense and Business, to have to do with a punctual finical Fop, that is too Mannerly, and does everything forsooth by Rule and Compass, especially where Quality, Relation, or Authority entitles him to Respect'.[48] Such stultifying attention to manners was also present in the subject matter and delivery of fops' conversation. Boyer believed Sir John Foppington to be a good example of a type of 'superficial Gentlemen [who] wear their Understanding like their Cloaths, always set and formal, and would no more Talk than dress out of Fashion'.[49]

Finally, fops' excessive attention to established social niceties led to their conduct being characterized as overly fastidious and trivial. For many satirists and conduct writers, such attention to social rules led to an excessive or exquisite politeness in which the desire to acquire a reputation for social refinement led certain fops not to 'polish' but to downplay a masculinity they considered brutish and incivil. The effects of this renunciation of established male roles could be seen in the time Sir John Foppington spent at the chocolate house conversing not about suitably 'male' issues of public interest, but about what were considered essentially 'feminine' subjects of fashion, romance and scandal. The degenerative effect of over-refinement was also apparent in the image of fops as physically delicate, another condition associated with the female rather than the male constitution. In certain representations of the type these weaknesses were described as the inevitably ridiculous consequence of a foppish lifestyle. However, many fops were depicted as regarding delicacy more favourably and cultivating it as a characteristic, indicative of an admirable level of refinement. Fops' delicacy was evident in a number of characteristics including susceptibility to illness, a diet of exotic and dainty foods, an avoidance of traditionally male activities such as smoking and drinking alcohol, and a sensitivity to conditions that others experienced without question. Boyer's Sir John Foppington, for example, displayed a typical degree of feebleness in his decision to travel to the chocolate house in a chair since 'he apprehends every breath of Air as much as if it were a Hurricane'.[50]

48 Boyer, *English Theophrastus*, p. 110.
49 Ibid., pp. 57–8.
50 Ibid., p. 53.

A male identity characterized by superficiality or delicacy was clearly at odds with more acceptable forms of masculinity characterized by a synthesis of modern refinement and traditional responsibilities. Men were repeatedly informed of the differences between superficial foppery and sincere refinement, and the attractiveness of this latter identity to mature and 'virtuous' women. This point was well made in the discussion of social types provided in the anonymous *Satyr on the Mall*. While vain women were attracted to the displays of 'Peacock-Fops', more responsible women – 'the FAIR, in whom good Sense and Taste United Shine' – would always reject such triviality in favour of 'The Man genteel, with Sense'; that is, a man who was equally acceptable, equally masculine, in the civilized urban spaces of both leisure and work.[51]

Conclusion

Eighteenth-century commentators drew attention to the stereotype of the fop for a variety of reasons. The fop was an obvious target for ridicule, providing periodical satirists and dramatists with a well-known character type, descriptions of which could always be used for entertaining and comic purposes. Few, however, could read a character sketch of the fop type without being aware of its place within a wider debate concerning standards of masculinity. Certain characteristics of the typical eighteenth-century fop, such as puniness, vanity and foolishness, had been prominent in early seventeenth-century stereotypes of deviant masculinity; however, the eighteenth century's undeniable fascination with fops represented more than a reiteration of long-running concerns over the declining standards of male recreations, blurring of social distinctions through fine dressing, and men's abnegation of public responsibilities. Early eighteenth-century representations of the fop underwent a shift, notably in terms of the stress that was placed on depicting fops as exhibitionistic social actors within a developing system of public social spaces. To critics of social change, fops illustrated in microcosm the declining standards of an urban culture given over to excessive levels of superficial socializing that left men either affected or enervated. To 'modernizing' social commentators keen to promote new levels of commercial development and social interaction as a source of national health and acceptable male conduct,

51 *Satyr on the Mall*, p. 10.

fops represented the potentially debilitating effects not of change *per se*, but of unregulated socio-economic change. The attention such writers gave to highlighting the hazards of unregulated refine-ment revealed their continued alertness to the potentially debilitat-ing effects of male self-improvement in its various forms. In this context, the fop functioned not to prevent, but to promote the development of new standards of male conduct by providing a con-spicuous and forceful image of failed masculinity. Foppish displays of intrusive and showy manners revealed the underside of a civiliz-ing process facilitated through participation in an increasingly influ-ential network of arenas for public assembly. References to fops as consciously or unconsciously wayward social actors mirrored, and helped to define, an image of early eighteenth-century masculinity measured, in part, in terms of acceptable behaviour within the mixed public space of the promenade, garden or theatre, or the predomin-antly male environment of the coffee-house.

A study of representations of the fop has obvious implications for historians interested in eighteenth-century notions of masculine identity. This chapter has questioned the thrust of an existing his-toriography, predominantly concerned with early modern attitudes to male homosexuality, which proposes that eighteenth-century conceptions of masculinity were principally determined by sexual activity, and specifically, by the gender of an individual's sexual partner. Rather, it has argued that the eighteenth-century reader of periodicals, social documentaries and behavioural literature would have understood the debate over acceptable and unacceptable forms of masculinity as focusing predominantly on men's social conduct, and would have identified discussions of the fop as part of this debate.

Research into representations of the fop also prompts us to think carefully about other aspects of eighteenth-century social and cul-tural history. For example, historians would be in error if they failed to acknowledge the problems that many early eighteenth-century commentators identified with the rise and dissemination of theories of politeness, especially given the nature of representa-tions of the fop, and the function of these descriptions in different literary categories. The fact that fops were ridiculed for their beha-viour in public is also of interest for developing the existing histor-ical model of 'separate spheres'. Links between gender definitions and spatial demarcations have typically been identified in accounts that chart the fashioning of an eighteenth-century, middle-class notion of femininity associated with domesticity and servitude located within the 'private' sphere of the home and its environs. Questions have recently been asked about the links between bourgeois female identity and the 'private' sphere, but the equally simple connection between masculine identity and the 'public' has gone unchallenged.[52] Depictions of fops remind us that men's participation in urban social spaces provided opportunities for confirming one's masculinity as well as for exposing oneself to ridicule, and, more importantly, that eighteenth-century notions of acceptable masculinity depended not only on participation but also on conduct within these arenas.

52 Assertions of the public/private framework include Vivien Jones, ed., *Women in the Eighteenth Century: Constructions of Femininity* (London and New York, 1990). Questions as to the suitability of this model for discussions of eighteenth-century studies and women's history in general are raised in Lawrence E. Klein, 'Gender and the public/private distinction in the eighteenth century: some questions about evidence and analytic procedure' *ECS* 29 (1995), pp. 97–109. Klein's principal concern is to question historians' equation of femininity and privacy, rather than masculinity and publicity.

CHAPTER THREE

The public life of actresses: prostitutes or ladies?

KIMBERLY CROUCH

The social position of actresses throughout the eighteenth century was without question problematic: actresses and the theatres in which they performed were obvious targets for criticism from both moral reformers intent on chastising the stage and satirical authors interested in relating scandal.[1] Either sort of author could criticize an actress as a whore, given the way she supported herself by displaying herself on stage.[2] Yet the perception of the actress varied with the perceiver, and she could be presented and understood to have far more in common with the aristocratic woman than with the prostitute. Positive commentators pointed to the education required to maintain a position on the stage, the actress's alliances with aristocratic men and women, and her ability to imitate the social élite.[3] In addition, the fact that her sometimes substantial income might allow her to purchase the accoutrements of gentility, such as fine clothes and a country estate, confirmed that actresses could mirror the social and economic life of the upper classes.[4] This chapter will consider the points at which the prostitute, the actress and the fine lady merged within the theatre and beyond. In doing so, it will suggest some of the ways that actresses exerted control over their private lives so as to affect their public reputations. By presenting herself as a whore and mocking the problematic nature of her condition, an actress could appeal to the broad spectrum of

1 I would like to thank Tracy C. Davis for her comments on this chapter.
2 Thomas Brown, *Amusements Serious and Comical, Calculated for the Meridian of London* (1700), p. 51.
3 John Oldmixon, *Life and Posthumous Works of A. Maynwaring* (1715), p. 43. William Egerton [Edmund Curll], *Faithful Memoirs of . . . Anne Oldfield* (1731), pp. 2, 23, 12.
4 Margaret Woffington and Hannah Pritchard purchased country estates with the proceeds of their theatrical incomes, in Teddington and Twickenham respectively.

the eighteenth-century audience. Alternatively, by presenting herself as having aristocratic qualities, sympathies and inclinations in
both public and private, an actress might inspire emulation. All
women, including actresses, had to be concerned with their public
image and how it might inspire contemporaries' approbation or disapproval. In this way, the two worlds of public and private became
indistinct, not only for actresses, but for anyone who could create
and present a particular public image.

Actresses took on the qualities and characteristics of the women
who drew the most attention to themselves in the theatrical audience:
the prostitutes known and ridiculed for seeking custom in the pit
and galleries, and the aristocratic women who displayed themselves
in the stage boxes. Eighteenth-century actresses could employ either
of these apparently antithetical images to improve their reputation
or to seek the audience's attention and acclaim. As the century progressed, more actresses were able to claim convincingly that they
were more closely allied to the aristocracy and other respectable
members of their audience than to prostitutes, although some actresses, such as Anne Catley, would continue to play up their licentious characteristics to appeal to the less cultivated portion of the
audience.[5] There were no hard and fast rules about the behaviour
of women within the theatre and the respectability, or lack thereof,
of actresses. By examining variations, differences and exceptions to
accepted parameters of female behaviour and asking how actresses
moved within and beyond those parameters, it is possible to shed
some light on the evolving condition of eighteenth-century women
generally and actresses in particular. At issue is how actresses could
influence their public reputation, often by emphasizing the way in
which they lived their private lives.

The actress as prostitute

Since the Restoration, the prominence of prostitutes seeking custom in the pit of the theatre had provided fodder for the pens of
pious and godly authors intent on closing the theatres and removing the occasion for sin that they offered.[6] David Roberts has argued

5 Leo Hughes, *The Drama's Patrons* (Austin, TX, 1971), p. 186.

6 James Wright, *Historia Histronica: An Historical Account of the English Stage, Shewing the
Ancient Use, Improvement, and Perfection of a Dramatic Representation, in this Nation. In a
Dialogue of Plays and Players* (1699), p. 6: 'Whereas of late, the Play-houses are so extremely
pestered with Vizard-Masks and their Trade . . . that many of the more civilized Part of the
Town are uneasy in the company and shun the Theatre as they would a House of Scandal.'

that such women were more discreet and their presence more fleeting than the literary sources would suggest. Yet the fact remains that authors critical and supportive of the stage admitted that the theatre, as a place where people of all sorts gathered, provided a logical place for prostitutes to work.[7] It was the continued presence of the punks and their gulls in the audience, and the fact that Restoration actresses such as Nell Gwynn had been famous for their off-stage alliances and their capriciousness in arranging them, that allowed the distinction between actresses and prostitutes to remain obscure throughout the eighteenth century.[8] Actresses were readily associated with prostitutes at the beginning of the century and players themselves were willing to joke about such confusion between the actress and the whore. More than one early eighteenth-century epilogue allowed that actresses could support themselves by selling their favours, should the reformers of manners succeed in closing the theatres.[9] For example, the epilogue to *The Modish Husband* noted that 'eighteen pence in velvet', or the mask that marked the prostitute, could gain an actress additional income.[10] The degree to which actresses were willing to equate their activities with those of prostitutes, and how long such associations were beneficial to actresses' professional status, deserve further discussion.

In 1710, *A Justification of the Letter to John Stanley* viciously lambasted the popular actress Anne Oldfield and defended her rival, Letitia Cross. The pamphlet suggested that Oldfield could easily fill the audience at her benefit performance with men who had been intimate with her. Additionally, she was charged with being overbearing and malicious in her professional relationships.[11] Such accusations of sexual incontinence and the sale of sexual favours were an obvious way to attack women who were well known in their capacity as professional actresses. Despite the fact that Oldfield's defenders would deny such rumours, claiming that the actress had never 'troubled any Lady's lawful Claim; and was far more constant than Millions in the conjugal Noose', her audience was willing to

7 David Roberts, *The Ladies: Female Patronage of Restoration Drama 1660–1700* (Oxford, 1989), p. 87.

8 'Punks' is eighteenth-century slang for prostitutes; gulls, for gullible, were their customers.

9 Judith Milhous, *Thomas Betterton and the Management of Lincoln's Inn Fields, 1695–1708* (Carbondale, IL, 1979), pp. 93, 139.

10 Pierre Danchin, ed., *Prologues and Epilogues of the Eighteenth Century 1701–1720*, 2 vols (Nancy, 1989), I, p. 63.

11 Judith Milhous and Robert Hume, 'Theatrical politics at Drury Lane' *Bulletin of Research in the Humanities* 85 (1982), pp. 421–2.

react to the more scandalous aspects of her fame.[12] In his correspondence of 1725, the poet James Thomson described the way
Oldfield 'twines her body and leers with her eyes most bewitch-
ingly' and supposed that she acted better in bed than on the stage.[13]
Other actresses famous in the first quarter of the century who were
celebrated for their sexual activity and had reputations for exchanging their sexual favours for a price include Lavinia Fenton and
Hester Santlow Booth.[14] By having a professional role that advertised and capitalized on their physical attractions as well as their
ability to appeal to the higher emotions of their audiences, these
early eighteenth-century actresses were easy targets for malicious
writers who presented them as no different from the prostitutes
known to work in the theatre.

Actresses as a group or type provoked the same charge of prostitution. Their actions and speech on stage were considered immodest, as was their supposed behaviour in their personal lives.[15]
One commentator compared the stage to the window of a toyshop
through which actresses could be seen and purchased.[16] The ease
with which actresses, both as individuals and as a category, were
associated with prostitutes in the first quarter of the eighteenth
century has been demonstrated; yet it is also important to indicate
how that association was successfully opposed by contemporaries
and how an alternative image was proposed, particularly in regard
to the way any given actress lived in private among her family and
social contacts. While the conflation of the actress with the whore
would remain in place throughout the century, even before 1725
that association was beginning to break down. The actress, with her
appeal to both women and men in the audience, received comments
and attention which suggested that the actress could also be considered a valuable and important addition to the school of virtue that
the theatre represented. A German visitor to London in 1710 presented a different image of the 'strumpet' Hester Santlow: 'She is
universally admired for her beauty, matchless figure and the unusual

12 William Chetwood, *General History of the Stage* (1749), p. 202.

13 Alan Dugald McKillop, ed., *James Thomson, Letters and Documents* (Lawrence, KS, 1958), pp. 7–8.

14 For Fenton, *Amorous Lover* ([1728]); for Booth, John Dennis, 'The character and conduct of John Edgar', in Edward Niles Hooker, ed., *The Critical Works of John Dennis* 2 vols (Baltimore, MD, 1943), II, p. 191.

15 William Law, *The Absolute Unlawfulness of the Stage Entertainment Fully Demonstrated* (1726), p. 29.

16 *The Laureate. Or, the Right Side of Colley Cibber, Esq. Not Written by Himself* (1740), pp. 92–3.

elegance of her dancing and acting, and she is visited by those of the highest fashion in England'.[17] The notion that Santlow received fashionable visitors provides a reasonable counterpoint to the idea that the actress was treated no differently than the prostitute. Similarly, Anne Oldfield's biographers complimented her on her alliances with the aristocracy and her personal qualities. Her accomplishments and personal characteristics were presented as suitably genteel and an appropriate example for women of quality to follow.[18]

In the second half of the century, a variety of publications still continued to equate the actress with the whore. The semi-pornographic biographies and scurrilous memoirs produced throughout the century are obvious examples. In these, actresses were featured as the heroines of scandalous stories. Anne Catley and Elizabeth Billington received the attention of such biographers, yet neither suffered any loss in popularity as a result. *An Answer to the Memoirs of Mrs. Billington* chortled that 'the malignant blow lately levelled at her proved futile and impotent', and she continued to be favoured by her audiences with only the occasional hiss regarding her activities off stage.[19] In addition to such memoirs, there were poems and pamphlets that continued to assert the same sorts of innuendoes regarding the lack of sexual virtue to be expected in a woman who used her skills at presenting herself publicly for financial recompense. Edward Thompson's *Meretriciad*, published in 1761, made the connection between actress and prostitute absolutely clear. He focused his venom on the most famous prostitutes and demi-reps of the capital and featured several well-known actresses among his subjects, including George Anne Bellamy and Nancy Dawson.[20] Poems like *Meretriciad* were guaranteed an audience for the way they derided public figures, including the actresses who were known for their professional activities on the stage. Yet the *Meretriciad* and other poems like it did not reserve their criticism for the way a particular actress handled herself on stage, but attacked her personal life. Thompson charged Bellamy for neglecting her children and ridiculed Dawson for her choice in lovers. Just as actresses could employ positive personal qualities to enhance their public reputations, so detractors of their

17 For Santlow as strumpet, see Hooker, *Critical Works of John Dennis*, II, p. 91; W.H. Quarrell and M. Mare, eds, *Z.C. Uffenbach: London in 1710* (1934), pp. 30–1.

18 *Authentick Memoirs of the Life of the Celebrated Actress, Mrs. Anne Oldfield . . . With Large Additions and Amendments* 3rd edn (1730), pp. 6, 33.

19 *An Answer to the Memoirs of Mrs. Billington, with the Life and Adventures of Richard Daly, Esq.* (1792), p. 65.

20 Edward Thompson, *Meretriciad: Revised, Corrected, and with Large Additions* 4th edn (1763), pp. 17–18.

style of living attempted to use more negative personal characteristics to denigrate them.

A consideration of how two actresses of different generations
were dealt with by authors whose intent was to ridicule them and
capitalize on their notoriety will illuminate how the conflation between actresses and prostitutes shifted over the course of the century. Certainly, by the end of the period, actresses could appeal to
their public through commemorative biographies celebrating their
aristocratic connections and maternal attributes, but it makes more
sense to compare publications of similar kinds and with compar-
able intentions. By the end of the century, authors with satirical or
critical aims were careful to make their innuendoes and descriptions
concerning sexual transgressions more subtly than their predecessors had done.

In 1728, Lavinia Fenton was the focus of a series of publications
that ridiculed her, her popularity on the stage following her success
in the *Beggar's Opera*, and her association and eventual marriage to
the Duke of Bolton. Her biography and other publications distinguished her from the 'common' prostitute, but her willingness to
exchange her sexual favours for gifts of money or in kind was made
clear:

> she is above asking for Money for dispensing her Favours; and yet
> not foolish as to surrender before she sees the glittering Bait, for by
> some pretty witty Tale, Smile, Parable, or Fable, she insinuates so
> finely, that her Sparks are ready to offer a Diamond Ring, a Green
> Purse, a Watch . . . or some valuable trinket.[21]

All of these publications recounted Fenton's reputed sexual activities with a series of men and ridiculed the Duke of Bolton for his
attempts to secure her person as his own.[22] Without exception, the
numerous publications that featured Fenton during 1728 concentrated on her sexual reputation rather than her skill on stage. Their
record of her numerous lovers and the lampoons she attracted
were not necessarily meant to be believed, but provided a convenient way to ridicule a woman whose private life was of interest to
readers, especially given her popularity on the stage and the prominence of her lover.

In the 1780s and 1790s, Elizabeth Farren followed Fenton's example by gaining the affections of a member of the nobility and
marrying him after his wife's death. However, the publications that

21 *The Life of Lavinia Beswick, alias Fenton, alias Polly Peachum* (1728), p. 34.
22 *A New Ballad Inscrib'd to Polly Peachum* ([1728]).

celebrated her professional capabilities and those that greeted her marriage to the Earl of Derby in 1797 were very different in tone and subject to those that had featured Lavinia Fenton in a previous generation. *Memoirs of the Countess of Derby* was written ostensibly as a tribute to Farren upon her retirement and marriage, yet was certainly intended to ridicule her. It was full of *double entendres* concerning sexual matters, but it did not associate the images of actress and prostitute as clearly as had the poems and biographical works about Fenton. Instead, Farren was criticized for sins less sexual in nature: ingratitude, ambition and parsimony. And, rather than relying solely on the image of actress as whore to sell copy, the author made fun of Derby for his own eccentricities.[23] Moreover, Farren, like other actresses of her generation, was the object of numerous complimentary notices in the press about her professional skills and personal qualities. She was acclaimed for her talents at representing a particular type of character on stage, her successes in maintaining friendships with the aristocracy and the personal attributes that secured her their favour. Her most constant defenders insisted that she had maintained her sexual purity before her marriage despite the fact that such commendations usually provoked derisive responses from satirists.[24]

The differences in attitudes toward actresses manifested in publications concerning Lavinia Fenton and Elizabeth Farren illustrate a shift in the way actresses were considered by the end of the century. Actresses increasingly aligned themselves with aristocratic women to defend themselves against the less flattering comparisons suggested in scurrilous biographies and the ever more scandalous paragraphs in periodicals. That the more flattering image was, in some ways, a successful one is evidenced by their inclusion in a range of social settings and the parallel prominence of publications that celebrated their talents instead of mocking their private lives. Although the direct association of actresses with prostitutes became less apparent as the century progressed, the fascination with popular actresses' private lives continued, thus demonstrating the difficulty of distinguishing a public life from a private one. For actresses, or any women with public reputations, a private life was impossible to maintain. Any personal details of lovers, children, or any social association beyond the realm of the theatre or within it, was of interest to the public.

23 Petronious Arbiter, *Memoirs of the Present Countess of Derby* 5th edn (1797), pp. 20–1.
24 Mary Pilkington, *Memoirs of Celebrated Female Characters* (1811), p. 142.

While it is true that by the end of the eighteenth century actresses were able to present themselves as worthy recipients of favourable attention from their wealthiest and most socially secure patrons, it is important to acknowledge that some actresses consciously emphasized the more notorious and promiscuous aspects of their reputations in order to appeal to a broader section of the audience. They continued the tradition of playing up the more bawdy elements of their personal reputation and the more general notion that actresses were women of easy virtue.[25] Actresses throughout the eighteenth century, such as Margaret Woffington (d. 1760) and Anne Catley (1745–89), relied on such attributes to secure their place in the public's consciousness and favour well after other actresses had begun to present themselves more decorously. Wearing breeches, speaking licentious prologues or epilogues, and specializing in particularly provocative roles were the most obvious ways an actress could play up her sexuality to appeal to an audience. Margaret Woffington was long acclaimed for her ability to 'lear you into a clap', but Anne Catley's career best demonstrates the way an actress could use her scandalous reputation to secure her audience, in spite of the reputedly improving repertoire of more circumspect plays.[26] Notorious from her first year on the stage, in 1762, for a court case brought by her father against her aristocratic lover, Catley became a popular subject for newspaper editors and print-makers to lampoon.[27] Yet she continued to be a popular performer in both Dublin and London throughout the 1770s and until her retirement in 1781. A review of her performances in 1773 lamented her popularity, in spite of the fact that she neglected the 'sensible' part of the audience, by 'learing to a set of creatures whom both as a woman and as an actress, she should long ago have learned to despise'.[28] In 1776 the diarist Sylas Neville recorded his own reaction to her:

> In the evening went ... to see the celebrated Miss Catley perform Lucy in the Beggar's Opera. She sings well & gives many of the songs uncommon expression, but she is vulgar to a degree even beyond what might be expected from the character & has all the appearance of an impudent battered woman of the Town.[29]

25 Elizabeth Howe, *The First English Actresses* (1992), p. 198; John Harold Wilson, *All the King's Ladies: Actresses of the Restoration* (Chicago, IL, 1958), pp. 85, 105.

26 *A Guide to the Stage* (1751), p. 14.

27 Miss Ambross, *The Life and Memoirs of the Late Miss Ann Catley, The Celebrated Actress* (1789), p. 27.

28 *The Macaroni and Theatrical Magazine*, April 1773, p. 292.

29 Basil Cozens-Hardy, ed., *The Diary of Sylas Neville, 1767–1788* (Oxford, 1950), pp. 254–5.

In spite of this polite disregard for her performances, Anne Catley was among the highest paid actresses of her generation. In 1770 her salary was 15 guineas a week, second only to the tragedienne Mary Ann Yates.[30] She remained at the top of the salary structure and earned £21 a week in her last season.[31] Although more serious critics derided the vulgarity and indecency of her performances, Catley's managers clearly thought her lucrative salary a fair exchange for the less particular audiences she brought to the theatre.

Charging a publicly prominent woman with selling her sexual favours was an easy way to attack her. Describing a woman as a whore was meant to be malicious and harmful to her reputation and social standing; however, the question remains as to how seriously such allegations were taken and if accusations of immoral behaviour might affect an individual actress's livelihood. The experience of the most famous actresses as well as some of their less popular rivals suggests that any publicity, whatever the author's intent, served to improve an actress's reputation, in the sense that it brought her public notice. By fostering the bawdy elements of their personal reputations Anne Catley and other actresses exerted some influence over their public reputations. Alternatively, defenders of a particular actress's virtue (or the actress herself) often printed supportive and celebratory verse in an attempt to control the perceived damage after scurrilous publications or paragraphs had been printed. In either case, audiences flocked to the theatres to see what the fuss was about. In addition, the expectations of immorality that accompanied the actress into the green room and onto the stage allowed her to be forgiven her reputed indiscretions. Throughout the century, similarities between actresses and prostitutes were readily admitted, and theatre historians have emphasized them to demonstrate the problematic nature of the theatre and the reputation of the women who worked there. However, the picture is more complicated than just a simple alignment of the actress and the whore, for the eighteenth-century actress could also present herself as a gentlewoman. While this more flattering comparison was increasingly common by the end of the century, it is important to mark the evolution of attitudes toward actresses that permitted its growing acceptance. In addition, this comparison of actresses to

30 *Town and Country Magazine*, Nov. 1770, p. 572.
31 Charles Beecher Hogan, ed., *The London Stage 1660–1800: A Calendar of Plays, Entertainments and Afterpieces Together with Casts, Box-Receipts and Contemporary Comment Compiled from the Playbills, Newspapers and Theatrical Diaries of the Period. Part 5, 1760–1800* 3 vols (Carbondale, IL, 1968), II, p. 47.

both whores and fine ladies raises further questions about reputations and images in the period. The distinctions between public and private become obscured if an actress could employ her 'private' qualities as a good mother or charitable benefactor to diffuse the more negative and 'public' image of a whorish actress. How actresses might compare themselves to fine ladies at the cost of making details of their personal lives matter for public consumption deserves further explanation.

The actress as aristocrat

Aristocratic and other upper-class women were essential components of the eighteenth-century audience. Like the prostitutes, aristocratic women in the audience provided a model of behaviour for actresses to appropriate. The prominence of ladies of quality in the audience was the bane of anti-theatrical pamphleteers, who thought their encouragement of other women 'to act smuttily' was neither suitable nor acceptable.[32] In 1726, William Law was horrified that 'Ladies' gave their names to support players' benefits, and complained that it was 'monstrous for Women to encourage a Number of Women in an immodest way of life'.[33] Dissecting this phrase underlines the difficulty of being able to define an image of women that was characteristic of a period or class. Law evidently felt that aristocratic women should preserve the rest of society from immoral behaviour, needed protection from immoral behaviour, and could instigate immoral behaviour. The fact that these three distinct ideas about women's behaviour and authority were contradictory did not concern him, but they do indicate some of the problems involved with characterizing prevailing attitudes within eighteenth-century society. Still, the attacks on aristocratic women patronizing the theatre by anti-theatrical writers not only demonstrate the prominence of women in the audience, but also suggest that such writers saw this sort of female aristocratic patronage as an obstacle to their own ends. If eminent women were willing to countenance the action of the stage in its unreformed state, then anti-theatrical writers had powerful opponents to their designs.

Actors and actresses throughout the century recognized the importance of their aristocratic, and particularly female aristocratic,

32 Jeremy Collier, *A Short View of the Immorality and Profaness of the English Stage* (1698), pp. 9, 13, 165.
33 Law, *Absolute Unlawfulness*, p. 29.

patrons in securing and protecting their livelihood from anti-
theatrical writers. Prologues and epilogues constantly appealed to
the generosity of 'The Ladies' for applause and approval.[34] In addition, individual performers used hints regarding such patronage to
enhance the reception of a particular play or production. By the
1730s, claims that benefits or particular performances were 'by Desire
of Several Ladies of Quality' were recognized as a form of puff and
Henry Fielding felt free to ridicule them as such in *Pasquin*.[35] Still,
both actresses and actors continued to use such notices of wealthy
feminine patronage to improve the presentation of their benefits
in advertisements throughout the century. If ladies were not mentioned as ordering the performance, they were encouraged to send
their servants early to secure their seats. Despite the trope that
women in general were inclined to vice rather than antithetical
to it, the opposite notion seems to have been far more prevalent
and persuasive, especially with regard to the success of the theatre.
As 'the best Patrons of Wit', the group of aristocratic women who
apparently encouraged theatre managers to revive Shakespeare's
plays were acknowledged and heralded in the pamphlet press.[36]
Not only did such women encourage a Shakespearian revival, but
in so doing they were said to discountenance 'whatever may prop-
agate low, slavish, and effeminate Manners'.[37] Women of the public
domain, aristocratic women as well as actresses, continued to be
objects of satiric comments on the basis of gender throughout the
century. Complimentary authors, however, pointed out their learning and other personal attributes to emphasize their importance as
patrons of the theatre and, as such, as nurturers of virtue.

How did gentlewomen act within the theatre; how was their
behaviour perceived; and how did they associate with the actresses
they considered worthy of their patronage? Evidence recorded in
correspondence and memoirs indicates that even aristocratic ladies
could be hissed out of countenance by the rest of the audience or
criticized in print should their actions interfere with the presentation of the play. In a letter to his wife in 1756, Henry Fox described
how Lady Coventry and Lady Rockingham, and two other women,

34 Danchin, ed., *Prologues and Epilogues*, I, p. xxxi.
35 Henry Fielding, *Pasquin: A Dramatic Satire on the Times, Being the Rehearsal of Two Plays*
(1736), p. 2.
36 Emmet L. Avery, 'The Shakespeare Ladies Club' *Shakespeare Quarterly* 7 (1956),
p. 153. See also Michael Dobson, *The Making of the National Poet: Shakespeare, Adaptation,
and Authorship, 1660–1769* (Oxford, 1992), pp. 150–4.
37 *The Case of our Present Theatrical Disputes* (1743), p. 44.

'made such an Uproar in the Stage Box' and angered or embarrassed the actress George Anne Bellamy so much that she left the stage.[38] This behaviour – on the part of the ladies, not on the part of the actress for deserting her post – earned them a rebuke from *The Old Maid*:

> If the lady who was guilty of this indecency, had no regard for humanity, or the civility due to an audience; yet one would imagine pride might have guarded her against a behaviour so very unbecoming to her rank . . . she not only condescended to the utmost meanness in thus attacking one of her own sex, who in that place was not allowed to return the insult, but that she put herself upon a level with the lowest of the audience, by such an imitation of their manners.[39]

Such criticism is noteworthy because it implies that women in the audience should serve the women on stage more politely than the rogues and servants in the galleries. By acting as 'four Drunken men', Lady Coventry and her associates subverted the social hierarchy and inverted their gender: in so doing they instituted confusion on stage and in the theatre.[40]

This encounter between these aristocratic women and the actress demonstrates the way in which aristocratic women could attempt to insult an actress and interfere with a production. More typical were cordial relations between actresses and their affluent patrons. In addition to noting that benefits were 'at the Desire of Several Ladies of Quality', actresses also directly acknowledged their patrons from the stage. Susannah Cibber, known for her sympathetic portrayal of pathetic characters, on one occasion curtsied three times to her acquaintances in the audience in the third act of Hamlet. This recognition of her benefactors provoked the ire of at least one critic:

> Pray, good Sir, ask her in what part of the Play it is said, that the Danish Ophelia (for she was then Ophelia and not Mrs. Cibber) is acquainted with so many British Ladies? . . . Pray tell Mrs. Cibber, that though her parading-it to the whole house, that she was honoured with the acquaintance of some persons of fashion, might be food for her pride, it was neither proof of her understanding, nor a mark of her respect for the rest of the audience.[41]

38 BL Add MS 51,415 (Holland House Papers), Henry Fox to Lady Caroline Fox, 16 Feb. 1756.
39 Mary Singleton, *The Old Maid*, 21 Feb. 1756, p. 89.
40 BL Add MS 51,415.
41 *Theatrical Review* (May 1763), p. 213.

Susannah Cibber was not the only actress to use her audience thus. Memoirs and autobiographies of actresses emphasized aristocratic alliances as a way of enhancing their popularity with the public.[42] By acknowledging and expressing appreciation for such alliances, individual actresses hoped to offset the more questionable aspects of their personal reputations and profession.

Actor-manager David Garrick's friendly relations with such women as the Lady Spencer and Lady Burlington have been acknowledged by biographers and historians.[43] Similar trends in fascination with particular female performers are apparent throughout the century, and culminated at the end of the period with the cult of Sarah Siddons, who, as Catherine Clive wryly supposed, had the 'whole world . . . to stand God fathers and God mothers' for her children.[44] Individual actresses, including both Clive and Siddons, were able to establish personal friendships with members of the aristocracy who had initially served as their patrons. At two centuries' remove, nuances in personal relationships are difficult to ascertain; however, it can be argued that members of the aristocracy, most secure in their own social position, were willing to associate with a variety of public personalities, including actresses. The nature and extent of individual relationships depended on the personalities involved, but performers at the most exalted levels were certainly encouraged by the social élite. For instance, Sir Gilbert Elliot regretted having missed the opportunity to meet Sarah Siddons at one ball, but did so at a dinner hosted by William Windham.[45] There, Elliot found the actress 'very beautiful in a room', and noted that she spoke modestly and well.[46] That Siddons was often included in select company is significant and is confirmed by other contemporary diaries as well as her own memoirs.[47] While it is difficult to determine at what point and with whom patronage of actresses by men and women of the aristocracy eased into social relationships, Sarah Siddons and other actresses such as Catherine

42 Catherine Clive was accused of similar inattention by Thomas Davies, *Memoirs of the Life of David Garrick* 2 vols (1780), II, pp. 191–2.

43 George Winchester Stone, Jr and George M. Kahrl, *David Garrick, A Critical Biography* (Carbondale, IL, 1979), p. 366.

44 E.W. Harcourt, ed., *The Harcourt Papers* 14 vols (Oxford, 1876–1905), VIII, p. 176: Clive to Earl Harcourt, 1785.

45 E.E.E. Elliot Murry-Kynynmound, ed., *Life and Letters of Sir Gilbert Elliot, 1751–1806* 3 vols (1884), I, p. 136.

46 Ibid., I, p. 152.

47 Mrs Henry Baring, ed., *The Diary of the Rt. Hon. William Windham 1784–1810* (1866), p. 293; Thomas Campbell, *The Life of Mrs. Siddons* 2 vols (1834), II, p. 117.

Clive were able to maintain a variety of contacts and alliances among the social élite.

It is also important to consider the ways in which actresses could mimic successfully aristocratic women on the stage. By modelling their behaviour on that of fine ladies, actresses could foster the notion that they were worthy of audience appreciation, both on the stage and off it. In addition, by dressing well on stage and in private, actresses could exert additional control over the way they were perceived by their public. While performing, actresses prided themselves on dressing fashionably, regardless of the specific part they played. Theatre critics such as John Hill lamented this lack of truth in representation and complained that chambermaids who were dressed as duchesses served to weaken the effects of drama. By further commenting that 'Mrs. Clive has a great many very good clothes', his critique shifted from the general to the particular.[48] The fact that Catherine Clive played the chambermaids and hoydens of her repertoire in the attire of a woman of quality did not trouble audiences as much as it bothered critics. Actresses throughout the period continued to dress at the height of fashion, especially in comedy. By doing so, they were able to give the audience hints of their financial well-being, for it is clear that actresses were, to some extent, responsible for their own clothes. Colley Cibber, in his preface to the *Provok'd Husband*, acknowledged that Anne Oldfield had provided her own 'Ornaments' and added that 'they seem'd in all Respects, the Paraphonalia of a Woman of Quality'.[49] Often, the best actresses were given a clothes allowance in addition to their salary, but the stage attire they purchased with such funds became their personal property, rather than the theatre's.[50] Established actresses took control of their stage apparel, and although they could be chastised in the papers as having 'forgot their engagement on stage and dress'd for a card party', they much preferred such critical comment to the alternative of appearing in the more humble and dated accoutrements of the company stock.[51] The actress Sophia Baddeley, when strongly encouraged to cut down on her expenses, reputedly answered, 'one may as well be dead as not in the fashion, and I am determined I will follow them all'.[52]

48 John Hill, *The Actor: A Treatise on the Art of Playing* (1750), pp. 223–4.

49 John Vanbrugh and Colley Cibber, *The Provok'd Husband* (1728), preface.

50 For further discussion of this topic, see Cecil Price, *Theatre in the Age of Garrick* (Oxford, 1973), pp. 44–7.

51 *Public Advertiser*, 4 Oct. 1782.

52 Elizabeth Steele, *Memoirs of Mrs. Sophia Baddeley* 3 vols (Dublin, 1787), II, p. 114.

Actresses used their freedom in selecting their own stage apparel to associate themselves further with women of quality. By dressing fashionably both on stage and off, they reinforced the idea that there was little to separate them from their most established and wealthy patrons. The debt that might result from maintaining a stylish appearance was feared considerably less than the potential loss in status that might be incurred by appearing behind the times.

Royalty and other aristocratic women, on occasion, sold their once-worn coronation robes or elaborate dresses to the theatres or gave them to particular actresses – a practice that could demonstrate how private individuals might use the stage to advertise their own good taste and financial well-being.[53] The actress Hannah Pritchard, whose family owned stay and dressmaking shops, was appointed as a dresser for Queen Charlotte for her wedding and coronation in 1761;[54] whereas George Anne Bellamy made the claim in her memoirs that she had been consulted by women of fashion for advice concerning dress for the 'birthday and fancy cloaths'.[55] Such reliance on actresses for fashionable consultation was not limited to the peculiarities of the court or the fancy dress of masquerades. By the end of the century, the actresses most successful at presenting themselves as well-dressed on stage were able to set fashion rather than follow it; they were emulated by aristocratic women instead of the reverse. Letitia Hawkins noted that Jane Barsanti set a new trend in petticoats in Dublin,[56] while Frances Abington, famous for her friendships among the aristocracy, in the Irish capital and in London, was also well known for the willingness of those ladies to follow her dress sense:

> As she possesses an exquisite taste, she is constantly employed in driving about the capital to give her advice concerning the modes and fashions of the day. She is called in like a physician, and recompensed as if she were an artist. . . . A great number of people of fashion treat her in the most familiar manner, and as if she were their equal.[57]

53 On the Duchess of York presenting Mrs Barry with her wedding suit, see Thomas Betterton [Edmund Curll], *History of the English Stage from the Restoration to the Present Time* (1741), p. 17; John Rich purchased a suit from the Princess Dowager of Wales for Mrs Woffington, George Anne Bellamy, *Apology for the Life of George Anne Bellamy, Late of Covent Garden Theatre* 6 vols (3rd edn, 1785), II, p. 206.

54 Anthony Vaughn, *Born to Please, Hannah Pritchard, Actress 1711–1768* (1979), p. 84.

55 George Anne Bellamy, *Apology for the Life of George Anne Bellamy, Late of Covent Garden Theatre* 3 vols (2nd edn, Dublin, 1785), I, p. 255.

56 Letitia Hawkins, *Anecdotes, Biographical Sketches and Memoirs* (1822), p. 219.

57 M. D'Archenholz, *A Picture of England, containing a description of the laws, customs, and manners of England, translated from French* 2 vols (1789), I, p. 110.

The change that took place during the century, from actresses accepting cast-off gowns from their patrons to patrons asking actresses' advice for dress, initially from caprice and then more seriously, suggests that actresses were so successful at taking on the characteristics of their wealthiest and most socially secure patrons that they became worthy of imitation. Fashionable dress and the effective use of it by actresses establishes another point at which the relationship between aristocratic women and actresses became more than the simple one between patron and patronized.

Dressing fashionably was not the only way an actress worked to convince her audience that she could be compared to and associated with her aristocratic patrons in the audience. In addition, the most popular and accomplished actresses were, by the last quarter of the eighteenth century, often the subjects of portraits that represented them as fashionably dressed women of quality. Initially, actresses were portrayed in character in paintings that were then reproduced as engravings for display and sale in printshops.[58] The sale of such prints encouraged attendance at the theatre and advertised the skills of the original painter and the engraver, as well as of the actress herself.[59] Joshua Reynolds's portrait and the engraving of Frances Abington as the comic muse recalls similar portraits of aristocratic women as other muses or figures of classical allegory. Abington's holding the mask of comedy marks the theatricality of her portrait, but its general pose – the subject standing in classical drapery with one arm resting on a table or altar – has little to distinguish it from Reynolds's later portrait of Lady Bampfylde.[60] Gainsborough's portraits of Sarah Siddons and Mary Robinson, and Thomas Lawrence's portrait of Elizabeth Farren, all present actresses as aristocratic women.

Conversely, aristocratic women were willing to be presented in more theatrical, even revealing postures that recalled the more exuberant theatrical portraits of the period. *Mrs. Hale as Euphrosyne*, commissioned for the music room at Harewood House, provokes speculation as to why portraits were painted in which presumably respectable women were represented in such a casual, almost

58 For a more complete discussion of theatrical portraits, their uses and their composition, see Shearer West, *The Image of the Actor* (New York, 1991), and idem, 'Theatrical portraits in the eighteenth century' (unpublished Ph.D. thesis, St Andrews University, 1986).

59 Christopher Lennox-Boyd, Guy Shaw and Sarah Halliwell, *Theatre in the Age of Garrick* (1994), pp. vi–viii.

60 Nicholas Penny, ed., *Reynolds* (1986), pp. 277–8.

suggestive manner.[61] The liveliness of the pose, as well as the purpose of the room in which the portrait was to hang, brought together the images of the private gentlewoman and the professional performer. It is important not to make too much of the latter point, but the freedom and form of these often revealing postures, in which the drapery clearly delineates both the shape of the body and the leg, suggest additional ways that aristocratic women were willing to follow where actresses had led. There remains an important distinction between portraits of actresses and those of aristocratic women in that the former would be reproduced as engravings and sold to a wider market. Portraits of aristocratic women, in contrast, would be engraved only for friends and family. However, one reproduction would also be on display in the artist's studio for the perusal of other clients. In this way the aristocratic woman's portrait was on view to the public, much like that of the image of the actress.[62] Actresses' portraits approximated those of aristocratic women and vice versa. That both categories of portraits, those of aristocratic women and of actresses, were intended for and meant to influence a public audience demonstrates another arena in which it becomes difficult to separate the worlds of public and private.

Portraits and the engravings taken from them also allowed actresses to disseminate their images. The comparison such images evoked between the actress and the aristocrat was one of many possible messages or implications. Although it could be argued that images of actresses were merely the means through which artists and patrons displayed their own ideas about such women, evidence can be offered which suggests that the subjects had some control over the way they were presented. In her authorized biography, Sarah Siddons claimed that she had been instrumental in organizing the pose and selecting the colours Joshua Reynolds used in his representation of her as the tragic muse.[63] By emphasizing her own contributions to the arrangement of the portrait, which received high critical acclaim, Siddons impressed the readers of her biography with her command of an art outside her own sphere. Actresses wanted it acknowledged that they had the intelligence and taste to direct the painting of their own portraits, just as their aristocratic

61 Ibid., pp. 228–9; Marcia Pointon, 'Graces, bacchantes and plain folk: order and excess in Reynolds' female portraiture', Restoration to Reform Seminar, Oxford, 18 Oct. 1993. A version of this paper is published in Marcia Pointon, *Strategies for Showing: Women, Possession, and Representation in English Visual Culture 1660–1800* (Oxford, 1997), ch. 5.

62 Marcia Pointon, *Hanging the Head: Portraiture and Social Formation in Eighteenth-Century England* (1993), pp. 41–3.

63 Campbell, *Life of Mrs. Siddons*, I, p. 243.

counterparts did. Similar reports about Dorothy Jordan, Mary Robinson and Elizabeth Inchbald's attempts to control the way they were portrayed confirm the point that actresses saw their portraits, even when they were displayed in a particular role, as an important part of the publicity that accompanied their road to fame.[64] By influencing how she was presented in portraits, an actress might exercise some control over the way her image was published and circulated. Emphasizing the parallels between her own image and that of her patrons, the actress responded to and approximated the image of the aristocratic woman.

The most obvious way that aristocratic women emulated the actions and habits of the professional actresses was in the private theatricals that flourished at the close of the eighteenth century. From the beginning of the century, activity that might be considered theatrical took place within the family circle. Speeches from plays were taught to young people so that they could display skills of the schoolroom in their parents' drawing rooms and within the confines of the family. This kind of youthful activity was strictly relegated to the family setting, however, and needs to be distinguished from the private theatricals lauded in publications such as *The World* and other printed papers. From the 1780s, noblemen such as Lord Barrymore and the Duke of Richmond built small theatres to meet the craze for such private theatricals. The productions sometimes involved a combination of sons and daughters of noble and gentry families together with professionals, although there were many variations in the way different private theatricals were conducted. Lord Barrymore employed actors and actresses to supplement a small number of male amateurs and he performed occasionally on the professional stage himself.[65] In contrast, no professionals were employed to supplement performances either for the Duke of Marlborough or the Duke of Richmond.[66] 'Private theatricals' is a potentially misleading description, as tickets were printed and acquired by numerous people. The theatre at Blenheim,

---

64 Claire Tomalin, *Mrs. Jordan's Profession: the story of a great actress and a future king* (London, 1995), p. 71; Gill Perry, 'Women in disguise: likeness, the grand style, and the conventions of feminine portraiture in the work of Sir Joshua Reynolds', in Gill Perry and Michael Rossington, eds, *Femininity and Masculinity in Eighteenth-Century Art and Culture* (Manchester, 1994), p. 34; Cecelia Macheski, 'Herself as heroine: portraits as autobiography of Elizabeth Inchbald', in Mary Ann Schofield and Cecelia Macheski, eds, *Curtain Calls: British and American Women and the Theatre 1660–1800* (Athens, OH, 1991), p. 47.

65 Anthony Pasquin, *The Life of the Late Earl of Barrymore Including a History of the Wargrave Theatricals and Original Notes of Eminent Persons* (1793), p. 18.

66 Sybil Rosenfeld, *Temples of Thespis: Some Private Theatricals in England and Wales, 1700–1830* (1978), pp. 35, 110.

for example, could accommodate almost 200 spectators, although claims were made that only the best company was admitted.[67] It would be more accurate to describe them as 'amateur' theatricals, although contemporaries used 'private' to emphasize the gentility of both the performers and the audience. Certainly, professional performers were recruited, both to augment the players and to provide assistance in the direction of such productions.[68] Elizabeth Farren provided such direction at Richmond House before her marriage in 1797, while retired actress Priscilla Hopkins Kemble assisted Lord and Lady Abercorn in 1803.[69] Kemble described her experiences to Elizabeth Inchbald:

> Our Friday Evening was most splendid, and to me in every way triumphant . . . the Prince of Wales, Duke and Duchess of Devonshire, Lady Melbourne and family, the Castlereaghs, Mr. and Mrs. Sheridan, Lady Westmoreland, and the Ladies Fane, Lady Ely, &c. The audience consisted of about seventy persons. . . . Nothing could be more brilliant: the whole theatricals under my direction, and, I do assure you, most excellently acted. Lady Cahir admirable in *Lady Contest*, and she was a blaze of diamonds! . . . Lord and Lady A. treated me with the most marked attention . . .[70]

Private theatricals and their popularity within particular sections of the élite suggest another way that aristocratic women and men appropriated the opportunity for the display of wealth offered by the stage, and which professional actresses already used to advantage. Given that aristocratic women were already accomplished at putting on their own display in the boxes of the theatre, the step to the stage was not very far, particularly in a context so inviting and socially secure as their own homes and among their own family networks.

Evidence in memoirs and contemporary periodicals proves that in certain circles aristocratic women performed under the direction of women they admired on the stage. However, critical comment concerning such amateur performances, both in published memoirs and the press, could be ambivalent and even harsh in its judgement of the aristocratic women who participated in what were considered unconventional endeavours. Some of the women most involved with amateur theatricals on a grand scale, as performers

67 Frederick Reynolds, *The Life and Times of Frederick Reynolds* 2 vols (1826), II, p. 4.
68 Pasquin, *The Life of the Late Earl of Barrymore*, p. 18.
69 *Universal and Daily Register*, 21 April 1787.
70 James Boaden, *Memoirs of Mrs. Inchbald* 2 vols (1833), II, pp. 67–9.

or producers, were already socially problematic. Lady Cecilia Johnstone, Mrs Hobart and the Margravine of Anspach were considered
eccentric, if not worse.[71] The first two women were caricatured by
James Gillray as presenting themselves disgracefully in a variety of
ways that reflected poorly on their sex, their age group and their
social position.[72] In each case theatrical activity provided an additional excuse for chastisement in the public papers and prints: 'Lady
Buckingham acted *Cowslip* in the *Agreeable Surprise* at Brandenburgh
House. The part of Mrs *Cheshire* would have been more in character.'[73] Yet each of these women was evidently encouraged by her
own social circle to pursue such amusements. Sustained by certain
members of the aristocracy, like the professional theatres, amateur
theatrical performances continued in spite of the troublesome aspects of their reputation, and suggest another avenue by which
aristocratic women emulated professional actresses.

It is, of course, clear that actresses were almost always defined
differently from their aristocratic patrons, although the difference
apparent to observers might be glossed over should circumstances
warrant it. When Hester Lynch Thrale (later Piozzi) met Fanny
Burney for the first time, she commented in her diary that the
novelist had the 'Grace of an Actress not a Woman of Fashion'.[74]
Thrale implied that she condescended to make Burney a friend
and companion, but Burney herself would have been astounded
that her manner reminded Thrale of an actress. Burney's own
consciousness of her moral correctness and decorum and her acute
awareness of the precariousness of actresses' moral reputations weigh
heavily in her journals and diaries.[75] Although Thrale appeared to
be expressing disdain, she befriended Burney in the 1770s and
1780s, and the two remained on good terms until they fell out over
Thrale's second marriage. Later, as Mrs Piozzi, she befriended Sarah
Siddons and her family and other theatrical personalities.[76] Given
the way that Piozzi constructed her own friendships and alliances,

71 Lady Cecilia Johnstone and Mrs Hobart (later Lady Buckinghamshire) were caricatured frequently by James Gillray for their friendship with the Prince of Wales. The
Margravine of Anspach was notorious for her divorce from Lord Craven to marry a minor
German prince. The couple returned to England where she was often mocked in the
public papers for the irregularities of her personal life.

72 Penny, *Reynolds*, pp. 390, 392.

73 *Bon-Ton Magazine*, June 1795, p. 156.

74 Katherine Balderston, ed., *Hester Lynch Thrale: Thraliana* 2 vols (Oxford, 1951), I,
p. 368.

75 Joyce Hemlow, *Fanny Burney* (Oxford, 1958), chs 5–7. See also James Clifford, *Hester
Lynch Piozzi* (2nd edn, with an introd. by Margaret Doody, Oxford, 1987), pp. 225–6.

76 Ibid., p. 398.

her criticism of Burney rings hollow. Hester Thrale Piozzi provides an example of an upper-class woman, obsessed with the superiority of her own ancestry, who in practice acted differently towards actresses than her writings might suggest.[77] Whatever rules might have existed concerning the intimacy of the relationship between a professional actress and a woman of quality, these might be readily bent or broken, depending on the circumstances and inclinations of the individual women involved.

In its accommodation of women from a range of socio-economic levels, the theatre provided a *mélange* of eighteenth-century society where a variety of activity was encouraged. The women in the audience who received the most attention from both the anti-theatrical press and the more complimentary publications were prostitutes and aristocratic women. It is clear that the theatre provided an appropriate place for prostitutes to seek custom. Aristocratic women, resplendent in the boxes with their dresses, headpieces and jewels, were made much of both in theatrical advertisements and in a press more critical of their patronage. Both classes of women, given their prominence in the audience, provided models of behaviour for actresses to follow. All of these women – prostitutes, aristocrats and actresses – lived on their own terms, in some ways free from the limitations set by conduct books or prescribed by society. Prostitutes, given their incommodious economic position, were often too poor to conform to any set of expectations regarding the nobility of their sex, should they have been aware of the standards of morality and sensibility defined by prescriptive authors. Aristocrats, who were in a considerably more powerful position, could set themselves above prescriptions on their behaviour and might conduct their lives according to their own judgement. Like actresses, their public image was important to them and aristocratic women could employ tools similar to those used by actresses to improve their public reputations. Actresses, associated with characteristics of both the prostitute and the aristocratic woman, could choose which model of behaviour to follow, after determining which best suited their capabilities and inclinations. In the grey area between aristocrat and whore, the actress was sometimes allowed and even forgiven for the freedoms of both.

77 Ibid., pp. xxi, xxv.

PART TWO

Work and poverty

CHAPTER FOUR

Women, work and the industrial revolution: female involvement in the English printing trades, c.1700–1840[1]

HANNAH BARKER

For many historians the industrial revolution marked a turning point in the history of women and work, as the impact of capitalism profoundly altered the status and role of the female workforce. In *Women Workers and the Industrial Revolution, 1750–1850*, a book first published over 60 years ago but which still dominates the field, Ivy Pinchbeck argues that the industrialization of the late eighteenth and early nineteenth centuries brought about a dramatic change in the nature of women's work. Pinchbeck asserts that the industrial revolution caused the separation of home and workplace, and thus forced women to look for work and wages outside the domestic setting that had previously witnessed the bulk of female economic activity.[2] Bridget Hill has subsequently adopted a similar interpretation, following in the tradition of Alice Clark's writing on the seventeenth century.[3] In *Women, Work and Sexual Politics in the Eighteenth Century*, Hill recounts how industrial capitalism sounded the death-knell of the 'family economy' and caused a significant shift in the patterns of women's work from around the mid-century onward.[4]

Although they agree about the importance of the impact of industrialization on the female workforce, Pinchbeck and Hill are

1 I am grateful to Rodney Barker, Elaine Chalus, David Eastwood, Ann Hughes, Joanna Innes, Paul Langford, Roey Sweet and Stephen Taylor for their comments on this chapter, to Tim Clayton and John Feather for their advice on locating women printers, and to John Landers for information concerning widowhood and mortality.
2 Ivy Pinchbeck, *Women Workers and the Industrial Revolution, 1750–1850* (1930).
3 Alice Clark, *Working Life of Women in the Seventeenth Century* (1919).
4 Bridget Hill, *Women, Work and Sexual Politics in Eighteenth-Century England* (Oxford, 1990). See also Pat Hudson and W.R. Lee, eds, *Women's Work and the Family Economy in Historical Perspective* (Manchester, 1990).

divided in their beliefs about its qualitative effects on women's lives. Pinchbeck asserts that 'women gained greatly by the transference of manufacture from the home to the factory', a process which, she argues, brought with it increased female economic and social independence.[5] Hill, on the other hand, mourns the disintegration of the family economy and with it a loss of status for women and their marginalization within the economy as a whole. Her 'pessimistic' view is echoed by others. Eric Richards has argued that the industrial revolution did not emancipate women, but led to a substantial diminution of their economic role as employment opportunities contracted.[6] Others have linked capitalism with patriarchy, describing them as dual structures in the creation of women's oppression. It has been claimed that the industrial revolution helped to promote separate spheres ideology, and with it such developments as restrictive labour practices and campaigns for the family wage, which served to redefine and revitalize patriarchal forces.[7] In contrast, Tilly and Scott agree that industrialization meant that women were increasingly earning an independent wage instead of contributing to the efforts of a family work team, but argue that they continued to perform the type of low-status, low-skilled jobs that had always characterized women's work.[8] They have been joined in this view by an increasing number of historians who stress the continuity of women's experience of work and socio-economic status during the pre-industrial and industrial periods of the eighteenth and nineteenth centuries, rather than seeing the industrial revolution as a time of fundamental change.[9]

5 Pinchbeck, *Women Workers*, p. 307.

6 Eric Richards, 'Women in the British economy since about 1700: an interpretation' *History* 59 (1974). Although for more complex interpretations see Jane Rendall, *Women in an Industrializing Society: England 1750–1880* (Oxford, 1990); Deborah Valenze, *The First Industrial Woman* (Oxford, 1995); and Pamela Sharpe, *Adapting to Capitalism: Working Women in the English Economy, 1700–1850* (Basingstoke, 1996).

7 Catherine Hall, 'The early formation of Victorian domestic ideology', in S. Burman, ed., *Fit Work For Women* (1979); H.I. Hartmann, 'The unhappy marriage of Marxism and feminism: towards a more progressive union' *Capital and Class* 8 (1979); M. Barratt, *Women's Oppression Today* (1980); S. Walby, *Patriarchy at Work* (Cambridge, 1986); S. Dex, 'Issues in gender and employment' *Social History* 13 (1988); H. Berenson, 'The "family wage" and working women's consciousness in Britain' *Politics and Society* 19 (1991); Sara Horrell and Jane Humphries, 'Women's labour force participation and the transition to the male-breadwinner family, 1790–1865' *EcHR* 48, 1 (1995).

8 Louise A. Tilly and Joan W. Scott, *Women, Work and Family* 2nd edn (New York, 1987), p. 77. See also Janet Thomas, 'Women and capitalism: oppression or emancipation?' *Comparative Studies in Society and History* 30 (1988).

9 Judith M. Bennett, ' "History that stands still": women's work in the European past' *FS* 14, 2 (1988); see also Maxine Berg, 'Women's work, mechanization and the early phases of industrialization in England', in R.E. Pahl, ed., *On Work: Historical, Comparative and*

One of the main reasons for this shift in emphasis in women's history has been a series of developments in the field of economic history, specifically the historiography of the industrial revolution. The argument for a transformation in women's work rests largely upon a model of British economic development that now appears outdated in two important respects: firstly, in the assumption that industrialization happened suddenly and dramatically between about 1780 and 1840, and secondly, that this process had a broadly uniform impact on all areas of the economy and produced an inevitable shift in the manufacturing process from the family workshop to the factory system. Most economic historians would now agree that the period of the industrial revolution was marked more by continuity than by revolutionary change, so that the very use of the term is called into question. It appears that industrialization in Britain was a gradual process that was diverse in its impact between regions, industries and over time;[10] moreover, it was not the case that working patterns altered overnight. The industrial revolution did not result in the propulsion of the bulk of the workforce into factories. Even by the mid nineteenth century, the factory was not the normal unit of production, employing probably fewer than 12 per cent of the workforce. As late as 1871, the average manufacturing establishment had less than twenty employees: a scenario far closer to the supposedly pre-industrial model of the family workshop than the huge factories attributed to the industrial age.[11]

Theoretical Approaches (Oxford, 1988); Katrina Honeyman and Jordan Goodman, 'Women's work, gender conflict, and labour markets in Europe, 1500–1900' *EcHR* 2nd ser., 44, 4 (1991); Amanda Vickery, 'Golden age to separate spheres? A review of the categories and chronology of English women's history' *HJ* 36, 2 (1993); Pamela Sharpe, 'Continuity and change: women's history and economic history in Britain' *EcHR* 48, 2 (1995).

10 See N.F.R. Crafts, *British Industrial Growth During the Industrial Revolution* (Oxford, 1985); E.A. Wrigley, *Continuity, Chance and Change: The Character of the Industrial Revolution in England* (Cambridge, 1989); Pat Hudson, *The Industrial Revolution* (1992); Patrick O'Brien and Roland Quinault, eds, *The Industrial Revolution and British Society* (Cambridge, 1993); Maxine Berg, *The Age of Manufactures, 1700–1820: Industry, innovation and work in Britain*, 2nd edn (1994). Although see also Maxine Berg, 'What difference did women's work make to the industrial revolution?' *HWJ* 35 (1993), where she argues that a better understanding of the level of women's and children's labour and the role of organizational and technological innovation during the industrial revolution might reveal more significant productivity gains in this period than recent research has allowed.

11 Raphael Samuel, 'Workshop of the world: steam power and hand technology in mid-Victorian Britain' *HWJ* 3 (1977); John Stevenson, 'Social aspects of the industrial revolution', in O'Brien and Quinault, eds, *Industrial Revolution and British Society*. Although Maxine Berg argues that women may have been used in disproportionate numbers in new technologies and methods of organization in the late eighteenth and early nineteenth centuries, thus contributing greatly to a dynamic industrial sector, she still maintains that 'too much emphasis has been given in histories of women's work to the factories': Berg, 'What difference did women's work make?'

Such reassessments of the nature of industrialization have profound implications for the history of women's work. One can no longer assume that women were necessarily forced out of the workplace at the end of the eighteenth century, as organized labour and the factory system acted to exclude female workers and prompted the associated rise of the male breadwinner; nor can it be supposed that the factory girl was representative of women workers, as women had to look for work outside the home and the family economy disintegrated. Instead, it is clear that industrialization in England was a gradual process that began long before the supposed watershed of the late eighteenth century, and that throughout the eighteenth century as a whole, the British economy was far more industrial than was once thought. In this context, the image of women working solely within the domestic setting in the period before the industrial revolution is likely to be a distortion. It seems probable that throughout the century, substantial numbers of women, whether single or married, went out of the home to work for wages.[12] All these factors emphasize the continuity in women's experience of work during the eighteenth and early nineteenth centuries, rather than suggesting a revolutionary break with the past.

Despite the fact that the traditional model of female labour in the eighteenth and early nineteenth centuries has been undermined, the patterns of women's work still remain obscure due to a lack of empirical research. This chapter seeks to redress this in part, by looking at women's involvement in one area of the eighteenth-century economy, the printing trades. This slightly ambiguous description can be used to encompass a wide variety of women associated with all aspects of eighteenth-century printing: from the very poorest hawker of pamphlets to the wealthy owner of a large printing and bookselling business, and from the untrained newspaper-seller to the highly skilled engraver, printer or typefounder. In addition, one finds women working as stationers, paper dealers and makers, publishers, newsagents and bookbinders, as book, print, map and music sellers, and as the owners of circulating libraries. The nature of available sources means that emphasis will be placed on those women towards the upper end of the scale, who were either in charge of a business, or who maintained a high profile within an enterprise. Concentrating on women of property constitutes a major diversion

---

12 Richard Wall, 'Women alone in English society' *Annales de Démographie Historique* (1981); Olwen Hufton, 'Women without men: widows and spinsters in Britain and France in the eighteenth century' *JFH* 9 (1984); Peter Earle, 'The female labour market in London in the late seventeenth and early eighteenth centuries' *EcHR* 2nd ser., 42, 3 (1989).

in a field that has been dominated by research on the labouring poor. Such shifts in focus in the historiography of women's work in the eighteenth century are essential, however, if we are to gain a fuller understanding of the subject.

The printing trades as a whole experienced great growth during the eighteenth century. The period witnessed a massive increase in the public appetite for printed matter of all kinds: a development linked to what has been dubbed the 'commercialization of culture'. James Raven has shown that a dramatic rise took place in the number of publications as the century progressed, and has noted a watershed in the 1780s.[13] In response to such increases in demand, the printing trades expanded accordingly. Ian Maxted has estimated that the number of individuals involved in the book trades in London rose steadily through the first three quarters of the century, with a sharp rise of around 50 per cent in the last quarter.[14] Outside the capital, a similar story of growth emerges, although the provinces were less active than London in the earlier part of the century.[15]

While not a new phenomenon in the eighteenth century, printing and its associated trades represent one of the century's most notable commercial successes. This, coupled with its geographical diversity (no town of any note was without at least one printing office in the second half of the century), means that the printing trades constitute a particularly interesting example of eighteenth-century economic development. Moreover, printing was almost exclusively an urban activity, and despite the overall size of the industry was conducted in small-scale enterprises employing anything from a single individual to, more typically, between five and twenty people.

Given the bias of research towards female labour in rural areas and the impact of the factory system upon women's work, an examination of women in the printing trades provides a useful counterbalance with which to judge their place in the economic life of eighteenth-century England. Although female involvement in the printing trades constituted a very small part of the labour market as a whole, as an example of small-scale urban manufacturing and retailing it may well be more representative, at least in terms of the non-agricultural economy, than some other types of women's work

13 James Raven, *Judging New Wealth: Popular Publishing and Responses to Commerce, 1750–1800* (Oxford, 1992), pp. 32–5.

14 Ian Maxted, *The London Book Trades, 1775–1800* (Woking, 1977).

15 Ian Maxted, *The Devon Book Trades: A Biographical Dictionary* (Exeter, 1991); C.J. Hunt, *The Booktrade in Northumberland and Durham to 1860* (Newcastle, 1975); John Feather, *The Provincial Book Trade in Eighteenth-Century England* (Cambridge, 1985).

that historians have examined. Moreover, the women under discussion derive from two other neglected groups, by virtue of their
(mostly) widowed status and their social class.

The significance of widows in economic life has certainly not
gone unnoticed by historians,[16] but remains largely unexplored, at
least in an urban context. This is unfortunate, given that an estimated 9 to 14 per cent of households were headed by women during
the seventeenth and eighteenth centuries,[17] and were likely to have
constituted a significant economic force. It seems that there was a
decline in the number of widows remarrying in the seventeenth
and eighteenth centuries in England, which would suggest that
their numbers and prominence increased.[18] However, there is little
evidence that this pattern of decreasing remarriage became more
marked during the eighteenth century. This is certainly not suggested by an examination of the lengths of time women ran businesses, which did not appear to increase towards the end of the
eighteenth century as one would expect if remarriage became rarer.
It therefore seems unlikely that an increasing inability or disinclina-
tion amongst widows to remarry as the century progressed would
have counterbalanced other factors and explained the continuity of
women's involvement in the printing trades that this chapter will
describe. It is also unlikely that there were simply more widows,
since there was an appreciable decline in mortality in the later eighteenth century, which meant that fewer marriages would have been
broken by the death of one of the partners.[19]

Most of the women under discussion in this chapter were property owners of the middling sorts. As has been noted, middle-class
women have been overlooked in a field that has focused almost exclusively on those further down the social scale;[20] yet there can be

16 Hill, *Women, Work and Sexual Politics*, pp. 153, 240–8; Wall, 'Women alone in English
society'; Hufton, 'Women without men'; Mary Prior, 'Women in the urban economy:
Oxford 1500–1800', in idem, ed., *Women in English Society, 1500–1800* (1985); Rendall,
Women in an Industrializing Society, pp. 27–30; Olwen Hufton, *The Prospect Before Her: A
History of Women in Western Europe, Volume One: 1500–1800* (1995).
17 Wall, 'Women alone in English society', p. 303.
18 Barbara J. Todd, 'The remarrying widow: a stereotype reconsidered', in Prior, ed.,
Women in English Society; Jeremy Boulton, 'London widowhood revisited: the decline of
female remarriage in the seventeenth and early eighteenth centuries' *CC* 3 (1990); Pamela
Sharpe, 'Literally spinsters: a new interpretation of local economy and demography in
Colyton in the seventeenth and eighteenth century' *EcHR* 44 (1991).
19 E.A. Wrigley and R.S. Schofield, *The Population History of England, 1541–1871: A
Reconstruction* (Cambridge, 1981), pp. 174–9.
20 Although see Leonore Davidoff and Catherine Hall, *Family Fortunes: Men and Women
of the English Middle Class, 1780–1850* (1987); Catherine Hall, 'Strains in the "firm of wife,
children and friends"? Middle-class women and employment in early nineteenth-century
England', in Hudson and Lee, eds, *Women's Work and the Family Economy*.

little doubt, in the light of recent historical work, about the increasing size and importance of the middle classes in eighteenth-century England.[21] As the country witnessed more rapid urban development, the middling sorts grew in numbers, wealth and prominence.

What has been written about middle-class women in this period implies that they were increasingly likely to dissociate themselves from the world of business as time progressed.[22] This may have been the case for women at higher levels of society, but a survey of the overall numbers of women heading businesses reveals a continuity of involvement in the printing trades in the eighteenth century, with no diminution in the female role over time. It was not until the second decade of the nineteenth century that the printing trades began to experience the sort of technical innovations that historians have claimed served to diminish the position of female workers in other industries. Yet even then, the introduction of the steam press and stereotyping does not appear to have had this impact, at least in the short term.[23]

Like the economic activity of women in general, the role which women played within the printing trades is not easy to identify. There are some particularly prominent individuals on whom historians of the London press in the earlier part of the century have already focused, notably those women involved in producing political propaganda under Walpole. The histories of women such as Sarah Nutt, Ann Dodd and Ann Baldwin are accessible because

21 See, among others, Neil McKendrick, John Brewer and J.H. Plumb, eds, *The Birth of a Consumer Society: The Commercialization of Eighteenth-Century England* (1982); Nicholas Rogers, *Whigs and Cities: Popular Politics in the Age of Walpole and Pitt* (Oxford, 1989); Davidoff and Hall, *Family Fortunes*; Peter Earle, *The Making of the English Middle Class* (1989); Paul Langford, *A Polite and Commercial People: England, 1727–1783* (Oxford, 1989); idem, *Public Life and the Propertied Englishman, 1689–1798* (Oxford, 1991); T. Koditschek, *Class Formation and Urban Industrial Society, Bradford 1750–1850* (Cambridge, 1990); Peter Borsay, ed., *The Eighteenth-Century English Town: A Reader in English Urban History, 1688–1820* (1990); J. Barry and C. Brooks, eds, *The Middling Sort of People: Culture, Society and Politics in England 1550–1800* (Basingstoke, 1992); special issue of *JBS: The making of the English middle class, c.1700–1850*, 2, 4 (1993); Dror Wahrman, *Imagining the Middle Class: The Political Representation of Class in Britain, c.1780–1840* (Cambridge, 1995); P.J. Corfield, *Power and the Professions in Britain, 1700–1850* (1995).

22 Alice Clark noted this development in the seventeenth century: *Working Life*. For a discussion of this trend (or lack of it) in the eighteenth century, see Pinchbeck, *Women Workers*, pp. 282–3; Hill, *Women, Work and Sexual Politics*; Prior, 'Women in the urban economy'; Pat Thane, 'The history of the gender division of labour in Britain: reflections on "herstory" in accounting: the first eighty years' *Accounting, Organizations and Society* 17, 3/4 (1992); Davidoff and Hall, *Family Fortunes*, ch. 6; Vickery, 'Golden age to separate spheres?'

23 However, Jane Rendall does argue that in the second half of the nineteenth century, and with the introduction of new composing machinery, one can find evidence of male workers seeking to exclude women from their profession: Rendall, *Women in an Industrializing Society*, pp. 65–6.

their activities often led to their prosecution by the authorities, which was recorded in state papers. At least one historian writing on this period views this variety and extent of female activity as being temporary and atypical.[24] This is unlikely to have been the case. More often than not, one suspects that women's involvement in the printing trades remains hidden (like that of many male employees) in businesses where only those in overall charge – generally men – had their details recorded for posterity: in trade directories, advertisements, poll books, biographical dictionaries and in guild membership, apprenticeship and bankruptcy lists. Notwithstanding the preponderance of men listed in such sources, however, they do throw up important information about some types of female activity, namely when women took charge of businesses and operated under their own names.

There is also some evidence of women lower down the social scale working throughout the century as employees and apprentices. For example, the Exeter printer, Andrew Brice, was noted for the large numbers of female printers who worked in his office.[25] In addition, women can be found working as hawkers or mercuries – the street-sellers of newspapers and pamphlets. However, women like Mrs Pierce, Frances Karver, Ann Mahoney and Susannah Wilcox, who worked in London in the 1740s,[26] or Mrs Drew, the Devonshire almanack-seller at the end of the century,[27] for the most part remain impossible to track down. One can also find records of female apprentices, but again, the information that can be gleaned from them is sketchy.[28]

In north-east England the printing trades were at their peak between about 1750 and 1850. It is hard to tell how typical this region was in relation to other provincial areas in the country. The Northumberland and Durham trades may well have been larger and were certainly better documented than was the case elsewhere; however, they do provide a useful case study for the examination of female involvement in the printing trades that follows, covering

24 Margaret Hunt, 'Hawkers, bawlers, and mercuries: women in the London press in the early Enlightenment', in Margaret Hunt, ed., *Women and the Enlightenment* (New York, 1984). Also Michael Harris, *London Newspapers in the Age of Walpole* (Cranbury, NJ, 1987). Cf. C.J. Mitchell's more broad-ranging study, 'Women in the eighteenth-century book trades', in O.M. Brock, ed., *Writers, Books, and Trade: An Eighteenth-Century Miscellany* (New York, 1994).
25 T.N. Brushfield, *The Life and Bibliography of Andrew Brice* ([Exeter?, 1888]), p. 43.
26 Harris, *London Newspapers in the Age of Walpole*, pp. 39–40.
27 Maxted, *Devon Book Trades*, p. 58.
28 See Ian Maxted, *The British Book Trades, 1710–1777* (Exeter, 1983).

the period 1700 to 1840. During this time 59 women headed print businesses in this area.[29] As might be expected, the total number of individuals (both men and women) who ran businesses in the printing trades increased steadily throughout the period: from 7 in the first decade of the eighteenth century to 37 between 1750 and 1759; to 79 in the last decade of the century; and, climbing rapidly at the start of the nineteenth century, to 250 between 1830 and 1839.

What is particularly interesting is the proportion of women to men over the whole period. Although it is clear that female involvement was relatively constant, averaging just over 8 per cent between 1700 and 1840, this figure was prone to some fluctuation. There was a clear peak between 1780 and 1809, when the proportion rose to between 10 and 13 per cent, thereafter dropping off slightly to around 8 per cent until the end of the period. This broad trend is also found in both Devon and Liverpool, where the numbers of women in the printing trades appear to increase markedly in the last two decades of the eighteenth century.[30] These findings do not support the claim that the industrial revolution acted to exclude women from the workplace, or at least from work of any status. Indeed, female involvement in skilled and responsible positions in the printing trades appears to be increasing at the very point where some historians argue that they should have been either forced out of the business or marginalized within it.

When one looks at the types of trade in which women in Northumberland and Durham were involved, rather than their numbers, it appears that gender may have influenced choice or opportunity of occupation, with women being more evident in retailing than in production. For the period as a whole, women were slightly more likely than men to work as booksellers and stationers, and this trend was far more marked in the case of circulating library owners, of

29 Much of this analysis is based upon Hunt's *Booktrade in Northumberland and Durham.* Most of his information for the earlier part of the eighteenth century was taken from newspaper advertisements, whilst for the last decades of the century, and the first decades of the nineteenth century, details were obtained from regional trade directories. The latter might be a more reliable source (although certainly not entirely dependable) and the results may be skewed slightly. Also, H.R. Plomer, *A Dictionary of the Printers and Booksellers Who Were at Work in England, Scotland and Ireland from 1688–1725* (Bibliographical Society, Oxford, 1922); H.R. Plomer, G.H. Bushnell and E. McDix, *A Dictionary of the Printers and Booksellers Who Were at Work in England, Scotland and Ireland From 1726 to 1775* (Bibliographical Society, Oxford, 1968); Maxted, *British Book Trades, 1710–1777.*

30 See Maxted, *Devon Book Trades*; J.S. Attwood, *Booksellers and Printers in Devon and Cornwall in the Seventeenth and Eighteenth Centuries* ([Exeter?], 1917); M.R. Perkin, ed., *The Book Trade in Liverpool to 1805: A Directory* (Liverpool Bibliographical Society Book Trade in the North West Project, Liverpool, 1981).

whom a majority were female. Conversely, women were less likely to
be printers and bookbinders;[31] however, female involvement in these
apparently more masculine preserves did not disappear as the period
progressed. Indeed, all the examples of women working as bookbinders and printers that were found dated from the period after
1780.

This occupational breakdown of women traced in Northumberland and Durham between 1700 and 1840 can be compared to that
of the much larger sample of 250 women found operating in the
printing trades in London during the eighteenth century.[32] Here,
a broadly similar story is told, with 70 women listed as stationers,
54 as booksellers, 45 as printers and 24 as bookbinders. Interestingly enough, the numbers of women printers and bookbinders
were spread across the century, but, as in the north-east, there was
a marked concentration towards the later decades; thus, although
the evidence suggests that women were more likely to take part
in the retail side of the printing trades, as booksellers, stationers
and the owners of circulating libraries, there is no proof that they
were pushed out of the more 'male' manufacturing professions like
bookbinding and printing as the century progressed: rather the
opposite seems to be true.

Of course, the question still remains as to why such gender-
based divisions existed in the first place. One likely, but partial,
explanation is that technically complex trades such as bookbinding
generally required practitioners to have undergone an apprenticeship. Although it appears that many women did receive training to
equip them for such jobs within a family business – in a type of
informal apprenticeship – they were far less likely than men to be
given such an education outside a familial setting. This meant that
while women could and did become bookbinders and printers, this
was less usual than was the case with men. On the other hand,
although retailing required a degree of skill, it did not demand the
same type of technical expertise as manufacturing jobs in the print
trades; thus, running a circulating library could be a largely female

31 The following list records the percentage of women involved in various trades compared with figures for both men and women. It should be noted that most individuals
involved in the printing trades were described as having more than one profession, bookselling and stationery-selling being typically linked, for example. Bookselling: 78% women,
70% women and men; stationers: 63% to 56%; circulating library owners: 63% to 16%;
printers: 30% to 44%; bookbinders: 17% to 35%.

32 Plomer, *Dictionary of . . . Printers and Booksellers . . . 1688–1725*; Plomer, Bushnell and
McDix, *Dictionary of . . . Printers and Booksellers . . . 1726 to 1775*; Maxted, *British Book Trades*;
Maxted, *London Book Trades, 1775–1800*.

concern because participants needed no specific technical skills, other than a general knowledge of both the book trade and good business practice, backed up by sufficient capital (such as that received in a legacy.)

As far as their method of entry into the printing trades is concerned, there is no doubt that many women did not do so 'independently', but took over a business upon the death of a male relative, usually a husband. (In this, they differed little from the large number of sons who followed their fathers into business.) Of a total of 437 women who have been identified as running some type of printing business in England in the eighteenth century, 155 can be positively identified as widows, whereas 14 inherited as daughters, 8 as sisters and 2 as nieces. The sum of 179 constitutes 41 per cent of the total, and the real proportion is likely to be higher still. What is interesting about such women is not how they came to be in possession of a business, but what they chose to do with it once they had it. Clearly there were several options open to them: to sell up, to employ someone else to run it for them, or to run it themselves. Evidence suggests that the last choice was a popular one. Although some women did pass on their inheritance, many appear to have stepped into the shoes of the previous owner. The ease with which they appear to have done so suggests a prior and substantial involvement in the operation of the business, and may also explain why many women chose to continue the business they had inherited along broadly the same lines as before.[33]

A good example of such a 'seamless' takeover is provided by the case of Mary Say. When her husband Charles died in 1775, she was left in charge of a large printing business in London. One of Charles Say's main undertakings had been to publish a daily newspaper, the *Gazetteer*, and upon his death the proprietors of this paper immediately contracted with his widow to continue the arrangement.[34] This she did for over twenty years, in addition to publishing at least four other titles.[35] Say worked as a printer until 1810, despite the fact

33 Cf. Natalie Zemon Davis's study of women and work in early modern France, 'Women in the crafts in sixteenth-century Lyon', in Barbara A. Hanawalt, ed., *Women and Work in Preindustrial Europe* (Bloomington, IN, 1986). Davis finds little evidence of a work identity among women in her study. They appeared to have little continuity in their work lives and would generally 'marry out' of their family's trade or re-marry into a different trade from their husband if widowed. However, she does note, interestingly, that printing may have been an exception.

34 Harris, *London Newspapers in the Age of Walpole*, p. 84.

35 A. Aspinall, 'Statistical accounts of the London newspapers in the eighteenth century' *English Historical Review* 63 (1948); PRO, C104/67–8 (records of the *Gazetteer*).

that she remarried in 1787.[36] Her new husband was a calico printer
named Edward Vint,[37] who seems to have remained uninvolved
with his wife's business. Indeed, she appears on imprints as Mary
Say until 1790, and thereafter as 'Mary Vint (late Say)': suggesting
a commercially inspired concern to hold on to the prestige of an
established business name over and above any desire to acknowledge
her change in status. What is known about her relations with the
owners of the *Gazetteer* reveals her to have been a tough business-
woman. During the 1790s she became critical of the paper's management, but when the proprietors attempted to oust her as the
Gazetteer's printer, accusing her of breach of contract, she launched
a counter-attack as a result of which she gained overall control of
the newspaper.[38]

Mary Say was not alone in the apparent ease with which she took
over her husband's business: many more examples can be found.
For example, Ann Baldwin was married to the London bookseller
and publisher, Richard Baldwin, until his death in 1698. She was
described by a contemporary as a 'help-meet' to her husband and
when widowed as skilled in her work.[39] She continued to run her
husband's business with vigour, publishing over 200 works in fifteen
years.[40] Elizabeth James, a London printer and pamphlet-seller,
succeeded her husband to the office of printer to the City of London in 1750.[41] Also in London, Mary Cooper carried on her husband's publishing business after his death, and produced a good
deal of material in the 1740s under her own name;[42] similarly,
Elizabeth Applebee inherited her husband's business in the same
period and published various newspapers over the next 30 years.[43]
In Cambridge, Sarah James ran a printing business for nine years
after she was widowed, before selling up in 1767.[44] In Norwich,
Frances Oliver ran her husband's bookselling business for 37 years

36 Maxted, *London Book Trades, 1775–1800*, pp. 198–9.

37 Robert L. Haig, *The Gazetteer, 1735–1797* (Carbondale, IL, 1960), p. 215.

38 Ibid., pp. 245–61.

39 *The Life and Errors of John Dunton* (1705), pp. 236, 260.

40 Leona Rostenberg, 'Richard and Anne Baldwin, Whig patriot publishers' *Papers of the Bibliographical Society of America* 47 (1953), p. 28.

41 Plomer, Bushnell and Dix, *Dictionary of . . . Printers and Booksellers . . . 1726 to 1775*, p. 138.

42 Herbert M. Atherton, *Political Prints in the Age of Hogarth* (Oxford, 1974), pp. 6–7.

43 Plomer, Bushnell and Dix, *Dictionary of . . . Printers and Booksellers . . . 1726 to 1775*, p. 7; Aspinall, 'Statistical accounts'.

44 Plomer, Bushnell and Dix, *Dictionary of . . . Printers and Booksellers . . . 1726 to 1775*, pp. 95, 253.

after his death in 1703.[45] In 1716, reports came from Exeter that a widow had taken over her husband's press and that she was publishing illicit material just as he had done.[46]

The workings of the Caslon typefoundry in London provide an interesting example of constant female involvement in the printing trades over many years. When William Caslon, the foundry's owner, died in 1778, the business was left to his wife and two young sons. Renamed 'Elizabeth Caslon and Sons', the foundry was conducted by Elizabeth for the next seventeen years until illness (soon followed by her death) prevented her from continuing. Elizabeth Caslon appears to have run the business well. She was also an active member of the Society of Typefounders, which was started in 1793.[47] Timperley's biographical dictionary praised her highly:

> Of Mrs. Caslon it would be improper to pass unnoticed. Her merit and ability in conducting a capital business during the life of her husband, and afterwards till her son was capable of managing it, was deserving of all praise. In quickness of understanding, and activity of execution, she left few equals among her sex.[48]

It was, in fact, not Elizabeth Caslon's son, Henry, who inherited the business, but her daughter-in-law, another Elizabeth. She had been widowed in 1788, and was left Henry's share in the foundry jointly with her infant son. Timperley is even more effusive in his praise of the second Mrs Caslon, whom he describes as being 'celebrated in the annals of type founding' and possessing 'an excellent understanding'.[49] Indeed, it appears that she did much to improve the commercial success of the foundry, including producing new fonts. In 1799 she purchased her mother-in-law's old share, presumably raising the capital with a loan and/or her share of past profits, which, in addition to the interest in the company left her by her husband, gave her effective ownership of the foundry.[50]

Other examples of prominent women in the printing trades can be found in Newcastle, where the Slack family had been operating

---

45 David Stoker, 'A History of the Norwich Book Trades, 1660–1760' (Library Association Thesis, 1976), pp. 281–2.

46 L. Blackburne to Parker, Exeter, 22 Dec. 1716: BL Stowe MS. 750, fos. 234–5. I am grateful to Stephen Taylor for this reference.

47 Maxted, *London Book Trades, 1775–1800*, p. 40; John Nichols, *Literary Anecdotes of the Eighteenth Century* 9 vols (1812–15), II, p. 357.

48 C.H. Timperley, *A Dictionary of Printers and Printing* (1839), p. 744.

49 Ibid., pp. 834–5.

50 Maxted, *London Book Trades, 1775–1800*, p. 40; Nichols, *Literary Anecdotes*, II, p. 357; Timperley, *Dictionary*, pp. 834–5.

from the middle of the eighteenth century. Elizabeth and Sarah Slack, the daughters of Thomas Slack, inherited his printing and publishing business upon his death in 1785. A few months later, Sarah married Solomon Hodgson, one of her father's apprentices, who then took over the business. It is unlikely that this formal transfer of authority – from Sarah Slack to her new husband – was matched by a real withdrawal from involvement on her part. Like her mother before her, Sarah was described as having worked hard to assist her husband in his work.[51] Moreover, upon Solomon Hodgson's death in 1800, Sarah assumed control in an impressive manner. A nineteenth-century historian of Newcastle remarked on her character and ability:

> Upon Solomon Hodgson's decease, the responsibility of carrying on his business and rearing a family of four or five children devolved upon his widow. Mrs. Hodgson was a woman of energy and resource. Brought up in the establishment, she knew its wants and capabilities, and she discharged the responsible duties which belonged to it with skill and intelligence. Six years before he died her husband had relinquished to John Bell the bookselling and stationery department of his business (conducted in the adjoining shop, facing Union Street) and confined himself to letterpress printing, and the publication of his newspaper. But Mrs. Hodgson, extending her connection, re-occupied the Union Street shop, and fitted up the united premises for increasing trade as a printer and publisher.[52]

Sarah Hodgson succeeded in making her printing firm one of the most important in Newcastle. Although she worked with both her sons once they came of age in 1806 and 1814, it is clear that she remained in overall charge of the business until her death from cholera in 1822.[53]

The Farley family, and in particular its female members, featured prominently in the print trade in Bristol. Brothers Samuel and Felix Farley were estranged and owned rival newspapers in the town. In 1753 both men died. Felix left his business to his wife Elizabeth, while Samuel was succeeded by his niece, Sarah. The two Farley newspapers were run by women for the next twenty years, and continued to display a fierce commercial rivalry. As one nineteenth-

---

51 James Hodgson, the younger, 'Thomas Slack of Newcastle, Printer, 1723–1784, founder of the "Newcastle Chronicle"' *Archaeologia Aeliana* 3rd ser., 17 (1920), p. 149; Hunt, *Booktrade in Northumberland and Durham*, p. 50.

52 Richard Welford, *Men of Mark 'Twixt Tyne and Tweed* 3 vols (1895), III, p. 547.

53 Ibid., III, pp. 547–8; Hunt, *Booktrade in Northumberland and Durham*, p. 50; E. Mackenzie, *A Descriptive and Historical Account of the Town and County of Newcastle Upon Tyne* 2 vols (Newcastle upon Tyne, 1827), II, p. 28.

century commentator noted, 'neither of the papers showed any lack of vigour while conducted by ladies'.[54] Indeed, such was the distinctiveness of Sarah Farley's management that, when her *Bristol Journal* was sold following her death in 1774, it was renamed *Sarah Farley's Bristol Journal* by its new owners.[55]

What these examples suggest is that women often played full and active roles in family businesses, which equipped them to take over completely if circumstances demanded. On the whole, the evidence for such female involvement is circumstantial, and based upon the high incidence of apparently successful transfers to women. While there are a few sources that comment directly upon the useful role played by wives in their husbands' printing businesses, there is a suggestion that wives did not always act as 'full' partners, but were more likely to take on certain duties than others, usually in the area of retailing.

James Lackington, the London bookseller, wrote of his second wife, Dorcas:

> My new wife's attachment to books was a very fortunate circumstance for us both, not only as it was a perpetual source of rational amusement, but also as it tended to promote my trade: her extreme love for books made her delight to be in the shop, so that she soon became perfectly acquainted with every part of it, and (as my stock increased) with other rooms where I kept books, and could readily get any article that was asked for. Accordingly, when I was out on business, my shop was well attended. This constant attention, and good usage, procured me many customers; and I soon perceived that I could sell double and treble the quantity of books if I had a larger stock.[56]

The letters of Isabella Strange, wife of the engraver, Robert Strange, show that she was left in sole charge of selling his publications while he was abroad during the 1760s.[57] Maria Wier can be found working as a bookbinder and restorer in France, London and Edinburgh between 1774 and 1816.[58] For some of this time she was employed with her husband, but it appears that she far outshone him in their trade:

54 John Latimer, *The Annals of Bristol in the Eighteenth Century* ([Bristol], 1893), p. 293.

55 Ibid., pp. 292–3; G.A. Cranfield, *The Development of the Provincial Newspaper 1700–1760* (Oxford, 1962), pp. 60–1; Plomer, Bushnell and Dix, *Dictionary of . . . Printers and Booksellers . . . 1726 to 1775*, pp. 89–90; D.F. Gallop, 'Chapters in the history of the provincial newspaper press, 1700–1855' (unpub. MA thesis, University of Reading, 1954), pp. 29ff.

56 James Lackington, *Memoirs of the Life of James Lackington* (1794), p. 326.

57 James Dennistoun, *Memoirs of Sir Robert Strange* 2 vols (1855), I, p. 311.

58 Maxted, *London Book Trades, 1775–1800*, p. 246.

Mrs. Wier, was celebrated as the most complete book restorer that ever lived . . . her skill in mending defective leaves was such, that, unless held up to the light, the renovation was imperceptible.[59]

Some historians have assumed that, despite often having the ability to do so, women only took control of a business when it was absolutely necessary.[60] It appears that women may have exercised a degree of choice in this area. Some women seem to have been content to hand over their responsibilities, either because they aspired to genteel status or because other pressures were brought to bear on them. When John Almon married the widow of William Parker in 1784, he took immediate control of Parker's newspaper, the *General Advertiser*.[61] There is no suggestion from his business correspondence after that date that his new wife played any part in the enterprise.[62] Other women kept their distance from the day-to-day workings of a business, while still exercising a degree of control. Mercy Blakeway was left a share in the *Salopian Journal* by her husband in 1796, and appears to have attended some of the paper's shareholders' meetings.[63] The records of the *Essex Chronicle* record that Elizabeth Griffin was a proprietor of the newspaper between 1777 and 1784.[64] Neither woman appears to have had to intervene in the affairs of the company she part-owned. This was not the case for a shareholder in another newspaper, the *Ipswich Journal*. In 1761, Elizabeth Craighton and her nephew, John Shave, were left the paper by her brother. It is not clear what role Elizabeth played in running the paper, but in 1769 their partnership was dissolved and Shave was left in charge, in exchange for providing an annuity for his aunt. Despite her seeming desire for a 'hands-off' relationship with the paper, Mrs Craighton fought back when Shave ran into financial troubles in the early 1770s and set up a rival paper with the help of another nephew, Stephen Jackson. Craighton's defence of her inheritance produced a bitter struggle that resulted both in a minor pamphlet war and in her eventual victory when Shave's paper folded in 1777.[65]

59 Timperley, *Dictionary*, p. 796.

60 See, for example, ibid., p. 744; Plomer, Bushnell and Dix, *Dictionary of . . . Printers and Booksellers . . . 1726 to 1775*, pp. 11, 117.

61 [John Almon], *Memoirs of a Late Eminent Bookseller* (1790), p. 125.

62 BL Add. MSS. 20733.

63 SRRU, D2713 (articles of agreement between Blakeway and the other proprietors of the *Salopian Journal*); MS 1923 (minutes of the shareholders' meetings).

64 ERO, Acc. 5197, D/F 66/1.

65 *The History of the Ipswich Journal for 150 Years* (Ipswich, 1875), p. 3; S.F. Watson, 'Some materials for a history of printing and publishing in Ipswich' *Proceedings of the Suffolk Institute of Archaeology and Natural History* 24 (1949), p. 206.

Other examples of female inheritance show women reorganizing businesses to meet their new circumstances. While continuing in the same trade as her husband, Sarah Baskerville scaled down the size of the operation she had inherited from him in 1775, and kept his typefoundry going by dispensing with the printing side of his business.[66] More frequently, reorganization meant taking on extra help, often in the shape of a male employee. By becoming, in effect, the senior partner and replacing her husband, a widow's former position was left vacant. This is what Ann Ward did when she succeeded her husband Caesar to run a large printing business in York in 1759. Although she remained in overall control and did not go into formal partnership, she took on the compositor, David Russell, to help manage affairs.[67] Elizabeth Newbery employed two managers in succession for the bookselling business she inherited from her husband and ran for over twenty years.[68] Mrs Virtue, the widow of a London stationer, took her husband's apprentice into partnership after her husband's death.[69] Elsewhere, women who had inherited businesses went into formal partnerships. Elizabeth Fielder, who had been left her husband's stationery business in the early 1760s, had a registered press with Charles Philp and William Galabin in 1805.[70] Ann Watts, a London printer, succeeded Clement Watts, trading alone between 1785 and 1794 and then with Edward Bridgewater until 1817.[71] Ann Pearson, the Birmingham printer and publisher, was in partnership with Samuel Aris in 1768, then with a Mr Coy, and finally with James Rollason in 1783.[72]

Far more commonly, women took members of their family, most frequently their sons, into partnership. The terms of the partnership usually appear to have left the mother in a permanently senior role, rather than seeing a son take over once he came of age. While it seems that women remained in the background when their husbands were alive, it does not appear that they were expected to slip back into the economic shadows once their sons reached adulthood. This suggests that age, as well as gender and social class, was a condition of economic power. For example, in Exeter Margery Yeo, whose husband died in 1707, traded with her son as Margery and

66 Plomer, Bushnell and Dix, *Dictionary of . . . Printers and Booksellers . . . 1726 to 1775*, pp. 17–18.

67 Robert Davies, *A Memoir of the York Press* (1868), pp. 261–311; YCA, Acc. 1663, M32 (Ann Ward's bill to the Yorkshire Association Movement, 1779).

68 Maxted, *London Book Trades, 1775–1800*, p. 160.

69 Nichols, *Literary Anecdotes*, III, pp. 431–5.

70 Maxted, *London Book Trades, 1775–1800*, p. 80.

71 Ibid., p. 240.

72 Joseph Hill, *Book-makers of Old Birmingham* (Birmingham, 1907), pp. 66–96.

Philip Yeo between 1708 and 1713, and thereafter under her name alone.[73] The London stationer, Sarah Smith, traded alone from 1753 to 1763, and as Sarah Smith and Son until 1792.[74] Mary Haydon, who ran the printing, bookselling and stationery business left her by her husband, Robert, in 1773, operated under the names M. & B. Haydon and M. Haydon and Son. Her son, Benjamin, ran the business on his own after his mother's death in 1791.[75] Margaret Angus, who inherited a printing, bookselling, bookbinding and stationery business from her husband in 1788, began to trade as M. Angus and Son from 1800 and continued to do so until her retirement in 1812.[76]

Alternatively, widows who did not have the necessary skill to step into their husbands' shoes might capitalize on their business in other ways. This was the case for the widows of three engravers: William Hogarth, the rather less famous William Wynne Ryland (although he did achieve a degree of notoriety in his day for being executed for forgery), and Frederick Nodder. After the deaths of these men, each of their widows continued in the print business selling copies of their husbands' works. Mary Ryland had shops in Oxford Street and New Bond Street for this purpose;[77] Elizabeth Nodder published Frederick Nodder's work for nearly twenty years after his death;[78] and Jane Hogarth employed the engraver, Richard Livesay, in order to publish more of her husband's works, and profited from a Hogarth revival in the 1780s.[79]

Most of the women who headed businesses in the printing trades seem not to have remarried. Their status as widows was a particularly independent one in comparison with that of married women or women who had never married. Under common law, they were treated as single women, 'femmes soles', rather than as married women, 'femmes couvertes', and as such they had an existence in the eyes of the law that was denied to those with husbands, who could not sue or be sued, form contracts or control property.[80] In addition, they had an increased status in many trade guilds. For

73 Maxted, *Devon Book Trades*, p. 148.
74 Maxted, *London Book Trades, 1775–1800*, p. 209.
75 Ibid., pp. 178–9.
76 Hunt, *Booktrade in Northumberland and Durham*, p. 3.
77 *Reminiscences of Henry Angelo* 2 vols (1828–30), I, p. 482.
78 Maxted, *London Book Trades, 1775–1800*, p. 163.
79 Ronald Paulson, *Hogarth*, Vol. III: *Art and Politics* (New Brunswick, NJ, 1993), pp. 433–8.
80 Lee Holcombe, *Wives and Property* (Oxford, 1983); Susan Staves, *Women's Separate Property in England, 1660–1833* (1990); Amy Louise Erickson, *Women and Property in Early Modern England* (1993).

example, the Stationers' Company in the City of London would allow the widow of a freeman to become a freewoman, which meant she had the right to take on apprentices and to hold a share in Stationers' Company stock.[81] During the eighteenth century, around 10 per cent of the masters in the Stationers' Company were women.[82]

The legal circumscription of married women did not necessarily reflect the experiences of all working women in the eighteenth century. In some towns, borough custom allowed married women 'femme sole' status so that they could trade independently of their husbands.[83] Mary Say, the London printer, exploited this provision along with others. Elizabeth Newbery inherited her husband's bookselling business in London at around the same time as Say, and continued to run it after she remarried.[84] Another London printer, Mary Fenner, was left a printshop when her husband William died in 1735. Despite her remarriage to the apothecary, James Waugh, she worked as a printer until her death.[85] Similarly, Jane Butter continued to run her late husband's Exeter bookshop under her own name, even after her remarriage in 1723 to another bookseller, Daniel Pring.[86] As these examples show, women did not have to remain unmarried after being widowed in order to hold on to a business, nor did remarriage automatically mean a loss of control. Moreover, there is at least one case where a woman did not even have to inherit in order to wield a sizeable degree of economic power. Hannah Humphrey, one of the most important printsellers and publishers of the late eighteenth century, was never married, and though she came from a family with links to the printing trades, she almost certainly built up her business on her own.[87]

As the preceding examples have shown, women who controlled print-related businesses did not all share the same experiences. Not all chose or were able to stay in the print trade, and of those who

81 Cyprian Blagden, *The Stationers' Company: A History, 1403–1959* (1960), p. 162.

82 Mitchell, 'Women in the . . . book trades', p. 29.

83 Mary Bateson, ed., *Borough Customs* 2 vols (1904–6), I, pp. 227–8; Mary Prior, 'Women and the urban economy: Oxford 1500–1800', in idem, ed., *Women in English Society*, pp. 102–3; Judith M. Bennett, 'Medieval women, modern women: across the great divide', in David Aers, ed., *Culture and History, 1350–1600: Essays on English Communities, Identities and Writing* (Hemel Hempstead, 1992), pp. 154–5. Both Prior and Bennett suggest that this practice became increasingly rare, although little systematic research on the subject appears to have been done.

84 Maxted, *London Book Trades, 1775–1800*, p. 160.

85 Ibid., p. 80; Nichols, *Literary Anecdotes*, III, pp. 602–3; Timperley, *Dictionary*, p. 835.

86 Maxted, *Devon Book Trades*, p. 108.

87 I am grateful to Tim Clayton for this reference: see his forthcoming book, *The Print in England, 1688–1802* (New Haven, CT, 1997). See also Maxted, *London Book Trades, 1775–1800*, p. 116.

did, some appear to have exercised more power than others; moreover, certain individuals demonstrated considerable skill and expertise in their trade while others did not. In spite of these differences, some important generalizations about the role of women in the printing trades can still be made. Firstly, there was a clear continuity of involvement throughout the eighteenth and early nineteenth centuries that appears to have been unaffected by the impact of the industrial revolution. Neither technological innovation nor the development of 'separate spheres' ideology appear to have made women less likely to play active roles in heading businesses. Secondly, it was almost certainly the case that women from printing trade families, widowed or not, were intimately concerned with the day-to-day operation of family businesses, even if their roles remained hidden until and unless they inherited and took charge.

There is evidence that some gender division of labour was in operation in the printing trades that made women more likely to take part in certain activities within printing than in others; however, such divisions were clearly not rigorously adhered to, since women can be found working in all areas of the printing trades throughout the period. Finally, although an examination of widows and other women who inherited business interests suggests a level of female involvement in the workplace among women as a whole that would have made them integral to economic life, it is evident that widows as a group enjoyed a degree and type of economic and social independence that other women generally did not experience. Although male economic power in these sorts of family businesses generally appears to have been pre-eminent, and was most obvious in the relationship between husbands and wives, it seems that some women, and widows in particular, could exercise control over male members of their families. Female economic power over men seems to have been typically expressed by widows over their sons.

Such important variations in women's experience of work and economic power should guard us against treating female workers in the eighteenth and early nineteenth centuries, even within one sector of the economy, as a homogeneous group. Rather, we need to explore what various and complicated factors – including gender, social class, marital status and occupation – influenced women's economic standing and workplace roles. As this chapter suggests, the resulting picture is unlikely to be a simple one.

CHAPTER FIVE

Women teachers and the expansion of girls' schooling in England, c.1760–1820

SUSAN SKEDD

The establishment of commercial schooling for girls and boys in the early seventeenth century and its expansion during the course of the eighteenth century completely changed the pattern of education in England. These new commercial schools were private ventures dependent on fees and run for the profit of their teachers: unlike the existing grammar and public schools, they were neither charitable nor endowed foundations. The majority of them accommodated boarding as well as day pupils, and appealed to parents wishing their children to benefit from a polite education. The new boys' academies were either classical academies kept by clergymen or university graduates, or mercantile and naval academies that offered a more practical education than the standard classical curriculum of the grammar schools.[1] The girls' schools were a greater educational innovation because for the first time they gave girls the opportunity of an extensive school education as an alternative to a private education in the home. The mixture of useful subjects – reading, writing and arithmetic – with polite accomplishments – French, dancing, drawing and music – taught at these girls' schools ensured their extraordinary popularity at a time when there was widespread interest in female education and a vigorous debate about the relative merits of public and private systems of education. Not only did the commercial schools provide a public education for

1 Research into commercial schooling for boys is virtually non-existent. The best account is in Margaret Bryant, *The London Experience of Secondary Education* (1986), chs 3–4. For the evolution of the grammar school and how it responded to the challenge set by the commercial schools, see Richard S. Tompson, *Classics or Charity? The Dilemma of the 18th-Century Grammar School* (Manchester, 1971).

girls, they also brought a new source of employment to women, in a profession that was far from private in character.

Teaching was a common occupation for women in Hanoverian England and running a school offered them the chance to manage their own businesses and the prospect of independence. It seems surprising, therefore, that the life and work of women teachers has been neglected by historians of the eighteenth and early nineteenth centuries.[2] The institutional focus of educational history has tended to overlook the commercial schools, which were mainly ephemeral organizations rarely surviving beyond two generations. In the absence of school records from the boarding and day schools, literary sources and autobiographical material have been used successfully by several historians to piece together a general history of girls' education in England prior to the foundation of elementary schools under the auspices of the National Society and the British and Foreign Society in the early nineteenth century.[3] Although attention has been drawn to eighteenth-century concerns about the popularity of boarding schools, and fears that girls were receiving an education unsuited to their rank and role in society,[4] the significance of teaching as a female profession has not been investigated in detail. Research on female work in seventeenth- and eighteenth-century England has concentrated on the lower rather than the middle ranks of society, in accordance with the assumption that opportunities for employment among women in the middling ranks diminished significantly over this period.[5] The late eighteenth and early nineteenth century has been identified as the crucial period

2 The significance of teaching as a middle-class profession received little discussion in Leonore Davidoff and Catherine Hall, *Family Fortunes: Men and Women of the English Middle Class 1780–1850* (1987).

3 Dorothy Gardiner, *English Girlhood at School: A Study of Women's Education Through Twelve Centuries* (Oxford, 1929): a pioneering work that has yet to be superseded; Elizabeth M.D. Morris, *The Education of Girls in England from 1600 to 1800* (unpublished MA thesis, University of London, 1926); Nicholas Hans, *New Trends in Education in the Eighteenth Century* (1951), ch. 10; Rosemary O'Day, *Education and Society, 1500–1800: Social Foundations of Education in Early Modern Britain* (1982); Bryant, *The London Experience*; Josephine Kamm, *Hope Deferred. Girls' Education in English History* (1965). For the schooling of working-class girls see Deborah Simonton, *The Education and Training of 18th century English Girls, with Special Reference to the Working Classes* (unpublished Ph.D. thesis, University of Essex, 1988).

4 P.J. Miller, 'Women's education, "self-improvement" and social mobility – a late eighteenth-century Debate' *British Journal of Educational Studies* 20 (1972), pp. 202–14; Morris, *Education of Girls*, pp. 159–60.

5 Alice Clark, *Working Life of Women in the Seventeenth Century* (1919); Ivy Pinchbeck, *Women Workers and the Industrial Revolution, 1750–1850* (1930; repr. 1969); Mary Prior, 'Women and the urban economy: Oxford 1500–1800', in Prior, ed., *Women in English Society, 1500–1800* (1985).

when attitudes towards women's role and responsibilities became imbued with the ideal of the domestic, leisured and private sphere, in opposition to the active and public life of men. This apparent trend seems to be directly contradicted by the expansion of girls' schooling and the corresponding increase in the number of women teachers in the eighteenth and early nineteenth centuries, and it is in this context that this chapter seeks to describe and discuss the work of the female teaching profession. The period 1760 to 1820 has been chosen here because the published literature and comment on female education of the time focused particularly on the growing popularity of the polite education provided by boarding schools, whereas after 1820 the public turned its attention to governesses and education in the home.

The importance of teaching as a source of female employment in eighteenth-century England can be shown by estimating the number of women teachers at work in schools and private homes. In the absence of census statistics on occupations during the period 1760 to 1820 it is worth referring to the table of female occupations compiled by Ivy Pinchbeck from the census information for 1841. A total of 30,150 women in England were counted as schoolmistresses, governesses and teachers, which shows teaching to have been the fifth most common occupation for women – after domestic service (712,493), cotton manufacture (115,425), dressmaking and millinery (89,079), and agricultural labour (35,262).[6] Any attempt to calculate the number of private governesses in the Hanoverian period must rest on extrapolation from the number of families of the rank likely to have employed a governess. The task of gauging how many women taught in schools is made possible, though not easy, by the existence of local and national trades directories and the advertisements that commercial schools placed in provincial and London newspapers. In this chapter, the extent of girls' schooling will be examined using the evidence of the school advertisements in one provincial newspaper, *Jackson's Oxford Journal*, the city's only newspaper during the period 1760 to 1820.[7] From its first issue in May 1753 to the end of 1820, a total of 315 establishments and individuals, of which 167 were located in Oxfordshire, advertised their teaching services in the newspaper. This sample of 167 educational establishments consisted of 121 schools – either boarding or day or both – and 32 peripatetic tutors, 21 of whom also gave lessons at

---

6 Pinchbeck, *Women Workers,* Appendix.

7 Unless otherwise stated, all the schools referred to in this article were located in Oxfordshire (post-1974 county boundaries have been used).

their own lodgings or houses. The nature of the remaining 14 establishments is unclear from their advertisements. Not all schools in existence during this period advertised or even were recorded in trades directories, and therefore the figures used in this chapter provide only a guide to the prevalence of girls' schools in Hanoverian England.[8] Measuring the number of schools in each decade shows a definite increase over the period that may be in part due to a growth in the practice of advertising, yet nonetheless gives an idea of the minimum number of schoolmistresses in business. As can be seen in Table 1, there were between 25 and 35 educational establishments in each decade in Oxfordshire from the 1760s to the 1800s, with 62 in the 1810s, of which 43 were located in the country towns and villages and 19 in Oxford itself.

The location of girls' schools in Hanoverian England provides another means of estimating how common an occupation teaching was for women. The first private schools for girls had developed in London in the early seventeenth century, primarily to educate daughters of City merchants and lawyers, and so were located either in the City or in the neighbouring village of Hackney. Margaret Bryant has shown that 'the capital had established its pre-eminent position as a centre for fashionable girls' schools even by the end of the seventeenth century', and that its pre-eminence continued in the eighteenth century as the industry expanded into the suburbs of Islington, Newington Green, Hammersmith, Chelsea and Kensington.[9] London predominated, not only on account of the size of its population, but also because of the Season, which brought many families to the capital and provided a convenient opportunity for daughters to be educated at one of the many schools or by the specialist masters. The perceived expertise and the fashionable reputation of London schools encouraged parents to send daughters away from home to experience a metropolitan education. Distance was not seen as an obstacle, for parents either took their daughters to town themselves or arranged for a family friend to accompany them to and from school at the beginning and end of each term. After the summer term in 1806 the daughters of two Gloucestershire families, the Cliffords of Frampton Court and the

8 This survey of Oxfordshire schooling can be compared with Zena Crook and Brian Simon, 'Private schools in Leicester and the county 1780–1840', in Simon, ed., *Education in Leicester 1540–1940* (Leicester, 1968); Derek Robson, *Some Aspects of Education in Cheshire in the 18th Century* (Manchester, 1966). An excellent study of educational provision in Scotland is Alexander Law, *Education in Edinburgh in the Eighteenth Century* (1965).
9 Bryant, *The London Experience*, p. 145; Morris, *Education of Girls*, pp. 139–40.

Table 1 Occurrence of educational establishments in Oxfordshire – City and County

	1750s	1760s	1770s	1780s	1790s	1800s	1810s
City	9	15	10	10	13	14	19
County	16	16	17	14	14	21	43
Total	25	31	27	27	27	35	62

Source: *Jackson's Oxford Journal*, 1753–1820.

Huntleys of Boxwell Court, travelled in the company of a fellow pupil and her father and aunt, from Mrs Warner's boarding school in Wandsworth to Gloucester where they were met by Mr Clifford and taken home to their own families.[10]

Spa towns and fashionable resorts were also popular locations for boarding and day schools, for they were able to draw custom from the seasonal visitors who had the money and leisure to indulge in a polite education for their daughters. Bath attracted schoolmistresses and pupils alike in great numbers, giving parents a wide choice of rival establishments. While the Revd John Penrose was in Bath to take the waters in May 1766, he and his wife looked for a suitable school for their fourteen-year-old daughter Dolly and so visited Mrs Pullaine's boarding school in Trim Street, which met with their approval in every respect. However, without making a decision, the Penroses returned home to Penryn, Cornwall, to consult with their friends. They worried about the expense of a fashionable education, but the following year they were back in Bath and soon decided on another school: Mrs Aldworth's boarding school in St John's Court.[11] Although London and Bath were noted for their numerous schools and tutors, they far from monopolized the market in girls' schooling. The evidence of the advertisements placed in *Jackson's Oxford Journal* indicates that a school education could be acquired in the provinces, even in small towns and villages across Oxfordshire as well as in the city of Oxford. Table 1 shows that the number of educational establishments in the county of Oxfordshire exceeded the number in Oxford itself in every decade except for the 1750s. This suggests that girls' schools were a feature

10 Glos. PRO, D149/F43 Correspondence of Nathaniel Clifford Esq. of Frampton Court, Glos., to Richard Huntley of Boxwell Court [May 1806] and 18 June 1806.

11 Brigitte Mitchell and Hubert Penrose, eds, *Letters from Bath 1766–1767 by the Rev. John Penrose* (Gloucester, 1983), pp. 146–7, 167.

of both rural and urban society in late eighteenth-century England. A countryside location was preferred by some parents on the grounds of their children's health and schoolmistresses capitalized on this anxiety by stressing in their advertisements the healthy properties of the air, the spaciousness of the school-house and grounds, and the scope for pleasant walks to be found at a country school.[12] The evidence for the location of girls' schools in Oxfordshire corresponds with J.H. Plumb's conclusion from his wider survey of commercial schools for boys and girls that 'these schools were to be found more frequently in the old county towns, and the surrounding districts, than in the new manufacturing towns'.[13] Confirmation of this can be found in Catherine Hutton's memoirs, in which she claimed that Birmingham in the early 1760s possessed possibly only the one day school, which she attended, and certainly no boarding schools. There were 'none nearer, I believe, than Worcester, Stratford, and Lichfield'; and so her fellow pupils from Mrs and Miss Sawyer's school were 'transplanted' to Worcester to complete their schooling.[14]

Schools were mainly dependent on the local population for their pupils, although some of the larger establishments attracted pupils from further afield, whether on the strength of a newspaper advertisement, a personal recommendation or a family connection. As has been stated above, the Penroses travelled from Cornwall to Bath to place their daughter in a school. Another family from the south-west, the Meins of Devonport, sent three daughters to the boarding school at Belvedere House in Bath, which was run in the 1790s by Miss Sophia Lee and her sisters, Harriet and Ann. Dr Thomas Mein RN chose the Misses Lee's school on the advice of Mrs Gambier, who was a resident of Bath and the widow of Admiral James Gambier, with whom Mein had served during the American War of Independence.[15] One schoolgirl, Martha Sherwood (née Butt), listed in her recollections the provenance of some of her fellow pupils at the Abbey House School in Reading in the early 1790s: four pupils came from local families near Henley and Maidenhead; four were daughters of London professionals; one was from

12 Miss Prichard's advertisement for her school in Stow-on-the-Wold, Glos., *JOJ*, 16 Oct. 1779; Mrs Talbot's advertisement for her school in Woodstock, Oxfordshire, *JOJ*, 5 Jan. 1788.

13 J.H. Plumb, 'The new world of children in eighteenth-century England' *PP* 67 (1974), p. 73.

14 Catherine Hutton Beale, ed., *Reminiscences of a Gentlewoman of the Last Century: Letters of Catherine Hutton* (Birmingham, 1891), pp. 3–5.

15 Francis Paget Hett, ed., *The Memoirs of Susan Sibbald (1786–1812)* (1926), pp. 32, 81.

Wiltshire; another from Jersey.[16] Martha Sherwood's own family
lived in Kidderminster, near Birmingham, and her father had chosen
the Abbey House School after he had visited Reading to see his
close friend Dr Richard Valpy, then the headmaster of Reading
School, who had taken him to see 'some sort of an exhibition' performed by the pupils of the Abbey School.[17] Schoolmistresses were
keen to encourage pupils' parents to persuade friends and family
to patronize their establishment. Wishing to show off the school to
a wider public, schoolmistresses such as the St Quintins in Reading,
the Lees in Bath, the Mores in Bristol and the Stephensons in London organized plays and exhibitions of dancing, music and drawing
to be performed by their pupils.[18] Schools also made use of family
connections to attract pupils whether they lived close by or at a
distance. Elizabeth Ham first went to school in her home village
of Haselbury Plucknett, Somerset, where she attended a boarding
school kept by the youngest of her father's sisters.[19] The actress
Frances Kemble was sent from her home in London when she was
five years old to attend her first school at the boarding school in
Bath kept by Mrs Twiss, who was her godmother and her father's
married sister.[20]

A schoolmistress would attempt to establish a reputation for good
teaching either locally or in a more distant community and placing
an advertisement in a London or provincial newspaper was a popular and effective method of promoting a school. Announcements
appeared regularly after the Christmas and Whitsun holidays to
remind parents when the new term was to begin and that payment
of all bills was due. A detailed prospectus would be printed in the
newspapers, and often also on handbills, in which the schoolmistress proclaimed the advantages of location, curriculum, fees and
ethos that her school enjoyed, in order to persuade parents to favour
her school over any other advertised on the same page. Competition for pupils was fierce and thus a guaranteed source of pupils
was a valuable asset for any school. Mrs Fenwick's boarding school
at Flint House in Greenwich developed profitable ties with several
West Indian settlers who entrusted her with the education of their

16 F.J. Harvey Darton, ed., *The Life and Times of Mrs Sherwood, from the Diaries of Capt. and Mrs Sherwood* (1910), pp. 124–31.

17 Ibid., p. 82.

18 Ibid., pp. 84–5, 144–5; Hett, ed., *Memoirs of Susan Sibbald*, pp. 60–5; M.G. Jones, *Hannah More* (Cambridge, 1952), p. 15; Clare Williams, ed., *Sophie in London – 1786 – the Diary of Sophie von la Roche* (1933), p. 246.

19 Eric Gillett, ed., *Elizabeth Ham by Herself 1783–1820* (1945), pp. 16–17.

20 Frances Ann Kemble, *Record of a Girlhood* 3 vols (1878), I, p. 20.

daughters: Jane Broadbelt and possibly Sarah Barrett Moulton –
the subject of Sir Thomas Lawrence's painting 'Pinkie' – were among
the Flint House pupils who sailed to England from the West Indies
in the 1790s.[21]

Some ambitious schoolmistresses deliberately distanced themselves from a local source of pupils by setting up schools in France.
With the aim of making French easier to learn for the pupils, several teachers in the mid-1780s moved to France, choosing premises
near a convenient port such as Calais or Boulogne and advertising their academies in London newspapers. Their announcements
emphasized the ease with which pupils could travel to the school
and sometimes gave specific details about the sailings between
England and France.[22] One of the main attractions of these French
schools was their comparative cheapness, which appealed to parents
worried about fees and schoolmistresses worried about their over-
heads. The advertisements for Montreuil school and the Protestant
school in Hautbourdin spelled out the financial advantages of an
education abroad, yet there is no evidence that these schools met
with any lasting success.[23] A full account of one impulsive teacher's
move to France has survived in the memoirs of Elizabeth Lachlan
(née Appleton) who describes how her schoolmistress, Miss Shepherd, took advantage of the Peace of Amiens to open a school 15
miles from Rouen in the autumn of 1802. On a brief holiday with
friends in Normandy during the summer, Miss Shepherd had been
impressed by the low cost of living in France, and after purchasing
a château and its contents for £50, she relinquished her boarding
school in Percy Street, London, and advertised the new venture.
Elizabeth Lachlan was one of the pupils who accompanied her to
France and she later recounted this extraordinary episode:

> All was decided: she [Miss Shepherd] made known her plans, drew
> up advertisements, applied to her friends, solicited the parents of
> her scholars, and in two months had the promise of between thirty
> and forty girls of respectable families, and of ten or twelve ladies, as
> parlour boarders.[24]

21 Geraldine Mozley, ed., *Letters to Jane from Jamaica 1786–96* (1938); Philip Kelly and
Ronald Hudson, 'New light on Sir Thomas Lawrence's "Pinkie"' *Huntington Library Quarterly* 28 (1964–5), pp. 255–61.

22 *The Daily Universal Register*, 19 Nov. 1787.

23 *The Daily Universal Register*, 4 June 1785, 17 June 1786.

24 *Jehovh-Jireh; or, The Provisions of a Faithful God: As Manifested in his Wonderful Dealings
with the late Mrs. Elizabeth Lachlan formerly of No. 6, Upper Portland Place, London written by
herself* (1850), pp. 20–1. Parlour boarders paid higher fees than ordinary boarders, enti-
tling them to a room of their own and to the privilege of receiving visits and sitting with

Within three months the new school crossed over to Dieppe and settled in the Château de Taillis, on the banks of the Seine. The novelty of the French school combined with her established reputation as a schoolmistress enabled Miss Shepherd to attract enough pupils to make the enterprise viable though very short-lived, for the onset of war soon brought them back to England. After the end of hostilities between England and France in 1815, one London schoolmistress established a boarding school in the rue d'Angoulême in Paris that consisted almost entirely of English pupils, including Frances Kemble. Miss Rowden had gained considerable experience in her profession before venturing on her Parisian enterprise. Her mother kept a school in Henley-on-Thames, Oxfordshire, at which Mary Wollstonecraft's sister Everina taught briefly as an assistant teacher in 1787. However, Miss Rowden herself had been sent to the St Quintin's school in Reading where she acquired not only an education but also a career, for she became a teacher and then headmistress at the school, which moved to Hans Place, Chelsea, in the early 1800s.[25]

Unlike the schools in France, which consisted entirely of boarders, day schools needed a local source of pupils for their survival, although some came from a distance to attend a day school and boarded with relatives or friends during the week. Of the 167 educational establishments in Oxfordshire, all 15 of the day schools were in Oxford and 14 of the 21 combined boarding and day schools were also located the city. A further 20 day schools were in Oxford, all run by specialist tutors who divided their time between giving private lessons at their lodgings and travelling to teach in private homes or at schools in the surrounding towns and villages. Several of the more elementary day schools in Oxford were conducted from lodgings, such as Mrs West's 'Genteel Day School' at Mr Palmer's Circulating Library in the High Street and Miss Hill's school for needlework and reading at Mrs Bird's house in Ship Lane.[26] The expenditure required to set up one of these day schools was small, needing only rent for the rooms and an initial outlay on fabric and needles for sewing and on books. Setting up a school of this type was a cheaper alternative to opening a shop, as there was no stock to buy in and a schoolmistress received her income quarterly or

their schoolmistress in the parlour. They were usually older pupils and were introduced into society by their schoolmistress who acted as their chaperone.

25 Kemble, *Record of a Girlhood*, I, p. 73; Ralph Wardle, ed., *The Collected Letters of Mary Wollstonecraft* (1979), pp. 158, 169.

26 *JOJ*, 16 Nov. 1793; 16 April 1796.

even weekly, as at Mrs and Miss Moores' school in Brewer Lane where 1s. a week was paid by each of their 'few little Ladies'.[27] These aspects of school teaching made it a common business for women to take up if their circumstances had changed, usually following the death of a husband or father, or after a business failure. Two Oxford schools provide illustration: in 1775 Anne and Sarah Law, the daughters of a deceased mercer, intended to open a reading school in lodgings opposite Carfax Church, and in 1795 Mrs S. Kennedy, widow of Revd W. Kennedy of Abingdon, opened a boarding and day school in Holywell.[28] The small premises needed for a day school also made it a possible second business for a family wishing to enlarge its income. The wife or daughter of Mr Gruchy, a silversmith, taught French 'carefully and expeditiously' to girls and boys at the family's house opposite the King's Arms: hoping to enhance her credentials as a French teacher, she styled herself Mrs De Gruchy in her advertisement.[29]

Boarding schools demanded greater investment of capital, time and attention from their schoolmistresses than day schools. As one experienced Bath schoolmistress wrote of her satisfying yet arduous profession:

> Truth to say, I do not believe that there can be found, in the whole range of civil society, a situation of so much anxiety, and occasional mortification, as that of a governess in a private school, however well organised or liberally patronised.[30]

Suitable premises had to be found that would provide sufficient accommodation for the boarders without becoming too expensive to maintain if the schoolmistress experienced difficulties in attracting pupils. The evidence from *Jackson's Oxford Journal* suggests that most new schools started as small enterprises and either extended their premises or moved to larger houses as they prospered. In 1805, after four years in Headington, Mrs Sydenham moved her boarding school to a house in Rose Hill that had 'Room to accommodate Ten more Pupils'; and in 1818 at Stadhampton Green, Miss Kent began her school in part of a house, and then later rented it in full, enabling her to accommodate more pupils, including two parlour boarders who enjoyed rooms of their own.[31] Mary Wollstonecraft was

27 *JOJ*, 4 Aug. 1792.
28 *JOJ*, 25 March 1775; 10 Jan. 1795.
29 *JOJ*, 5 Sept. 1767.
30 Frances Broadhurst, *A Word in Favor of Female Schools: Addressed to Parents, Guardians, and the Public at Large* (1826), pp. 1–2.
31 *JOJ*, 13 April 1805; 7 Nov. 1818.

less fortunate in her attempt to establish a boarding school. After failing to attract any pupils in Islington, she and her sisters rented a spacious house in Newington Green in 1785 that guaranteed the custom of a few pupils, yet the burden of rent and servants' wages soon forced her to take in lodgers in addition to her boarders.[32] While Wollstonecraft was not alone among schoolmistresses in her failure to find enough pupils to make the school viable, she was particularly handicapped by her ignorance of the practicalities of running a school and by her inexperience in teaching. Her father's erratic career and declining fortunes had disrupted her own formal education, so that she had spent only two or three years at a school in Beverley, in the East Riding of Yorkshire. This contrasts with the experience of her schoolfriend Jane Arden, who had stayed at school until she was sixteen or seventeen years old and had then spent six years as a governess before opening a school with her sister in Bath in 1781. Following the marriage of her sister, in 1784 Jane Arden returned home to Beverley where she ran a boarding school for sixteen years.[33] Unlike Wollstonecraft, who knew few people in either Islington or Newington Green, Arden set up her second school in her home town where there were family and friends to provide references for her character and to find pupils through their local contacts.

The financial risk involved in establishing a girls' school was lessened where there had been a school conducted on the same premises previously or at least in the same town or village. In several of the Oxfordshire schools the business was handed over from the old schoolmistress to the new, and with it the pupils, whose parents were encouraged to honour the new management with their patronage. The boarding school at Ewelme started by Miss Mason in 1791 was run by four successive schoolmistresses until 1818, when Mrs and the Misses Hills moved to Long Wittenham. No sooner had the Hills left Ewelme than a replacement school appeared under the management of Miss Alnutt. Ewelme was also home to a long-lived boys' commercial academy that was kept by Mr James Garlick and his wife from the mid-1810s until Mrs Garlick's death in 1875.[34] Miss Alnutt's school occupied the premises that had previously housed the Garlick academy, which had moved to Ewelme Manor

32 Claire Tomalin, *The Life and Death of Mary Wollstonecraft* (1992), pp. 45, 48–9.

33 Wardle, ed., *The Collected Letters of Mary Wollstonecraft*, Appendix B.

34 *JOJ*, 7 May 1791; 3 Jan. 1795; 14 Jan. 1797; 6 July 1792; 16 July 1808; 4 July 1818; Kate Tiller, 'A 19th-century village boarding school: the Garlick School at Ewelme' *Oxoniensia* 57 (1992), pp. 331–7.

House.[35] This change-over neatly illustrates the similarities in size and type of enterprise undertaken in girls' and boys' schools of this period. One of Oxford's most successful teachers, Miss Randall, ran two schools in the city centre between 1789 and 1803, separated by a brief attempt to set up a school in Kidlington during 1795 and 1796. Within six months of her marriage to Mr Johnson she had resigned her Holywell Street school to Mrs Cooper, whom she recommended to all her patrons. Under the guidance of this new but experienced schoolmistress, the school continued in Oxford for ten years before Mrs Cooper moved to Cheltenham where she remained in the teaching business for at least another eight years.[36] These two examples suggest that girls' boarding schools could become stable businesses, both in Oxford, where there was considerable competition, and in a small village such as Ewelme, which had fewer than 5,000 inhabitants according to the 1801 Census. Particular buildings could become firmly associated with the schooling of girls, as proved to be the case with North Weston House, near Thame in Oxfordshire. This large medieval and Elizabethan manor house, with its chapel still surviving, was home to a succession of boarding schools during most of the years from 1785 to 1816.[37] Belvedere House in Bath gained its reputation as a fashionable boarding school under the care of the Lee sisters in the 1780s and 1790s, and on their retirement in 1803 passed into the hands of Mr Thomas and Mrs Frances Broadhurst, who kept a school in the same grand building for the next 30 years.[38]

Schools, like other common businesses, could provide employment for a whole family and become established family concerns. Some 34 of the 167 educational establishments in Oxfordshire involved more than one member of the same family for all or part of their lives. The most usual partnerships were between two sisters or between a mother and her daughters: at Mr Towle's house in Penny-Farthing Street, Oxford, first his wife and then his daughters ran a boarding school, at which he taught music and dancing.[39] A gradual transition of the business from mother to daughter was the usual pattern in these family-run schools. Another example is

35 *JOJ*, 3 July 1819.
36 *JOJ*, 21 Feb. 1789; 25 April 1795; 2 July 1796; 2 April 1803; 13 Nov. 1813; 8 July 1820.
37 *JOJ*, 22 Oct. 1785; 21 Jan. 1792; 16 July 1808; 13 July 1816; Jennifer Sherwood and Nicholas Pevsner, *The Buildings of England. Oxfordshire* (Harmondsworth, 1990), p. 818.
38 Trevor Fawcett, 'Leevites and others' *History of Bath Research Group Newsletter* 23 (1994), pp. 5–6; Broadhurst, *A Word in Favor of Female Schools*, p. 1.
39 *JOJ*, 22 Oct. 1774; 18 Sept. 1779.

provided by Mrs Wells, who opened a boarding school in Witney in July 1800 and who by 1808 was being assisted by her daughters. Her death in 1813 led to the following newspaper announcement:

> The Misses WELLS, encouraged by the many assurances of support received since the lamented death of their late Mother, beg to inform their friends they purpose continuing the SEMINARY; and as from the declining health of their Mother for some years past the duties of the School have devolved on them, they flatter themselves, by adhering to the same system, a continued confidence will be merited and reposed in the Establishment which has hitherto been enjoyed.[40]

It was a more unusual circumstance for a relation to take over a school when not directly involved in its management, but this took place in a Holywell Street school in Oxford in 1813. When Mrs S. Wall[41] died in that year, her boarding school was taken over by her daughter, Mrs C. Wall, who had arrived from London to continue the establishment. Under its new management the school moved twice within Oxford and was still in existence in July 1819.[42] There appear to be no instances in Oxfordshire of a family-run school continuing beyond a second generation.

Some of the most renowned boarding schools in Hanoverian England were family enterprises run by sisters: notable examples being the Misses More's school in Bristol, the Misses Lee's school in Bath, and the Misses Stephenson's school in Queen's Square, London. The More sisters started their school in 1757 to provide themselves with the living that their impoverished schoolmaster father could not guarantee for them. It proved to be such a success that they were able to retire from the business in 1790, leaving one of their pupils, Miss Selina Mills, to carry it on.[43] The Lees opened their first school in December 1780 after their father, the actor-manager John Lee, had contracted a serious illness which led to his death in 1781. The successful run in London of Sophia Lee's play, *The Chapter of Accidents*, enabled the sisters to move their school to a better location in Bath, where they quickly acquired 23

---

40 *JOJ*, 5 July 1800; 16 July 1808; 25 April 1812.

41 Either Mrs C. Wall was Mrs S. Wall's daughter-in-law or she was her unmarried daughter who preferred to use 'Mrs' as a courtesy title.

42 *JOJ*, 20 March 1813; 10 July 1819.

43 Selina Mills was later joined by her sisters who continued the school after her marriage to Zachary Macaulay c.1796; the school was still active in 1808. The elopement of one wealthy pupil, Miss Clark, with a Bristol surgeon named Perry in March 1791 seems not to have damaged the school's reputation, in spite of the widespread coverage of the episode in the national and local press.

boarders.[44] Unlike the More sisters and the Lee sisters, the Misses Stephenson had no financial need to earn a living and yet turned over their large house and its neighbour in Queen's Square to the boarding and educating of some 220 pupils. According to the German novelist and educationalist, Sophie von la Roche, who visited the school in 1786, the sisters, despite charging annual fees of 100 guineas, attracted so many pupils because 'as they were known to be persons of merit, the best children were entrusted to them to receive all the good tuition which they themselves had obtained during their education'.[45] Although the spectacular success of the Stephensons' school owed much to their fortune and rank, it cannot be ignored as an example of how effectively four unmarried women could create a thriving business out of teaching girls. If a boarding school attracted enough pupils, it provided its schoolmistress with a comfortable and regular income from the annual fees. In the Oxfordshire schools fees averaged between 12 and 20 guineas per boarder, while they could be as much as 80 or 100 guineas at a prestigious school in Bath or London.[46]

Many schoolmistresses who had not benefited from a family association with teaching started their careers and learned the skills of their trade as either pupils, half-boarders or assistant teachers in an established school. The most common and often the only qualification that a teacher could rely on was her own experience of a school education, which in itself was often seen as an investment for future employment: Elizabeth Ham's aunt opened her school in Haselbury with the intention of turning the advantage of her school education to some account.[47] A girl could embark on a more deliberate course of apprenticeship by becoming a half-boarder. A half-boarder was an older pupil, usually aged between fourteen and eighteen, who received tuition in some subjects yet also supervised the younger children in their lessons. A schoolmistress would engage one or two half-boarders as apprentices and was paid a premium to train them for the teaching profession. One advertisement placed by an anonymous school in 1817 gives details of the terms typical in such an apprenticeship:

> In a respectable BOARDING SCHOOL there is a VACANCY for a
> YOUNG LADY, as an APPRENTICE for three years, to be further

44 Fawcett, 'Leevites and others', p. 6.

45 Williams, ed., *Sophie in London*, p. 92.

46 Mrs and Miss Twiss's boarding school in Bath charged 80 guineas per annum with 5 guineas for the entrance fee: *JOJ*, 16 Nov. 1816.

47 Gillett, ed., *Elizabeth Ham*, p. 16.

instructed in the necessary branches of education to qualify her for
a Teacher or Governess. Premium, 50 Guineas.[48]

The distinction between a half-boarder and an assistant teacher
was often very slight as some assistant teachers were articled and
therefore bound to the school for a certain number of years. The
apprentice who joined Mrs Lardner's school at Newland House,
near Witney, clearly worked as an assistant for she undertook the
French, Music and Geography departments within a few months of
her engagement.[49] Assistant teachers in girls' schools, like ushers in
grammar schools and boys' academies, could soon gain sufficient
experience of the teaching business to be able to set up on their
own. Miss Matilda Smith left her post as the head assistant teacher
at North-Weston House School to open a boarding and day school
in Oxford in 1802.[50] When Mrs Richings opened a boarding school
in Wallingford in October 1804 she referred to her previous teaching post, which served as her principal qualification:

> Mrs. R. having been for Eight Years Assistant at a principal Boarding
> School at Oxford, trusts she is in every Respect competent to the
> Undertaking, and assures her Friends that nothing on her Part shall
> be omitted to give them complete Satisfaction.[51]

Just as an apprenticed half-boarder or assistant was qualified to
become either a schoolmistress or a private governess, so a governess
such as Jane Arden was able to use her teaching skills in a school.
Henrietta Edsall, Miss Randall and Miss Rackstrow had all been
governesses in private households before they began their schools
in Oxford in 1780, 1789 and 1811 respectively.[52]

These instances of women leaving positions as governesses to
become schoolmistresses raise some interesting questions about the
motives that led women to teach. The relative merits of governesses
or boarding schools were often discussed in print during the late
eighteenth century, but only from the point of view of parents
wishing to decide which would provide the best education for their
daughters and not from the point of view of a young woman wishing to know which would provide her with the better living. A fortunate governess could enjoy the security of being part of a private
household, but her salary offered little chance of independence

48 *JOJ*, 13 Sept. 1817.
49 *JOJ*, 1 Jan. 1820; 8 July 1820.
50 *JOJ*, 9 Oct. 1802.
51 *JOJ*, 8 Sept. 1804.
52 *JOJ*, 21 Feb. 1789; 6 May 1780; 27 April 1811.

once her pupils had grown up. In the absence of any guaranteed
pension, she would have to look for a new position every decade or
so. By contrast, the livelihood of a schoolmistress depended largely
on her own exertions: though failure was a common enough occurrence, if the school kept going there was always the prospect of new
pupils. In the young Mary Wollstonecraft's opinion there was no
doubt as to which was preferable. In a letter of 1780 she warmly
encouraged Jane Arden in her proposal to start a school:

> I have ever approved of your plan, and it would give me great pleasure
> to find that you and your sister could contrive to live together; – let
> not some small difficulties intimidate you, I beseech you; – struggle
> with any obstacles rather than go into a state of dependence: – I
> speak feelingly, – I have felt the weight, and w^d have you by all means
> avoid it. – Your employm^t tho a troublesome one, is very necessary,
> and you have the opportunity of doing much good, by instilling
> good principles into the young and the ignorant, and at the close of
> life you'll have the pleasure to think that you have not lived in vain,
> and, believe me, this reflection is worth a life of care. . . .[53]

It must be noted that Wollstonecraft had yet to experience at first
hand the 'small difficulties' of which she wrote. At this point, she
had worked only as a paid companion and it was this that had given
her such a loathing of 'a state of dependence'. In the event, Jane
Arden's successful career as a schoolmistress was to bring her the
satisfaction that her friend wished for her so early on in their lives.
The famous Misses Stephenson similarly were motivated by the desire
to lead a worthwhile life and, according to Sophie von la Roche's
account, 'felt themselves called upon to be of some use; so they
decided to avoid the reproach of leading a useless existence by
bringing up young women'.[54]

Teaching evidently could offer women something more rewarding
than a mere means of subsistence. To dismiss teaching as nothing
more than the last resort of destitute but genteel women would be
to ignore the fact that keeping a school not only could be lucrative
but also could secure a woman's respectability and give her a sense
of usefulness and purpose in life. Certainly Susan and Mary Parker,
the illegitimate daughters of Dr Erasmus Darwin, enjoyed lifelong
careers as a result of their father having set them up in a school
of their own at Ashbourne, Derbyshire, in 1794.[55] In her memoirs,

53 Wardle, ed., *The Collected Letters of Mary Wollstonecraft*, p. 72, Mary Wollstonecraft to
Jane Arden, c.April–June 1780.
54 Williams, ed., *Sophie in London*, p. 92.
55 Desmond King-Hele, *Doctor of Revolution. The Life and Genius of Erasmus Darwin* (1977),
pp. 234–7.

the actress Mary Robinson (née Darby) took a positive view of her mother's decision to open a boarding school in the early 1770s. Deserted by her husband and fearing financial ruin, Mrs Darby rented a convenient house in Little Chelsea, London, engaged assistants and appointed the fourteen-year-old Mary as English teacher: 'an occupation that flattered my self-love, and impressed my mind with a sort of domestic consequence'. In a few months Mrs Darby had acquired ten or twelve pupils, but at this hopeful time, 'just at a period when an honourable independence promised to cheer the days of an unexampled parent', her feckless husband returned to deplore 'the public mode which his wife had adopted of revealing to the world her unprotected situation' and ordered her to give up the school.[56] Teaching provided an income and a respected profession for Mrs Elizabeth Cumyns, who was schoolmistress of the 'high-prized' boarding school in Kensington that educated three of Hester Thrale's daughters in the 1770s. An unfortunate life had forced Mrs Cumyns to take up teaching, which Mrs Thrale, a girlhood friend, regretted was 'a Situation considerably below her Abilities', even though she had the highest opinion of her friend's aptitude for such work.[57] Mrs St Quintin (née Pitts) was another woman who became a teacher as a consequence of a sudden change in her circumstances. She had been brought up by her rich uncle and educated in the expectation of inheriting his fortune, but when he died the fortune was willed to a housekeeper; consequently, Miss Pitts entered into a partnership with her own schoolmistress at the Abbey House School in Reading.[58]

A common comment made about school teaching during this period was that it was an occupation taken up only by women who had failed to marry and secure a living through their husbands' businesses or private incomes. It is evident from the Oxfordshire sample of schools that, though many spinsters and widows were schoolmistresses and teachers, marriage did not always curtail a woman's teaching career or remove its necessity. It was certainly the case that some married women continued their schools for only a year or six months after marrying, but there were a number for whom marriage seemed to make little difference to their business. Mary Thurland had been a schoolmistress for eight years in Kidlington before she married, and under her new name of Wyatt she moved her school to St Aldate's in Oxford in 1772, then onto

56 Mary Robinson, *Memoirs of the Late Mrs. Robinson, written by herself* (1803), pp. 39–43.
57 Hester Thrale, *'The Family Book' 1764–78* in Mary Thrale, ed., *The Thrales of Streatham Park* (1977), p. 86, 3 March 1774.
58 Darton, ed., *Mrs Sherwood*, p. 123.

Wood-Eaton in 1780, and finally to the Parsonage House at Begbrook in 1786.[59] The Banbury boarding and day school established by Miss Shelton (later Dury) in 1774 remained at the same premises on the Green after her marriage in 1792, and 24 years later she was joined in the business by her daughter, Miss Dury. Her daughter had faded from the scene by the time that Mrs Dury resigned the school into the care of Miss Isaac and Miss Cook, but Mrs Dury continued to give 'her maternal attention to the domestic comfort and improvement of the young Ladies' until the end of our period in 1820. The school was still in business in 1830, over 55 years after she had first moved to Banbury following a brief attempt to start a school with her sister in Bloxham.[60] Neither Mr Wyatt nor Mr Dury feature in the advertisements for their wives' schools, and in the few examples in Oxfordshire of husband-and-wife teams, the husband taught the boys, the wife the girls.

Nevertheless, other sources show that it was not unknown for a husband to assist his wife in her girls' school. At her boarding school in Camden Place, Bath, Mrs Twiss was assisted by her husband and three daughters: Mr Twiss had earlier devoted himself to giving their daughters an extensive education which they used to advantage when they started teaching in the school.[61] When Miss Pitts, the schoolmistress and former pupil of the Abbey House School in Reading, married the French master, Dominique de St Quintin, the school came under their joint management, and together they raised its reputation.[62] Two instances in the early nineteenth century of a husband supporting in print his wife's educational enterprise provide further evidence that the business of running a girls' school was not exclusively female. The education given to pupils at Mrs Florian's boarding school in Leytonstone was described at length in an advertisement at the end of one of her husband's textbooks, entitled *An Elementary Course of the Sciences and Philosophy*, which was published in 1806. Mrs Florian presumably taught 'the occupations and accomplishments particularly belonging to the female sex', while Mr J.B. Florian-Jolly instructed the girls in a more adventurous curriculum:

> The elements of Geometry and Trigonometry are also taught as far as is requisite for a perfect intelligence of the principles of Astronomy,

59 *JOJ*, 27 April 1765; 27 June 1772; 12 Aug. 1780; 1 July 1786.
60 *JOJ*, 13 Nov. 1773; 11 June 1774; 24 March 1792; 13 July 1816; 26 June 1819; 1 July 1820; *Pigot & Co.'s Commercial Directory* 1830.
61 Kemble, *Record of a Girlhood*, I, pp. 20–1.
62 Darton, ed., *Mrs Sherwood*, p. 123.

of the geographical knowledge of our globe and of Natural Philosophy, which are illustrated by experiments and machines. The young
ladies enter at the same time on a complete course of universal history and geography, ancient and modern (according to Mr Florian's
Chronological Views). Each epoch of history is illustrated by a geographical map, made by the pupils themselves. . . .[63]

In 1808 Thomas Broadhurst published some of the Sunday lectures
he delivered to his wife's pupils under the title of *Advice to Young
Ladies, on the Improvement of the Mind, and the Conduct of Life*, which
contained an outline of the educational methods practised by the
Broadhursts at the Belvedere House school in Bath. Jane Arden
found similar support for her teaching in her husband, Mr Gardiner,
whom she married mid-career in 1797. Together they moved the
school from Beverley to Elsham Hall in Lincolnshire in 1800, and
then on to the more secluded Ashby Hall in 1814, where she continued the school until within a few years of her death in 1840.[64]

Notwithstanding these isolated examples of husbands who shared
with their wives the organization or promotion of a school, the
financial and administrative aspects of most girls' schools were the
responsibility of their female heads. In addition to the inevitable
risks taken in setting up a business and seeking sufficient numbers
of pupils, the daily organization of a boarding school resembled
the management of a sizeable household. Schools ranged from
half a dozen boarders, as at Mrs Field's Holywell House school in
Oxford, to some 60 or 70 pupils, as at the Abbey House School in
Reading or the Lees' school in Bath.[65] The feeding, washing and
clothing of the pupils, aged between five and eighteen, necessitated
several kitchen and maid servants. In such a large business as the
Stephensons' school, the sisters divided the responsibilities: 'one
took over correspondence with receipts and expenditure; another
the whole domestic side; the third superintended masters and private lady tutors, of whom there were twelve'.[66] In many schools
the assistant teachers supervised the pupils throughout the day,
whether in lessons, at prayers, at play, or on the daily walk, and at
night slept in the pupils' dormitories. Both the quality of domestic
management and the level of discipline varied between schools. At
the Misses West's school in Tiverton, Devon, Elizabeth Ham was

63 Quoted in Hans, *New Trends in Education*, pp. 204–5.
64 Everilda Anne Gardiner, *Recollections of a Beloved Mother* (1842), pp. 6–8, 26.
65 *JOJ*, 10 Jan. 1818; Darton, ed., *Mrs Sherwood*, p. 124; Hett, ed., *Memoirs of Susan Sibbald*, pp. 35–6.
66 Williams, ed., *Sophie in London*, p. 92.

half-starved on a diet of meagre dinners and hot water, while the pupils at the Manor House school in York practised 'every sort of dissimulation' to thwart the 'petty despotism' of the school rules.[67] By contrast, Susan Mein's memory of the Lees' school was of an efficient regime that encouraged pupils to apply themselves to their studies and yet was swift to expel the one disruptive pupil. Food was plentiful and appetizing and 'there was no want of good living at Belvedere House'; it is unsurprising that every place was filled at such a successfully managed school.[68]

The actual teaching duties of boarding schools invariably involved some visiting tutors who gave individual and joint lessons in particular subjects that were paid for separately and in addition to the basic school fees. These specialist tutors had originally derived their living from teaching in private households, but since the expansion in commercial schooling they had combined their engagements as private tutors with their work as visiting tutors at one or more schools. Girls' and boys' schools alike engaged visiting teachers to give lessons principally in the polite accomplishments of French, dancing, music and drawing, with fencing an additional option for boys. The accounts of the Hertfordshire music master, Thomas Green, record that in addition to his private pupils he taught music and drawing to pupils at four boys' schools and five girls' schools during his career from 1744 to 1790.[69] The majority of specialist tutors in the eighteenth century were men, and the division of teaching according to gender was strongest in the subjects of writing and arithmetic. It is significant that the only woman to advertise lessons in writing in *Jackson's Oxford Journal* during this period was the widow of a former master in writing and arithmetic, one Professor Bliss, whose business in making and selling pens Mrs Bliss also continued after his death.[70] The dominance of male expertise in teaching the specialist subjects meant that schoolmistresses had to engage a number of masters in order to offer a full curriculum for their pupils, yet the masters were similarly dependent on the girls' schools as sources of work. Concerns were expressed in print as to the propriety of male tutors instructing girls and the educationalist Priscilla Wakefield argued that girls should be taught by their own sex and not by masters:

67 Gillett, ed., *Elizabeth Ham*, p. 39; *Autobiography of Mrs Fletcher, of Edinburgh, with Selections from her letters and other Family Memorials, Compiled and Arranged by the Survivor of her Family* (Carlisle, 1874), p. 18.

68 Hett, ed., *Memoirs of Susan Sibbald*, pp. 38, 45, 32.

69 Gillian Sheldrick, ed., 'The accounts of Thomas Green, music teacher and tuner of musical instruments, 1742–90' *Hertfordshire Record Society* 8 (1992), Appendix 3.

70 *JOJ*, 5 April 1766; 14 March 1767; 1 Oct. 1768.

Surely it can never be denied, that the instruction of girls in every department of knowledge or art, is a fair field for the exercise of female talents. Is it compatible with propriety or decency, that the persons of girls advancing towards maturity, should be exposed to the wanton eye of a dancing-master? Are not the fascinating tones of music as dangerous as the graces of dancing, in exciting the tender emotions? Women only therefore, should be permitted to instruct the sex in these seductive arts. It ought to be their privilege to do so in every other. Nature has imposed no invincible barrier to their acquisition and communication of languages, arithmetic, writing, drawing, geography, or any science which is proper for girls to learn.[71]

Nonetheless, masters continued to be engaged by schoolmistresses and parents throughout the period, and thus the education of girls, whether in the home or at a boarding school, was not as a rule confined to a purely female or familial sphere during the eighteenth and early nineteenth centuries.

Over the course of this period women teachers expanded the basic school curriculum of reading and needlework to include lessons in grammar and literature, both English and French, history, chronology, geography and the globes. Less common subjects such as classical mythology, natural philosophy and Italian were sometimes added to the list of subjects taught by the schoolmistress or her assistant. While the majority of schools concentrated on educating their pupils in the elegant accomplishments, two in Oxfordshire in the 1760s and 1770s offered specialist tuition in more housewifely pursuits. Mary Vevers of Woodstock schooled her pupils in the arts of pickling, preserving and pastry-making as well as in English, French and needlework, and Mrs Mansfield counted such household subjects as extras to be paid for separately at her boarding school in Heath.[72] By the 1790s a large number of girls' schools offered tuition in music, dancing and drawing from their resident female staff in addition to standard lessons given by masters. This development of a more knowledgeable female teaching profession showed the possibility of realizing Priscilla Wakefield's demand. An advertisement from 1819 described how girls would benefit from the more qualified female teachers then resident in Miss Clarke's seminary at Adderbury:

she has engaged competent Assistants in the house, in the departments of Music and Drawing; by which means the progress of her pupils in those accomplishments will be much accelerated, and greater

71 Priscilla Wakefield, *Reflections on the Present Condition of the Female Sex; with Suggestions for its Improvement* (1798; 2nd edn 1817), pp. 49–50.
72 *JOJ*, 24 Sept. 1763; 20 Feb. 1779.

accuracy attained, from their practice being under the immediate
inspection of their instructors. The French language is constantly
spoken in her establishment.[73]

The Lee sisters' school in Bath prided itself on the expertise of its
female teachers. Apart from the four sisters themselves and their
three resident assistants, three of the visiting tutors were women:
Mrs Oakes taught the piano; the celebrated Miss Fleming arrived
in her own sedan-chair to teach minuets and figure-dances each
Wednesday; and Mademoiselle La Mercier taught the basic positions
and steps separately. The only male tutors to attend the school were
the writing and arithmetic master, Mr Perks, and the drawing master,
Monsieur Becker.[74] The increasing availability of an extensive education for girls during the late eighteenth century led to women
teachers possessing skills in a wider range of subjects than formerly
had been the case, further reducing the need to engage male tutors.

In order to determine the quality of schooling offered by women
teachers in the late Hanoverian period it is useful to compare schools
in terms of their resources and teaching standards. In her autobiography Eliza Fletcher presents a poor picture of the four years
she spent in the early 1780s under the supervision of Mrs Forster
at the Manor House school in York, where 'nothing useful could be
learned' and 'lessons were said by rote, without being understood'.
The daily reading lesson was two chapters of the Bible read out by
two pupils, while the library matched the teaching in its inadequacy:
'four volumes of the Spectator constituted our whole school library'.[75] Elizabeth Ham's education at the Misses West's school in
Tiverton in the 1790s was similarly hindered by poor teaching:

> Our studies were not very extensive, nor very edifying. We learnt by
> rote either from the Dictionary, the Grammar, or Geography. Wrote
> no exercises, nor were asked any questions about our lessons. We
> read from the Bible in the morning, and the History of England or
> Rome in the afternoon. A Master came to teach us writing and cyph-
> ering from eleven to twelve, and a Dancing master twice a week.[76]

Writing about her education from the perspective of the mid
nineteenth century, Elizabeth Ham expressed her astonishment at
'how little qualification was thought on in these days. Not one of

---

73 *JOJ*, 26 June 1819.
74 Hett, ed., *The Memoirs of Susan Sibbald*, pp. 44–5; Fawcett, 'Leevites and others',
p. 6.
75 *Autobiography of Mrs Fletcher*, pp. 17–18.
76 Gillett, ed., *Elizabeth Ham*, p. 40.

the Governesses it was my fate to be placed under knew as much of education as could now be found in any Mistress of any Charity School.'[77] By contrast, Elizabeth Lachlan experienced a high standard of teaching at Miss Shepherd's boarding school in Percy Street, London, which she attended in the late 1790s and early 1800s. In one subject, French, the combined efforts of a specialist master and the resident teacher ensured that most of the pupils could speak French fluently. This skill was put to immediate use when the school moved to France in 1802. On arriving in Dieppe, the first party of schoolgirls, accompanied by their schoolmistress's mother, Mrs Shepherd, were called upon to arrange accommodation, transport and the payment of bills since their chaperone could not speak a word of French: 'we schoolgirls, who had long been familiarised to it [French], under French people's tuition, managed the little business we had to transact'.[78]

The Twiss family, the Lee sisters and the More sisters all presided over schools where the teaching was of a high standard, and where the pupils had sufficient books, amusements and musical instruments to keep them busy throughout their school days. Jane Arden dedicated her life to the improvement of her pupils. She continually added to the school library by buying the most approved books for young people in English, French and Italian. When she retired from teaching in the late 1830s there were 2,800 volumes in the library. These included a number of her own works which she had written initially for the use of her pupils but had soon had published, with considerable success: her *English Exercises* passed through three editions. That Jane Arden was both an able writer and a conscientious teacher who excelled in her profession was made clear in her daughter's *Recollections of a Beloved Mother*: 'Almost every branch of female education occupied her pen to a considerable extent. Indefatigable were her efforts to benefit her pupils: even her English, French and Italian *games*, which she wrote for their instruction and amusement, amounted to about a hundred.'[79]

The rapidly expanding market in educational works and textbooks offered many schoolteachers the opportunity to publicize their teaching methods and to acquire more pupils while providing them with an additional source of income. Two famous women writers who had been schoolteachers, Hannah More and Mary Wollstonecraft,

77 Ibid., p. 42.
78 *Jehovh-Jireh*, pp. 16, 19, 22.
79 Gardiner, *Recollections*, pp. 26, 27–8.

published works on the principles of female education as well as books suitable for use in the classroom, like More's play, *The Search After Happiness*, and Wollstonecraft's anthology for girls, *The Female Reader*.[80] Frances Broadhurst wrote a spirited defence of a school education for girls, and the anonymous author of *A Legacy of Affection, Advice & Instruction* offered practical advice on teaching and running a school that was based on her own long experience as a schoolmistress in the late eighteenth and early nineteenth centuries.[81] Anne Murry's *Mentoria: or, the Young Ladies Instructor*, published in 1778, was one of the most popular educational manuals in the Hanoverian period; it reached its ninth edition in 1791. Murry's imaginary dialogues between a governess and her pupils were probably drawn from the lessons she gave at her school at Tottenham High Cross in London.[82] Even Mrs Ellin Devis, the schoolmistress of a fashionable London boarding school in Upper Wimpole Street, published the textbooks on English grammar and geography that she had written for her school pupils, whose numbers had included several young aristocratic ladies as well as Maria Edgeworth.[83] Some of the earliest school textbooks on scientific subjects were written by Mrs Margaret Bryan, who ran a succession of schools in Blackheath, Hyde Park Corner and possibly in Margate from 1795 to 1816. Mrs Bryan was encouraged to publish her 1797 *Lectures on Astronomy* by Dr Charles Hutton, then Professor of Mathematics at Woolwich Royal Military Academy, yet many of her readers were female: her *Lectures on Natural Philosophy* were subscribed to by 157 women, including seven of her pupils at Bryan House, before they were printed in 1806.[84]

80 Hannah More, *The Search After Happiness: A Pastoral Drama* (1773), *Essays on various subjects* (1777), *Strictures on the Modern System of Female Education* (1799); Mary Wollstonecraft, *Thoughts on the Education of Daughters* (1787), *The Female Reader, or, Miscellaneous Pieces, in Prose and Verse; Selected from the Best Writers, and Disposed under Proper Heads* (1789).

81 Broadhurst, *A Word in Favor of Female Schools*; Anon., *A Legacy of Affection, Advice & Instruction, from a retired Governess to the present pupils of an establishment near London for female education, which she conducted upwards of forty years* (1827).

82 Ann Murry, *Mentoria: or, the Young Ladies' Instructor, in Familiar Conversations on Moral and Entertaining Subjects: Calculated to improve Young Minds in the Essential, as well as Ornamental Parts of Female Education* (1778); in 1785 Miss Ann Murry moved her school to Hampstead and advertised the move in *The Daily Universal Register* (28 June).

83 Ellin Devis, *The Accidence; or First Rudiments of English Grammar. Designed for the Use of Young Ladies* 3rd edn (1777), *Miscellaneous Lessons designed for the Use of Young Ladies. On a New Plan* (1782), *An Introduction to Geography; for the Use of Mrs Devis's Little Society* (c.1790); Mrs Warenne Blake, *An Irish Beauty of the Regency, compiled from 'Mes Souvenirs' – the unpublished journals of the Hon. Mrs Calvert 1789–1822* (1911), pp. 24, 37; Marilyn Butler, *Maria Edgeworth: A Literary Biography* (Oxford, 1972), pp. 71–3.

84 Bryan published two additional books: *Conversations on Chemistry* 2 vols (1806) and *Comprehensive Astronomical Class Book* (1815), as described in Hans, *New Trends in Education*, pp. 203–4.

In spite of the published criticism[85] of boarding and day schools for girls on moral, social and educational grounds, which some of the schools evidently justified, girls' schools remained an important part of the educational scene and a vital source of business and employment for Hanoverian women. In the words of Mrs Frances Broadhurst,

> Much has been written against ladies' schools, and nothing, as far as I am aware has been said in reply to such accusations: because, in spite of all the invective, they continue to flourish.[86]

The very popularity of school education was a female teacher's principal security for her livelihood. The growing preference for governesses in the early nineteenth century did not reduce the number of public girls' schools in existence, but rather increased the overall number of teaching positions open to women. In short, the gradual realization at all levels of society that girls as well as boys deserved a more formal and extensive schooling than could be provided in the home by parents or siblings resulted in a greater demand for teachers, both male and female. As has been shown in this chapter, teaching duties in girls' schools were divided along gender lines, but this division was weakening by the end of the period as women teachers became more qualified to teach subjects that had previously been the preserve of male tutors. The fee-paying girls' school was principally a female institution, and yet it shared many of the characteristics of contemporary commercial boys' schools. Even though the domestic and private character of girls' schools was frequently emphasized in their advertisements, essentially they were public institutions that thrived on publicity and reputation. The social circle of both pupils and teachers within a school was not determined by considerations of family, locality or rank, but of business and income: a school community would be composed of women from differing backgrounds. The practicalities of establishing and conducting a school business were the same for male and female teachers yet the opportunity to initiate a business of their own or to inherit a thriving business from a fellow teacher was surely of greater significance for women than for men. Teaching was one of the few occupations open to women that freed them – at least in part – from dependence on male influence and expertise, and at the same time offered them a livelihood that was not confined to a private or a domestic sphere.

---

85 One of the most virulent attacks on boarding schools was made by J. Louis Chirol, *An Enquiry into the Best System of Female Education; or Boarding School and Home Education Attentively Considered* (1809).

86 Broadhurst, *A Word in Favor of Female Schools*, p. 8.

CHAPTER SIX

Poor women, the parish and the politics of poverty

RICHARD CONNORS

On Tuesday 13 July 1756 Elizabeth Elless, a single woman, died in the village of East Hoathley in Sussex. Such circumstances hardly make her unique, for sudden and unexpected death in the early modern period was ever-present and hardly discriminatory, even of the young.[1] But Elless's tale, recorded for posterity by a certain Thomas Turner,[2] illustrates more than the harsh mortality regime with which historical demographers have made us familiar.[3] Her life, or more accurately her death, was unique and is worthy of examination, for it provides historians with a plethora of information about society and social obligations and expectations in mid eighteenth century England; moreover, her particular circumstances shed light upon the relationship between the poor and parochial

---

1 See P. Aries, *The Hour of Our Death* (Oxford, 1991); P. Spierenburg, *The Broken Spell: A Cultural and Anthropological History of Preindustrial Europe* (1991), ch. 5; C. Gittings, *Death, Burial and the Individual in Early Modern England* (1984); T. Laqueur, 'Bodies, death and pauper funerals' *Representations* 1 (1983), pp. 109–31; S. Ryan Johansson, 'Welfare, mortality, and gender. Continuity and change in explanations for male/female mortality differences over three centuries' *CC* 6, 2 (1991), pp. 135–77; B.A. Doebler, *'Rooted Sorrow': Dying in Early Modern England* (Rutherford, NJ, 1994); and E. Schor, *Bearing the Dead: the British Culture of Mourning From the Enlightenment to Victoria* (Princeton, NJ, 1994).

2 *The diary of Thomas Turner, 1754–1765*, ed. D. Vaisey (Oxford, 1984) (hereafter *Thomas Turner, diary*), p. 50.

3 On this voluminous subject see, for example, E.A. Wrigley and R.S. Schofield, *The Population History of England, 1541–1871: A Reconstruction* (Cambridge, 1989), pp. 228–36, 248–53, 412–17; J. Walter and R.S. Schofield, eds, *Famine, Disease and the Social Order in Early Modern Society* (Cambridge, 1989); L. Bonfield, R.M. Smith and K. Wrightson, eds, *The World We Have Gained: Histories of Population and Social Structure* (Oxford, 1986); D. Levine, *Reproducing Families: The Political Economy of English Population History* (Cambridge, 1987); and M. Anderson, 'The social implications of demographic change', in F.M.L. Thompson, ed., *The Cambridge Social History of Britain 1750–1950* 3 vols (Cambridge, 1990), II, pp. 1–70.

authority in a society where over 80 per cent of those classed as poor were women.[4]

Recent historical debates on gender relations in the past, and particularly those concerning women and work, have great significance for placing the experience of pauper women within broader historical contexts.[5] While separate spheres has proved a compelling conceptual framework for many scholars and has gone some way to 'assert[ing] the wider historical significance of gender',[6] it has recently come under close scrutiny and criticism from numerous quarters. Notwithstanding the fact that debate upon the validity of the dichotomy between public and private continues to rage,[7] it seems increasingly evident that 'at no time in the preindustrial past was there a golden age when women were not confined – either by prevailing notions of separate spheres, complementarity, or partnership, or by the institutional structures and mentalities created by patriarchy – to marginal, unskilled and poorly paid work'.[8] To this voice of dissent can be added those of Judith Bennett, Linda Colley, Linda Kerber, Olwen Hufton, Janet Thomas, Amanda Vickery, Lyndal Roper and Richard Trexler.[9] Much of their recent

4 These statistics are drawn from D. Valenze, *The First Industrial Woman* (Oxford, 1995), pp. 15–16; C. Shammas, 'The world women knew: women workers in the north of England during the seventeenth century', in R.S. Dunn and M.M. Dunn, eds, *The World of William Penn* (Philadelphia, PA, 1986), pp. 99–114, here at p. 112; P. Lindert, 'English occupations, 1670–1811' *Journal of Economic History* 40 (1980), pp. 685–712, here at p. 703; and P. Sharpe, 'Literally spinsters: a new interpretation of local economy and demography in Colyton in the seventeenth and eighteenth centuries' *EcHR* 44 (1991), pp. 46–65, esp. pp. 57–62.

5 For summaries of this literature see P. Sharpe, 'Continuity and change: women's history and economic history in Britain' *EcHR* 48, 2 (1995), pp. 353–69; K. Honeyman and J. Goodman, 'Women's work, gender conflict, and labour markets in Europe, 1500–1900' *EcHR* 2nd ser., 44, 4 (1991), pp. 608–28; O. Hufton, 'Women in history: early modern Europe' *PP* 101 (1983), pp. 125–41; and J.W. Scott, 'Women in history: the modern period' *PP* 101 (1983), pp. 141–57.

6 A. Vickery, 'Golden age to separate spheres? A review of the categories and chronology of English women's history' *HJ* 36, 2 (1993), pp. 383–414, here at p. 413.

7 See, for example, L.E. Klein, 'Gender and the public/private distinction in the eighteenth century: some questions about evidence and analytic procedure' *ECS* 29, 1 (1995), pp. 97–109; L. Davidoff and C. Hall, *Family Fortunes: Men and Women of the English Middle Class, 1780–1850* (1987); and D. Goodman, 'Public sphere and private life: towards a synthesis of current historiographical approaches to the old regime' *History and Theory* 31 (1992), pp. 1–20.

8 D. Bythell, 'Women in the workforce', in P. O'Brien and R. Quinault, eds, *The Industrial Revolution and British Society* (Cambridge, 1993), p. 34.

9 J. Bennett, '"History that stands still": women's work in the European past' *FS* 14, 2 (1988), pp. 269–83; L. Colley, *Britons: Forging the Nation, 1707–1837* (New Haven, CT, and London, 1992), pp. 238–81; L. Kerber, 'Separate spheres, female worlds, woman's place: the rhetoric of women's history' *JAH* 75, 1 (1988), pp. 9–39; Hufton, 'Women in history'; J. Thomas, 'Women and capitalism: oppression or emancipation? A review article'

research seems to indicate that for the vast majority of women living between 1500 and 1800 the rhythms of everyday material life, of
social obligation and expectation remained much the same.[10] For,
as Janet Todd reminds us, 'at the bottom levels of the rural population where most women existed, life was a remorseless struggle
against poverty, a foraging for food and firewood, and an unremit-
ting war against disease and lice'.[11] Despite the development of these
differing historiographical interpretations – and an increasing interest in *alltagsgeschichte*, the history of everyday life – this contentious
research has done a great deal to draw women out from the archival
shadows, to cast light upon their experiences and to place them
more centrally upon the historical stage.[12]

Notwithstanding this interest in women's history, the experience
of poor and pauper women has received little attention by scholars
toiling in the Hanoverian field.[13] This is not to say that nothing has
been written,[14] but that more research needs to be done on the
poorer sorts and their history needs to be written 'from a more self-
consciously past-centred approach which seeks to insert the speech
and action [of women] back into the fluid structure of mentalities
that shaped them'.[15] By integrating contemporary attitudes towards

Comparative Studies in Social History 30 (1990), pp. 534–49; Vickery, 'Golden age to separate spheres?'; idem, 'The neglected century: writing the history of eighteenth-century
women' *GH* 3 (1991), pp. 211–19; L. Roper, *Oedipus and the Devil: Witchcraft, Sexuality and
Religion in Early Modern Europe* (1994); and R. Trexler, *Sex and Conquest: Gendered Violence,
Political Order, and the European Conquest of the Americas* (Ithaca, NY, 1995).

10 O. Hufton, *The Prospect Before Her: A History of Women in Western Europe, Volume One:
1500–1800* (1995); and A. Fletcher, *Gender, Sex & Subordination in England, 1500–1800*
(New Haven, CT, 1995).

11 J. Todd, 'The belaced and the beliced' *Times Higher Educational Supplement*, 16 Feb.
1996, p. 22.

12 On the purposes of *alltagsgeschichte*, see A. Ludtke, *The History of Everyday Life: Recon-
structing Historical Experiences and Ways of Life* (Princeton, NJ, 1995); and P. Burke, 'Over-
ture: the new history, its past and future', in P. Burke, ed., *New Perspectives on Historical
Writing* (University Park, PA, 1991), pp. 1–23, particularly pp. 8–12.

13 For the controversial concept of 'experience' in historical writing, see J.W. Scott,
'Experience', in J. Butler and J.W. Scott, eds, *Feminists Theorize the Political* (New York,
1992), pp. 22–40; idem, *Gender and the Politics of History* (New York, 1988), pp. 4–5, 18–
22, 68–71; E. Varikas, 'Gender, experience and subjectivity: the Tilly-Scott disagreement'
New Left Review 211 (1995), pp. 89–101; and D. Cannadine, 'The way we lived then' *Times
Literary Supplement*, 7–13 Sept. 1990, pp. 935–6.

14 On poor women see K.D.M. Snell, *Annals of the Labouring Poor: Social Change and
Agrarian England 1660–1900* (Cambridge, 1985); B. Hill, ed., *Eighteenth-Century Women: An
Anthology* (1984), pp. 156–76; Valenze, *The First Industrial Woman*, pp. 13–47; A.L. Erickson,
Women and Property in Early Modern England (1993), pp. 200–3; S. Amussen, *An Ordered Society:
Gender and Class in Early Modern England* (Oxford, 1988), pp. 67–94; and D. Andrew, *Philan-
thropy and Police: London Charity in the Eighteenth Century* (Princeton, NJ, 1989), pp. 115–27.

15 M. Gaskill, 'Witchcraft and power in early modern England: the case of Margaret
Moore', in J. Kermode and G. Walker, eds, *Women, Crime and the Courts in Early Modern
England* (1994), p. 127.

poverty with the existing literature on pauper women, and by elaborating upon their relationship with authorities of the Hanoverian state through a number of specific case studies,[16] this chapter seeks to redress this historiographical imbalance and consciously seeks to rescue poor women from what E.P. Thompson famously termed 'the enormous condescension of posterity'.[17] The study of the lives of women such as Elizabeth Elless clearly illustrates that sweeping generalizations about womens' experiences often conceal more than they reveal. Therefore, while this chapter focuses upon the lives and material misfortunes of a number of women – their microhistories – it also seeks to intersect with macrohistorical subjects of separate spheres, poverty and poor relief, the authority of the state in Hanoverian society and the implications that these intersections have for gender history.

Elizabeth Elless's untimely and somewhat suspicious demise in 1756 threw the village of East Hoathley into turmoil, and the village officials – overseers of the poor and churchwardens – into a quandary. It precipitated a deluge of accusation and dispute that held significant legal implications for the parish in general and its parochial officeholders in particular. Central to the case was the question of whether or not Elless had been murdered, and secondly, whether parochial officers had been complicit or merely negligent in not preventing the death of a person chargeable to the parish. However, this was a case surrounded by squalor rather than sensationalism; it had more to do, in the final analysis, with the Poor Laws than with the bloody code of the criminal law.

Historians are fortunate that Elizabeth Elless's story was recorded by Thomas Turner, one of the key players in those tragic events of July 1756, since his diary gives a voice – albeit secondhand – to a poor and unfortunate woman whose life would otherwise have left no imprint on the historical record.[18] Turner was the local shopkeeper,

16 On the 'state' see J. Brewer, *The Sinews of Power: War, Money and the English State, 1688–1783* (1989); L. Davidson, T. Hitchcock, T. Keirn and R.B. Shoemaker, 'The reactive state: English governance and society, 1689–1750', in L. Davidson *et al.*, *Stilling the Grumbling Hive: The Response to Social and Economic Problems in England, 1689–1750* (Stroud, 1992), pp. xi–liv; M. Braddick, 'State formation and social change in early modern England: a problem stated and approaches suggested' *Social History* 16, 1 (1991), pp. 1–17; idem, 'The early modern English state and the question of differentiation, from 1550–1700' *Comparative Studies in Society and History* 38, 1 (1996), pp. 92–111; M. Mann, *Sources of Social Power: Volume I* (Cambridge, 1986); P. Corrigan and D. Sayer, *The Great Arch: English State Formation as Cultural Revolution* (Oxford, 1985); and J.R. Kent, 'The centre and the localities: state formation and parish government in England, circa 1640–1740' *HJ* 38, 2 (1995), pp. 363–404.

17 E.P. Thompson, *The Making of the English Working Class* (1980 edn), p. 12.

18 The following discussion on Elizabeth Elless is based on information in *Thomas Turner, diary*, pp. 47–54.

sometimes undertaker, schoolmaster, tax-gatherer, churchwarden and overseer of the poor of East Hoathley. The village lay on the edge of the Weald seven miles north of Lewes and was of some importance in the local Sussex economy. It was also of wider political significance for it lay on the western bounds of Halland House, the Sussex estate of the Whig grandee Thomas Holles-Pelham, the first Duke of Newcastle. Apart from tales of boisterous parties, cricket matches, cock-fighting and horse-racing, Turner's diary offers glimpses of social relations in his village and of the events surrounding the life and death of Elizabeth Elless.[19]

Roughly a fortnight before her death, Elless came to the attention of overseers of the poor, for she was pregnant and approximately three weeks from full term. On 3 July 1756 Elless acknowledged to Turner and his colleague Jeremiah French that she was indeed 'with child', but she was unwilling to divulge the identity of the father to parish officials. Turner and French were no doubt anxious to ascertain this information, for it might in all probability have exonerated the parish from assuming any responsibility for the child. If the father was known, the task of maintaining the child and being responsible for his or her welfare would pass onto the father's shoulders. Instead of naming anyone, Elless agreed to accompany Turner and French to see a Justice of the Peace to swear, on oath, her parish of settlement. All of this was to be transacted despite the fact that Turner was already convinced that she belonged to the parish of East Hoathley and was, therefore, legally entitled to parochial relief. Turner's actions were motivated by his hope that she might be convinced, during the process, to declare the father of the as yet unborn child. That afternoon, and with the assistance of French's servant – James Shoesmith – she was carried to Lewes to be heard by a Justice. Upon their arrival, Elless was duly examined by Edward Verral, the Justice's Clerk, and it was determined that she was indeed chargeable to the parish and that there was no need for her to meet with a JP. Efforts were renewed to gain from Elless information about the paternity of the child, but again they 'could not prevail on her to confess the father ... though [they] tried all ways to come to the knowledge of him'. The day had proven expensive for East Hoathley, for not only had the trip and examination cost nearly five shillings, but the parish had also assumed responsibility for maintaining Elless and her unborn child.

---

19 On Turner and his familial relations see also N. Tadmor, 'The concept of the household-family in eighteenth-century England' *PP* 151 (1996), pp. 111–40.

At this point the tale takes a tragic turn, for on 13 July, Turner notes that Elless suddenly died. Immediately thereafter, one of the villagers – Peter Adams, a labourer – voiced his concern over the fact that Turner and French had taken her to Lewes. Because of their actions and Elless's subsequent death, Adams declared that they ought to be fined. While the actions of Turner and French had not necessarily precipitated her death, Adams's accusation of misconduct did in fact have considerable legal merit. Had they actually presented Elless before a Justice at Lewes on 3 July as they had planned, they would have been violating 6 George II, c. 31, which declared it illegal 'for any justice or justices of the peace to send for any woman whatsoever before she shall be delivered, and one month after, in order to her being examined concerning her pregnancy, or supposed pregnancy, or to compel any woman before she shall be delivered to answer any questions relating to her pregnancy'.[20]

Turner and French were, therefore, fortunate that Elless's examination in Lewes had not been conducted by a Justice of the Peace. Ironically, the statute, 'an Act for the relief of parishes and other places from such charges as may arise from bastard children both within the same', had been drawn up to assist parishes by enabling overseers to present pregnant and unmarried women before a Justice to swear the identity of the father. Women were offered some consideration in light of their circumstances by the law, but its intention was clear: while the moral weight of the legislation was directed at the 'single woman . . . delivered of a bastard child', the deterrent force behind the legislation was targetted at the putative father, for he was to be immediately apprehended and committed to prison unless he gave recognizances, in accordance with 18 Elizabeth, c. 3, to assume economic responsibility, or offer 'sufficient surety', for the welfare of the child.[21] These economic concerns were rendered academic for the overseers of East Hoathley upon the death of Elizabeth Elless; nonetheless, her tragic circumstances clearly affected Turner and others in the village.[22]

In the light of Adams's inflammatory remarks, and 'as the affair had occasioned much talk', Turner and his colleagues, encouraged by the rector Thomas Porter, concluded that 'it was the parish's duty

---

20 D. Pickering, *The Statutes at Large, from Magna Carta to the end of the fifteenth Parliament of Great Britain* (London, 1733), XVI, pp. 425–6.

21 Ibid., XVI, pp. 425–6.

22 References 'concerning the unhappy affair of poor Elizabeth Elless' recur in the days following her death. See *Thomas Turner, diary*, pp. 51, 54, 71.

to examine into the death of this poor creature [Elless] . . . and have her opened [conduct an autopsy]'. This decision was not taken lightly and most of the principal inhabitants of East Hoathley were consulted before the medical examination was ordered. The circumstances surrounding her death were suspicious and the parish officers, Turner included, suspected that Elless had either been poisoned, or that she had died of complications arising from efforts to terminate her pregnancy. Witnesses acknowledged that Elless had been well until she returned from an evening walk on the 12th, but later that night she 'was taken with a violent vomiting and purging and continued so all night until Tuesday 5 o'clock, at which time she expired'. Moreover, during the illness Elless 'never had any pangs or throes like labour, nor no external symptoms whatever, and complained of great heat, and was afflicted with an uncommon drought'. During the whole period of her illness, neither a midwife nor an apothecary was called, nor was the assistance of any neighbours sought to help Elless. Such behaviour ran counter to contemporary medical practices and to the social mores of neighbourly obligation.[23] Peter Adams had been with Elless for most of the day, however, and villagers recounted seeing them together the previous evening in 'a very remote and obscure place in a wood'.

This familiarity, coupled with the facts that Adams had already fathered an illegitimate child by another woman in the village, and that his wife was also pregnant, further raised suspicions and increased the gossiping among the villagers.[24] It was, therefore, agreed that a post mortem should be conducted on 15 July by a local surgeon, Dr Snelling, with the assistance of a man-midwife, Dr Davy, in

23 For discussions on childbirth see R. Houlbrooke, *English Family Life, 1576–1716* (Oxford, 1988), pp. 101–32; A. Laurence, *Women in England 1500–1760* (1994), pp. 75–86; Hill, ed., *Eighteenth-Century Women*, pp. 104–7; Hufton, *The Prospect Before Her*, pp. 173–89; K. Wrightson, *English Society, 1580–1680* (1982), pp. 104–8; B.S. Anderson and J.P. Zinsser, *A History of Their Own: Women in Europe from Prehistory to the Present* 2 vols (New York, 1988), I, pp. 104–12, 419–24; R.G. Fuchs, *Poor and Pregnant in Paris* (New Brunswick, NJ, 1992), pp. 112–25. On hospitality and neighbourliness see F. Heal, *Hospitality in Early Modern England* (Oxford, 1990); idem, 'The idea of hospitality in early modern England' *PP* 102 (1984), pp. 66–93; Wrightson, *English Society*, pp. 51–7; and K. Wrightson and D. Levine, *Poverty and Piety in an English Village: Terling, 1525–1700* rev. edn (Oxford, 1995), pp. 99–109.

24 For an excellent consideration of the implications of gossip on community relations, see S. Hindle, 'The shaming of Margaret Knowsley: gossip, gender and the experience of authority in early modern England' *CC* 9, 3 (1994), pp. 391–419. Also see D. Underdown, 'The taming of the scold: the enforcement of patriarchal authority in early modern England', in A. Fletcher and J. Stevenson, eds, *Order and Disorder in Early Modern England* (Cambridge, 1985), pp. 116–36; and L. Gowing, 'Gender and the language of insult in early modern London' *HWJ* 35 (1993), pp. 1–31.

the hope of determining 'whether she or any one else had administered anything to deprive her or the child of life'.[25] Turner and the local nurse were present for the autopsy which revealed that Elless would have given birth to a female child within days and that though there was little sign of poisoning – the vomiting and purging might have evicted it from her body – the practitioners agreed that 'circumstances looked very dark and all corroborated together to give room for suspicion'. The doctors concluded, 'so far as they could judge', that Elless died from 'a bilious colic'. Numerous inhabitants of East Hoathley suspected that Peter Adams had been intimately involved, not only with Elizabeth Elless, but also in the events that culminated in her demise. For instance, on 5 November 1756 the Reverend Thomas Porter confronted Adams publicly on the matter of Elless's death and strong words were exchanged. Turner confided in his diary that 'it must astonish almost any thinking person to see with what audaciousness the poor hardened wretch [Adams] behaves, for he seems to glory in and give encouragement to crimes of the deepest dye'.[26] Inconclusive as the autopsy was, there was, however, little more that could be done to ascertain the truth behind the deaths of Elless and her daughter, and only time would mask the social disturbance occasioned in East Hoathley by the events of 3–14 July 1756.

What are we to make of this case? In itself Elizabeth Elless's experience is worth recounting, for it reveals the fragility of life for many in eighteenth-century England. In all probability, Elless, perhaps with the assistance of Adams, had attempted to terminate her pregnancy with tragic results. At a precarious stage in her lifecycle – poor, pregnant and single – and clearly with no or very little material assistance from the putative father, Elless had accepted the risk of inducing a miscarriage. For those of us living in an age of death control, when modern medicine has forbidden, concealed and effaced death, or removed it from public view and muted it in our consciousness, it is important to recognize the implications of a far more volatile mortality regime upon the nature of Hanoverian

---

25 On the subject of midwifery, see D. Harley, 'Provincial Midwives in England: Lancashire and Cheshire, 1660–1760', in H. Marland, ed., *The Art of Midwifery: Early Modern Midwives in Europe* (London, 1993), pp. 27–48: I. Loudon, *Medical Care and the General Practitioner, 1750–1850* (Oxford, 1986); B.B. Schnorrenberg, 'Is Childbirth Any Place for a Woman? The Decline of Midwifery in Eighteenth-Century England', *Studies in Eighteenth-Century Culture*, 10 (1981), pp. 393–408; M.C. Versluysen, 'Midwives, Medical Men and "poor women labouring of child": Lying-in Hospitals in Eighteenth-Century London', in H. Roberts, ed., *Women, Health and Reproduction* (London, 1981), pp. 18–49.

26 *Thomas Turner, diary*, p. 71.

society.[27] It was in such an environment that Elless lived and died, one in which 'few could hope to live out the biblical span . . . [and] . . . that for most [like Elizabeth Elless] death came both unexpected and untimely, cutting them off quite literally in the midst of life'.[28]

Not only does Elless's case remind us that the poor were most susceptible to a harsh mortality regime, but, more importantly, it illustrates the power relationship and tensions between paupers (Elless) and their social and political superiors (Turner and his colleagues) in the thousands of parishes of eighteenth-century England. Unique this case certainly was in its circumstances and outcome, but overseers throughout England often dealt with poor and pregnant women. This owes much to the fact that early modern English social policy was founded upon a close relationship – quite literally face to face, as Peter Laslett has reminded scholars – between the parochial and patriarchal authorities and the labouring and destitute poor who lived within the bounds of their jurisdiction, the parish.[29] This point is well illustrated by the fact that Elless and Turner discussed her circumstances in detail in both East Hoathley and in Lewes. Furthermore, the Settlement and Poor Laws laid down strictures on how such cases should be handled.[30] In reality, a conglomeration of early modern statutes collectively dealt with issues of poverty, but these were often interpreted flexibly in the locality by people like the overseer of the poor and the Clerk to the Justice of the Peace, like Turner and Verral respectively, thereby rendering generalizations about social welfare problematic.[31]

27 These ideas are drawn from: Aries, *The Hour of Our Death*, pp. 602–14; N. Elias, *The Civilizing Process* 2 vols (English trans., Oxford, 1981–2); Spierenburg, *The Broken Spell*, pp. 125–62; Gittings, *Death, Burial and the Individual*; and K. Thomas, *Religion and the Decline of Magic* (1971).

28 K. Wrightson and D. Levine, 'Death in Whickham', in Walter and Schofield, eds, *Famine, Disease and the Social Order*, p. 129.

29 This concept is discussed in some detail in P. Laslett, *The World We Have Lost – Further explored* 3rd edn (1983), pp. 202–4, 213–14, 335. Also see D. Eastwood, 'The republic in the village: parish and poor at Bampton, 1780–1834' *Journal of Regional and Local Studies* 12 (1992), pp. 18–28.

30 The following discussion on the Poor Laws is drawn from: R. Burn, *The History of the Poor Laws: with Observations* (1764); Sir F.M. Eden, *The State of the Poor* 3 vols (1797), esp. vol. I. Also see R. Connors, 'The politics of poverty in eighteenth-century England', in R. Connors and C. Jones, eds, *Souls of State and Empire: Essays in Memory of Philip Lawson* (forthcoming, 1997); S. and B. Webb, *English Poor Law History. Part I: The Old Poor Law* (1963 edn); P. Slack, *Poverty and Policy in Tudor and Stuart England* (1988); idem, *The English Poor Law 1531–1782* (1990); and M.J. Daunton, *Progress and Poverty: An Economic and Social History of Britain 1700–1850* (Oxford, 1995), pp. 447–74.

31 On the Poor Laws and the locality, see A. Fletcher, *Reform in the Provinces* (New Haven, CT, 1986), pp. 183–228; D. Underdown, *Fire from Heaven: Life in an English Town in the Seventeenth Century* (New York, 1992), pp. 61–71; M. Barker-Read, 'The treatment of the aged poor in five selected West Kent parishes from Settlement to Speenhamland

Nevertheless, it is clear that a pauper who desired relief, whether female or male, had in the first instance to approach the parish overseer. He was expected and required by law to investigate and to acquaint himself with the appellant's particular circumstances, his or her financial situation and to determine whether the plea for parish assistance was in fact legitimate. For nearly a century after the passage of 43 Elizabeth I, c. 2 in 1601, overseers were allowed to dole out moneys collected through parochial taxation from the parish coffers as they saw fit. In 1693, however, legislation required that relief only be given, except in times of emergency, upon the authority of a Justice of the Peace. In 1722, it was further enacted that paupers had to approach their Overseers before they could appeal to a Justice for parochial assistance. In keeping with the Laws of Settlement (1662 and 1697), the Justice was required to hear sworn testimony so as to determine the pauper's parish of settlement. Once this task had been completed, the pauper was entitled to relief – but only from the parish of settlement. That accomplished (if possible, for this could prove particularly contentious if more than one parish was involved or if the prospective recipient had dependants), the pauper was duly relieved or removed to the parish of declared settlement.

This was the procedure that Thomas Turner and his colleagues had been eager to complete when they escorted Elizabeth Elless to Lewes on 3 July 1756. Their conduct on that afternoon was certainly suspect, in that taking a pregnant woman before a JP at that stage in her pregnancy was illegal, but their actions seem restrained when compared to examples found by Dorothy Marshall in various other parish accounts. For instance, one overseer's account lists disbursements 'geaven to a poore woman that was in labor carrying of her away .. 2–0'; and likewise, in 1722, 'to a big bellyd woman several days and nights at nursing at Robinsons, and conveying her to Chigivill after she had gathered strength to prevent her lying in here, she fell to pieces in 2 or 3 days there ..17–7'.[32] Such cases reveal, as does the experience of Elizabeth Elless, the paradoxical

---

(1662–1797)' (unpub. Ph.D. thesis, Open University, 1988); J.M. Shaw, 'The development of the local Poor Law Acts, 1696–1833 with particular reference to the incorporated hundreds of East Anglia' (unpub. Ph.D. thesis, University of East Anglia, 1989); A. Tomkins, 'The experience of urban poverty: a comparison of Oxford and Shrewsbury 1740–70' (unpub. D.Phil. thesis, Oxford, 1994); and W. Newman Brown, 'The receipt of poor relief and family situation: Aldenham, Hertfordshire 1630–90', in R.M. Smith, ed., *Land, Kinship and Life-Cycle* (Cambridge, 1984), pp. 405–22, to list but a few works in a growing field.

32 *The Poor Book of Westbury on Trym*, ed. H.J. Wilkins (1910), p. 53, and the *History of Leyton*, ed. J. Kennedy (1894), p. 159, both cited in D. Marshall, *The English Poor in the Eighteenth Century* (1969 edn), p. 212.

nature of the Poor Law; 'providing relief, enforcing discipline, an expression of communal responsibility yet a potent reminder of social distance'.[33] Moreover, the Settlement Laws reinforced the patriarchal nature of society by ensuring that a child took his or her father's parish of settlement and that a married woman took that of her husband. The laws produced a massive amount of litigation between parishes, and disputes often focused upon unmarried women and widowed or abandoned women with children living in parishes without legal claims to parochial relief.[34] This also owed something to the fact that poor women were more likely to become dependent upon the parish for long-term relief. This was in part because bearing children – particularly illegitimate children – made it more difficult for them to gain employment, but it also resulted from the harsh realities of the workplace.[35] Simply put, work for poor and marginalized women throughout early modern England and Europe was, and always had been, 'low-skilled, low-status and low-paying'.[36]

33 K. Wrightson, 'The social order of early modern England', in Bonfield, Smith and Wrightson, eds, *The World We Have Gained*, pp. 177–202, here at p. 201.

34 Confusing and contentious to contemporaries, the Poor Laws have proven equally controversial to historians. For recent discussions on the significance and intent of Settlement Law, consult Snell, *Annals of the Labouring Poor*; idem, 'Settlement, poor law and the rural historian: new approaches and opportunities' *Rural History* 3 (1992), pp. 145–72; idem, 'Pauper settlement and the right to poor relief in England and Wales' *CC* 6 (1991), pp. 375–415; N. Landau, 'The eighteenth century context of the laws of settlement' *CC* 6 (1991), pp. 417–39; idem, 'The regulation of immigration, economic structures and definitions of the poor in eighteenth century England' *HJ* 33 (1990), pp. 541–72; idem, 'The laws of settlement and the surveillence of immigration in eighteenth-century Kent' *CC* 3 (1988), pp. 391–420; P. Rushton, 'The poor law, the parish and the community in north-east England, 1600–1800' *Northern History* 25 (1989), pp. 135–52; and R. Wells, 'Migration, the law, and parochial policy in eighteenth and early nineteenth-century southern England' *Southern History* 15 (1993), pp. 86–139.

35 On this subject see Roper, *Oedipus and the Devil*, pp. 1–34; T. Laqueur, *Making Sex: Body and Gender from the Greeks to Freud* (Cambridge, MA, 1992); and Vickery, 'The neglected century', p. 217, who notes that 'throughout the eighteenth-century British Atlantic empire, women's lives were circumscribed by biology, law, economics, morality and custom'. For a discussion of the impact of illegitimacy in Hanoverian England, see A. Wilson, 'Illegitimacy and its implications in mid-eighteenth century London: the evidence of the Foundling Hospital' *CC* 4 (1989), pp. 103–64.

36 Bennett, ' "History that stands still" ', p. 278. Also see A. Clark, *Working Life of Women in the Seventeenth Century* 3rd edn, intro. by A.L. Erickson (1992); I. Pinchbeck, *Women Workers and the Industrial Revolution, 1750–1850* 2nd edn (1969); L.A. Tilly and J.W. Scott, *Women, Work and Family* (New York, 1987); L.A. Tilly, *Industrialization and Gender Inequality* (Washington, 1993); L. Charles and L. Duffin, eds, *Women and Work in Pre-industrial England* (Beckenham, 1985); P. Earle, 'The female labour market in London in the late seventeenth and early eighteenth centuries' *EcHR* 2nd ser., 42, 3 (1989), pp. 328–53; M. Berg, 'What difference did women's work make to the industrial revolution?' *HWJ* 35 (1993), pp. 22–44; idem, 'Women's work, mechanization and the early phases of industrialization in England', in P. Joyce, ed., *The Historical Meaning of Work* (Cambridge, 1987),

It is important to realize that those on poor relief or on the margins of poverty endured life as participants of an 'economy of makeshifts'.[37] They scraped together a subsistence income from a variety of sources, such as casual labour, day jobs, charitable donations, begging, petty crime, loans, common and use rights and, of course, the parish chest. Changing conditions of the poor were not only tied to the vagaries of under- and unemployment and new industrial modes of production, they were also linked to an erosion of traditional use-rights, which undermined their position within a moral economy of provision, and also to the weakening of the common rights that reinforced the family economy.[38] Research by Edward Thompson and Bob Bushaway on custom, by Peter King on gleaning and Jeanette Neeson on enclosure, powerfully illustrate the physical and personal consequences of these forces on Hanoverian society and the labouring poor in particular.[39] In periods of economic crisis between a third and a half of the population could be forced onto parish relief.[40] Therefore, the importance of the

pp. 64–98; Hill, *Women, Work and Sexual Politics*; P. Hudson and W.R. Lee, eds, *Women's Work and the Family Economy in Historical Perspective* (Manchester, 1990); C. Middleton, 'The familiar fate of the formulae: gender divisions in the history of wage labour', in R.E. Pahl, ed., *On Work* (Oxford, 1988), pp. 21–47; J. Rendall, *Women in an Industrializing Society: England, 1750–1880* (Oxford, 1990); S. Rose, 'Proto-industry, women's work and the household economy in the transition to industrial capitalism' *JFH* 13 (1988), pp. 181–93; and P. Sharpe, *Adapting to Capitalism: Working Women in the English Economy, 1700–1850* (Basingstoke, 1996).

37 The term is taken from O. Hufton, *The Poor of Eighteenth Century France* (Oxford, 1974), ch. 3.

38 On this subject consider E.P. Thompson, 'The moral economy of the English crowd in the eighteenth century' *PP* 50 (1971), pp. 76–136; R.B. Outhwaite, *Dearth, Public Policy and Social Disturbance in England, 1550–1800* (1991); K. Wrightson and J. Walter, 'Dearth and the social order in early modern England', *PP* 71 (1976), pp. 22–42; and J. Walter, 'The social economy of dearth in early modern England', in Walter and Schofield, eds, *Famine, Disease and the Social Order*, pp. 75–128.

39 See E.P. Thompson, *Customs in Common* (1991); B. Bushaway, *By Rite: Custom, Ceremony and Community in England 1700–1880* (1982); P. King, 'Customary rights and women's earnings: the importance of gleaning to the rural labouring poor, 1750–1850' *EcHR* 44 (1991), pp. 461–476; idem, 'Gleaners, farmers and the failure of legal sanctions, 1750–1850' *PP* 125 (1989), pp. 116–50; J. Neeson, *Commoners: Common Right, Enclosure and Social Change in England, 1700–1820* (Cambridge, 1993); and J. Humphries, 'Enclosures, common rights and women: the proletarianisation of families in the late eighteenth and early nineteenth centuries' *Journal of Economic History* 50 (1990), pp. 17–42. On custom also see T. Stretton, 'Women, custom and equity in the courts of requests', in Kermode and Walker, eds, *Women, Crime and the Courts*, pp. 170–89.

40 Gregory King calculated that 51% of the population in 1696 did not have sufficient wherewithal to support themselves. See G. Holmes, 'Gregory King and the social structure of pre-industrial England' *Transactions of the Royal Historical Society* 27 (1977), pp. 41–68. Also see R.W. Malcolmson, *Life and Labour in England, 1700–1780* (London, 1981), pp. 11–21, 77–80; Rushton, 'The poor law', pp. 142–6; J. Rule, 'Land of lost content? The

Poor Laws in facilitating the transition from the catastrophic to the 'non-catastrophic world',[41] and in providing 'relief at critical stages in the lifecycles of the labouring poor', should not be underestimated.[42] When account is taken of recent research suggesting that as many as 86 per cent of those classed as poor in 1755 were women,[43] it becomes increasingly obvious that they often had little choice but to turn to the parish for assistance. We see this clearly in the experiences of a number of women in Hackney, a satellite hamlet north and east of London.

On 13 December 1731, Elizabeth Stamper, widow, petitioned Henry Norris, Samuel Tyssen and Alexander Garrett, Justices of the Peace for Hackney, for relief.[44] Her request, punctuated by the fact that she had children and was pregnant at the time, was duly met and she summarily received a sum of two shillings, to be continued for the following four weeks. At the same Petty Sessions the Justices heard the case of Mary Johnston, 'she being in great want and having two children to provide for and her husband having left her in want'.[45] In the process of examination it became evident that Johnston's parish of settlement was in fact in Boden, Cheshire, and therefore that Hackney had – according to Settlement Law – no long-term legal responsibility for her or her family. Nevertheless, the Justices ordered that the churchwardens pay her two shillings and sixpence to alleviate her distress. In both instances, the parish had been called upon to tend to the material needs of those in distress and privation. This payment was generous, but the harsh reality of Johnston's plight was made clear one week later when the

eighteenth-century Poor Law' *Revue Française de Civilisation Britannique* 6, 2 (1991), pp. 7–26, esp. pp. 7–11; D. Hay, 'War, dearth and theft in the eighteenth century: the record of the English courts' *PP* 95 (1982), pp. 135–44, 158–60; and J. Innes, 'Social problems: poverty and marginality in eighteenth-century England', an unpublished essay, pp. 25–31. I would like to thank Joanna Innes for allowing me to see this important unpublished paper.

41 D.E. Eversley, 'The home market and economic growth in England, 1750–1780', in E.L. Jones and G.E. Mingay, eds, *Land, Labour and Population in the Industrial Revolution* (1967), p. 255. Eversley goes so far as to state that 'after 1740, for the first time, more people live in the non-catastrophic world. Food, shelter, and clothing became a certain expectation. Calamitous death became rare.'

42 K. Wrightson and D. Levine, *The Making of an Industrial Society: Whickham 1560–1765* (Oxford, 1991), pp. 351–5; and T. Wales, 'Poverty, poor relief and the life-cycle: some evidence from seventeenth-century Norfolk', in Smith, ed., *Land, Kinship and Life-Cycle*, pp. 351–404.

43 See footnote 4.

44 *Justice in Eighteenth-Century Hackney: The Justicing Notebook of Henry Norris and the Hackney Petty Sessions Book*, ed. R. Paley (1991) (hereafter, *Norris Notebook*), case 424. On Elizabeth Stamper see cases 424, 439, 460, 548.

45 *Norris Notebook*, case 425; also see 433, from which the following discussion is drawn.

Justices allocated her a further twelve shillings on the condition that she leave the parish and never trouble Hackney again.

These two cases would be unremarkable were they not so typical of the treatment of pauper women in not only Hackney, but all over England during the eighteenth century. Through differing, yet similarly unfortunate, circumstances, both Stamper and Johnston had been driven into the hands of the parish, and both, in the first instance, had been refused the right to poor relief. It is because of the initial refusal of relief that these women and their families ever appeared – upon appeal – before Justice Norris at Quarter Sessions. Until the 1690s, paupers had habitually presented their petitions for relief before Justices at Quarter Sessions. Upon hearing the case the JP would make a ruling and the orders of the court – for relief, incarceration or employment, among other things – would be carried out by parish officials.[46] However, once individual justices were authorized to handle cases of this nature, petitions to sessions from paupers diminished and Quarter Sessions in the specific context of the Poor Laws became, for all intents and purposes, a Court of Appeal.[47]

Thus, from the 1690s onwards cases appear in Justices' notebooks of paupers asking for relief, arrears to their pensions, and orders from the courts that the overseers of the parishes be compelled to respect rightful settlements and entitlement to relief. Justice Norris and his colleagues on the bench at Petty Sessions in Hackney dealt with a substantial number of such cases. According to his justicing notebooks, which cover the period from October 1731 until August 1753, Norris dealt with 786 cases, of which 99, or 13 per cent, were appeals for poor relief.[48] Thus, Norris spent an impressive part of his job and time as a JP dealing with the intricacies of Settlement Law and parish politics. Focusing upon the 99 appeals for relief and analysing them further reveals a distinct asymmetry: 18 appeals were made by males; 37 were made by single females; 30 were made by women with children; 12 were made by families; and 2 were made on behalf of children. Not only were single women (this includes widows and spinsters) the highest category, but by combining all the categories that included women, 80

46 On Justices of the Peace, see N. Landau, *The Justices of the Peace 1679–1760* (Berkeley, CA, 1984); L.K.J. Glassey, *Politics and the Appointment of Justices of the Peace* (Oxford, 1979); R. Shoemaker, *Prosecution and Punishment: Petty Crime and the Law in London and Rural Middlesex, 1660–1725* (Cambridge, 1991); and J.M. Beattie, *Crime and the Courts in England, 1660–1800* (Oxford, 1986).

47 3 William and Mary c. 11.

48 *Norris Notebook*, pp. 71–201.

per cent of the cases involved women directly. In the majority, 67 per cent, women were the principal appellants. These statistics are remarkably similar to calculations made by other scholars seeking to gauge the scale of pauperism amongst women in the early modern period.[49] The picture that emerges from the Hackney Sessions is one of widespread deprivation, and while poverty did not discriminate between men and women (there are numerous cases of destitute males), the number of cases involving single women (37 per cent) and women with children (30 per cent) is indeed striking.[50]

Let us return to the case of Elizabeth Stamper to illustrate this impression. Shortly before Christmas 1731 she received a lump sum payment of five shillings and a further two shillings per week, 'she having lately laid in and having two children'. In February, the parish was ordered to provide Widow Stamper with ten shillings, 'to put her into a way of business'. The intention was, no doubt, to assist her in finding employment, perhaps with the hope of eliminating the grinding poverty under which she and her children laboured, but certainly with the desire to remove her from the parish relief lists.[51] Clearly this plan failed, for by the summer her two children had died. On 19 June 1732, Justice Norris ordered the parish overseers to pay 'eight shillings towards the burying of her two children'.[52] In other cases the results were not so tragic. For instance, on 1 May 1732, Justices Norris, Tyssen and Oakey presided over a Quarter Sessions in which a number of appeals by women were heard. Their orders included: three shillings for Elizabeth Bartmaker, 'she having two children to provide for'; one shilling for Margaret Bolton 'for two weeks to come her husband being in Goal and she in want'; and 'two shillings/week to Susannah Durant, she having two children'.[53]

The parochial system not only provided pensions to female and male paupers and their families, it also sought to provide employment for the idle and destitute. One way in which poor women were readily employed by the parishes, and by which the theoretical dichotomy between public/private spheres was undermined, was in the field of medical provision. Women participated in the public sphere as employees of the parish in various capacities: as

49 See footnote 4.
50 On this subject also see O. Hufton, 'Women without men: widows and spinsters in Britain and France in the eighteenth century' *JFH* 9 (1984), pp. 355–76.
51 *Norris Notebook*, cases 439 and 460.
52 Ibid., case 548.
53 Ibid., cases 525, 526, 527.

nurses, maid-servants, labourers, caretakers and caregivers. As local representatives – employees of an intrusive state – they entered into the private domain of hearth and home dispensing relief and medicines. It has been argued by others that these forms of employment and activity projected a paternalist social policy that 'confounded the private with the public sphere at the very time that the state assumed new functions and women remained excluded from public office'.[54] In May 1732, Justice Norris ordered overseers to pay Martha Baxter, widow, one shilling per week 'towards the maintenance of Elinor Kingsland, widow, incapable of working for her living'. Likewise on the same day, Mary Kirby received 'eight shillings for nursing and maintaining Thomas Cawne for two weeks he being Lunatick'.[55] Further evidence of such action is provided in July 1732 when Mary Wingood was paid 'twelve shillings for nursing maintaining and Lodging two Poor Travellers that were taken dangerously ill'. At the same sessions, 'Amy Butling afflicted with the Rhumatysm be put into St Thomas's Hospital for cure', and finally, Mary Kirby (again), received 'thirty shillings for nursing and maintaining Elizabeth George for four weeks in her laying Inn and eight shillings for nursing and maintaining her daughter Sarah for four weeks to this day'.[56]

Both the Justices and the Overseers of the Poor undoubtedly saw the benefits of such a system of relief and medical provision. While those in need of medical assistance were taken care of in the parish, and at minimum expenditure, poor women were set to work and paid for their employment rather than for their maintenance alone. Not only did this employment benefit the parish, the infirm and the poor, but it served as a work-scheme which reinforced rather than undermined the family economy, and it did not threaten existing labour pools in other menial trades. Moreover, as Diane Willen has shown for the sixteenth and seventeenth centuries, this participation by women in public matters – medical provision and the dispensation of poor relief – did not challenge patriarchy or traditional hierarchies since these women continued to live on the fringes of power and remained bound by their employment to an economy of

54 D. Willen, 'Women in the public sphere in early modern England: the case of the urban working poor' *Sixteenth Century Journal* 19 (1988), pp. 559–75. Also see M.E. Fissell, *Patients, Power and the Poor in Eighteenth Century Bristol* (Cambridge, 1991); and P. Rushton, 'Lunatics and idiots: mental disability, the community, and the poor law in north-east England, 1600–1800' *Medical History* 32 (1988), pp. 34–50.

55 *Norris Notebook*, cases 538 and 539.

56 Ibid., cases 562, 568 and 576. Other cases combining medical provision to paupers and employment to poor women include 401, 448, 475, 528 and 663.

makeshifts.[57] Men remained in positions of social and political power as Justices of the Peace, Overseers of the Poor and churchwardens – yet paradoxically, this authority was, at times, mediated in the parishes by women as servants of the parochial administration. Moreover, these patriarchal structures also remained intact because a disproportionate amount of relief was distributed to women (for various social, cultural, demographic and economic reasons) since they made up the vast majority of those deemed deserving poor.

Such a litany of disbursements and medical employments seemingly reveals a parochial system that was generous and acutely aware of social and economic obligation. There is some truth to such a conclusion; nevertheless, it was also discriminatory and harsh at times. A striking contrast to the cases in Hackney is offered by an examination that took place in Nantwich, Cheshire, on 26 December 1751. Upon examination of Sarah Davies, a single woman with an illegitimate child, taken before Justice James Croxton, it was decided she should be committed to the House of Correction until further notice.[58] In her deposition, Davies confided that she had been born in the parish of St James, Bristol, and that seven years earlier, in 1745, she had dressed in men's clothing and made her way to London where she had bound herself as apprentice – to go to sea – to Captain John Hasseck for five years. Using the alias John Davies she had sailed to Jamaica but after six months in the service of Hasseck she had run away and had been a sailor on numerous other vessels. Davies's luck turned from bad to worse on 1 November 1751 when the ship she was serving on foundered in the Bay of Biscay. Fortunately, she and thirteen crew members were plucked to safety by another ship headed for Sunderland and she was brought ashore in that port on 18 November. Thereafter Davies set out begging and wandering. Desperate for food and shelter, she had arrived on 16 December in the township of Eccleston, and on the same day had been delivered safely of a healthy daughter. The court concluded that this child had been chargeable to Eccleston since her birth, and would continue to be so thereafter. Sarah Davies was an outsider, unknown and thus undeserving. She was incarcerated and dealt with harshly because she did not have a claim to settlement and was, therefore, entitled neither to parochial relief nor to a great deal of neighbourly compassion.

57 Willen, 'Women in the public sphere', pp. 558–60, 573–5.

58 *Quarter Sessions Records, County Palatine of Chester, 1559–1760*, eds J.H.E. Bennett and J.C. Dewhurst (Vol. 94, 1940), p. 221. The following information is also drawn from this source.

This chapter has discussed only a few illustrations of the interaction between pauper women and local authorities of the Hanoverian state. Here the worlds of rich and poor, the rulers and the ruled, met – yet they interacted according to a set of orderly and stylized procedures, and within a face-to-face society and community rather than an impersonal and bureaucratic system.[59] The players – be they Justices, witnesses, overseers of the poor or paupers – understood well the importance of this ritual-laden social minuet and most played their parts at Petty and Quarter Sessions according to the community-orientated expectations and conventions of mid-eighteenth-century law and society. While the law, the social order and deference were parts of this equation, so too were expectations of benevolence, reciprocity and relief. Therefore, negotiations at Petty and Quarter Sessions for the relief of poverty were as much community-based 'rituals of inclusion', to appropriate Thomas Laqueur's phrase, as they were struggles between contending images of the deserving and undeserving poor.[60] The social welfare system, embodied in the Poor Laws, was founded upon a hierarchical and patriarchal recognition of eligibility and responsibility, but at the same time it was discretionary and exclusive.[61] On the one hand the right of settlement identified membership in the parish community, the right to relief and, perhaps, even neighbourly hospitality and Christian compassion. On the other hand settlement also identified those to be excluded from the parish, it delineated the undeserving poor and quite literally 'the other' – those who were not part of the community.[62] As Keith Wrightson has recently reminded us, 'the system identified and isolated the poor as a group: stressing their otherness; markedly reinforcing the moral differentiation of the deserving and the undeserving; defining the boundaries of the community by the recognition of settlement and entitlement'.[63]

59 Eastwood, 'The republic in the village', p. 18, notes that the 'governing style in most parishes ... was personal rather than bureaucratic, with word of mouth rather than detailed written records being the essential currency of parish administration'.

60 This is an adaptation of the phrase to be found in Laqueur, 'Bodies, death and funerals', pp. 112–14.

61 On the exclusive nature of the Poor Laws, see S. Hindle, 'The politics of exclusion: power, poor relief and social relations in Frampton (Lincolnshire), c. 1600–1800' (*HJ*, forthcoming). I would like to thank Steve Hindle for sharing his ideas with me in advance of publication.

62 On 'the other' see Colley, *Britons*.

63 K. Wrightson, 'The politics of the parish in early modern England', in A. Fox, P. Griffiths and S. Hindle, eds, *The Experience of Authority in Early Modern England* (London, 1996), pp. 10–46, here at p. 21. I would like to thank Keith Wrightson and the editors for allowing me to see this piece in typescript.

The case of Sarah Davies testifies to such an impression of the early modern English social welfare system.

From evidence in numerous Justices' notebooks, it is clear that the relief system was completely discretionary, but that the right of settlement was legally binding, not only on the poor but on the parishes too – as Elless's case illustrates and as Thomas Turner knew only too well. Of this there can be little doubt. Poor women fully recognized this legal right and were not merely passive recipients of poor relief.[64] Occasionally pauper women challenged and confronted local Poor Law authorities, overseers of the poor and churchwardens in the courts of law, so as to obtain and protect their right to parish assistance. In such circumstances, the Justices of the Peace became crucial players since the day-to-day maintenance of the social welfare system ultimately rested upon their shoulders. Theoretically JPs were responsible for the appointment of parish officials, but in practice, they seem to have given the parishes more latitude than the statutes instructed. Still, parish officials were accountable to the JPs. The notebook of William Hunt, a JP in Wiltshire, makes fascinating reading on these points, for frozen in his notes are the daily dramas of face-to-face governance.[65] Hunt repeatedly dealt with removal orders, bastardy cases, petty crimes, assault and property offences – the stock-in-trade of a Justice's workload.

While it is important not to exaggerate the number of appeals by paupers to the JP for redress of grievances, Hunt's notebook contains a number of references to his having summoned the overseers to account for their treatment of poor women. In most of the cases, Hunt sided with the appellant. For example, on 8 April 1745 Hunt 'granted a summons for the overseers of the poor of Tilshead to appear and show cause why they would not relieve Francis Whitely and Mary Found, paupers of the said parish. They obeyed the summons and relieved them.' Furthermore, on 4 May 1745 another action was taken, 'against the parish officers of Urchfont at the complaint of Anne Whitely, a pauper, for relief. She was relieved without appearence and the summons returned.' A similar set of circumstances presented themselves on 13 June 1745 when Hunt granted another summons 'on the complaint of Mary Pettit of Earl Stoke against the parish officers of the same for them to relieve her. Upon their appearing, they allowed her 6 d. a week'.[66] It is striking that

64 On this subject also see D. Hey, *The Fiery Blades of Hallamshire: Sheffield and its Neighbourhood, 1660–1740* (Leicester, 1991), pp. 236–7; and A. Fletcher, *Reform in the Provinces: The Government of Stuart England* (1986), p. 188.

65 *The Justicing Notebook of William Hunt 1744–1749*, ed. E. Crittall (Devizes, 1982).

66 Ibid., pp. 180, 214, 223–4, 236.

these women, all paupers in the eyes of the law, understood so well the intricacies of settlement and had the courage to challenge the judgements of their social superiors publicly in the courts.

Such actions in both Hackney and Wiltshire run against the grain of some Marxist and feminist interpretations of the Hanoverian social and legal systems.[67] It could be contended that these cases have little to do with the women themselves and more to do with Justices wishing to assert their authority upon wayward local officials. This suggestion seems doubtful, since the rest of Hunt's diary and Norris's notebook reveal an impressive degree of coordination between them and officials in the parishes within their jurisdictions. It could also be argued that the legal system had to favour occasionally the appeals of the poor, if only to make the legal system appear as though it were fair and applicable to all. At best, such a cynical perspective merely misrepresents the capacities of the legal system in Hanoverian England; at worst it undermines the agency and historical credibility of the people under consideration. In an age ever conscious of property rights, a lawful settlement acted as, perhaps, the only legal recourse paupers could use to express their membership within the community and parish. While other use-rights in the agricultural and textiles industries were increasingly coming under threat in the eighteenth century, for poor and destitute women the right to relief through legal settlement remained. Moreover, for their own reasons, some motivated by self-interest, others by paternal or humanitarian sentiment, the political élite recognized these rights of relief. Thus, individual cases like those of Elizabeth Elless, Sarah Davies and their Wiltshire counterparts Anne Whitley and Mary Found were considered against this background of expectation and use-right.[68] William Hunt and his colleagues on the Bench dealt constantly with these cases and often reminded local officials of their parochial responsibilities. This

67 This view of the law is brilliantly elucidated in D. Hay *et al.*, *Albion's Fatal Tree* (1975); E.P. Thompson, *Whigs and Hunters* (1975); and P. Linebaugh, *The London Hanged: Crime and Civil Society in the Eighteenth Century* (1991). For a critique of this approach to the law, see P. Langbein, 'Albion's fatal flaws' *PP* 98 (1983), pp. 96–120, and for a summary of recent writing on the subject consult J. Innes and J. Styles, 'The crime wave: recent writing on crime and criminal justice in eighteenth-century England', in A. Wilson, ed., *Rethinking Social History: English Society 1570–1920 and its Interpretations* (Manchester, 1993), pp. 201–65.

68 For another example of expectation see G.L. Hudson, 'Negotiating for blood money: war widows and the courts in seventeenth-century England', in Kermode and Walker, eds, *Women, Crime and the Courts*, pp. 146–69, which considers demands by widows for state pensions; and E. Chalus, 'Patronage and protection: women in English political life, 1754–90' (unpublished paper, 1993), which discusses appeals for patronage at higher social levels during the later eighteenth century. I would like to thank Elaine Chalus for

phenomenon is also noticeable in Thomas Turner's East Hoathley. During his four years' tenure as overseer of the poor, Turner had to allocate poor relief, handle vagrants and settlement cases – often as a representative of the parish at Quarter Sessions – keep the parish accounts and certificates, and have his books scrutinized by both the vestrymen and the JPs. This process was the result of 17 George II, c. 3, a 1743 statute that made it mandatory to publicize the poor rates. Turner seems to have been diligent in his duties, often agonizing over the plight of those he dealt with as an overseer, as Elless's case illustrates; however, even he was called to appear before a Justice on 4 March 1757 to explain why he had refused relief to beggars, and to defend his parish against the accusation of 'use[ing] the poor so hardly'.[69]

The experiences of individuals such as Elizabeth Elless and Sarah Davies reveal an economic vulnerability that should lacerate complacency from those of us who inhabit the non-catastrophic world and should help to discredit romanticized notions of a 'bon vieux temps' for women in pre-industrial society. At the same time, it should also be clear that the relationship between women and parish authority – the personal face of the Hanoverian state – cannot be reduced to overarching generalities. The fact that these women appealed to Quarter Sessions and took an active part in the administration of poor relief seriously questions modern historiographical assumptions about the dichotomy of a public/private separate spheres ideology and its unqualified application to Hanoverian society. Pauper women approached the courts and challenged local authorities with the expectation of redress of grievances and in some cases with positive results. Parochial authorities responded to the plight of the poor through a sense of duty and legal responsibility, but also because of the paupers' personal circumstances. This was a male-dominated and at times daunting legal world, yet these poor women were not deterred from making their concerns and circumstances known to the parish. Admittedly, many other women undoubtedly suffered in silence and those who approached the Bench did so in the face of grinding poverty and acute distress. Yet

making this important paper available to me. Similar behaviour by women and men can be found in the Walpole correspondence: see Cambridge University Library, Cholmondeley Houghton MSS, Ch (H) MSS 80/2, 3, 26, 33, 34, 50, 64, 78, 92, 117, 135, 136, 152, 163, 181, 184, 187, 192, 199, 208, 218, 228, 249, 253, 267, 281, 289, 290, 305, 319, 321, 322, 336, 341, 353, 359, 361, 367, 373, 389, 398, 405, 407, 425, 429, 451, 459, 469, 479, 481 and 492.
69 *Thomas Turner, diary,* pp. 90–1.

it is also evident that men accepted and, perhaps, even expected women to be part of the social welfare machine. At the lowest levels of the welfare structure, pauper women were an integral part of the state apparatus. Such participation helped to blur the distinctions between public and private spheres. Based upon the life experiences of the women considered in this chapter, it is clear, therefore, that 'both the public and the private in early modern England were permeable concepts in thought' and that gender relationships were 'constantly under negotiation'.[70] Moreover, the true position of women in Hanoverian society was far more complex than literature, the law, tradition and custom suggest to twentieth-century scholars. Women did raise their voices and participate in the public sphere, and they did so with the same ingenuity they needed to survive the strain of the harsh economic and demographic regimes which the vast majority of eighteenth-century women faced every day of their brief lives.

---

70 P. Crawford, 'Public duty, conscience, and women in early modern England', in J. Morrill, P. Slack and D. Woolf, eds, *Public Duty and Private Conscience in Seventeenth-Century England* (Oxford, 1993), pp. 57–76, here at p. 57.

PART THREE

Politics and the political élite

CHAPTER SEVEN

'That epidemical Madness': women and electoral politics in the late eighteenth century[1]

ELAINE CHALUS

Five months before the 1768 general election, Lord Breadalbane complained to his daughter, Marchioness Grey, that the 'Rage of Electioneering' had already infected Scotland, and that the 'epidemical Madness' of the upcoming elections was more virulent than ever.[2] At the same time in London, Mrs Sarah Osborn observed wryly, 'Cards & Elections are the only Subjects';[3] and Lady Spencer, writing from Althorp, remarked, 'we are all Election Mad just at present'.[4] When elections swept the country, they dominated conversation, personal correspondence and the press. As national politicization was spurred by improvements in transportation and communication, and a steady stream of highly politicized events took place, the peaks of political excitement became higher and more all-encompassing. Particularly heated campaigns made the most impact and could generate interest well down the social scale. For the political élite,[5] close kin relationships and political connections created an intimacy that had long encouraged periodic bursts of election-related political excitement. For women who were members of the political

1 I would like to thank Hannah Barker, Joanna Innes, Paul Langford, Mark Pottle and Roey Sweet for their comments on this chapter prior to publication. I would also like to thank the Trustees of the Chatsworth Settlement for generously allowing me to consult the Devonshire Papers, Chatsworth House, and the Duke of Beaufort for permission to use the Badminton Muniments.
2 WP L30/9/17/125 Breadalbane to Marchioness Grey, Edinburgh, 10 Nov. 1767.
3 Bodl. Ms. North D.11, f. 94, Sarah Osborn to Guilford, London, 7 November 1767.
4 GP PRO 30/29/4/3/43 f. 348d, Lady Spencer to Lady Susan Stewart, Althorp, 9 Nov. [1767]. Georgiana (née Poyntz), the wife of the 1st Earl Spencer, is referred to as Lady Spencer throughout; her daughter-in-law, Lavinia, is indicated by name to avoid confusion.
5 As used here, the 'political élite' extends from the upper echelons of the middling sort through the aristocracy, those groups most involved in local and national politics.

élite,[6] electoral politics were a fact of life. Not only did the familial and factional nature of politics ensure their political awareness and encourage their interest, but the personal and social nature of the eighteenth-century political world often required their active participation.

Women's involvement in electoral politics has thus far received little attention from political or women's historians. It is telling that Karl von den Steinen's essay, 'The discovery of women in eighteenth-century political life', published in 1979, remains the only attempt to synthesize eighteenth-century women's political experience.[7] As women were barred by custom from voting or holding seats in Parliament, political historians have presumed that they could not have been political actors and that women's participation was limited, anomalous and ultimately secondary to men's.[8] Women's historians, whose long-standing assumptions that women and politics were mutually distinct categories prior to the suffrage movement have been reinforced by the popular separate spheres model, are only just beginning to revise this argument.[9] The teleology of women's history has discouraged research by accepting, almost without question, that a widespread cultural misogyny excluded all but a few exceptional élite women from political life. As even these women acted in support of men, their participation is considered indirect, unaccountable and unquantifiable. Their electoral involvement is assumed to have always been sporadic, but decreasingly acceptable

6 By birth or marriage. Unless otherwise specified, this chapter deals only with women who were members of the political élite.

7 Karl von den Steinen, 'The discovery of women in eighteenth-century political life', in Barbara Kanner, ed., *The Women of England From Anglo-Saxon Times to the Present* (Hamden, CT, 1979), pp. 229–58.

8 The trivialization of women's political involvement has a long history. Grego, in 1886, dismissed female canvassing as 'the seductive wiles of female charms and persuasions'; a century later, O'Gorman referred to it as 'public flaunting of fairly innocent sexual and sartorial behaviour'. J. Grego, *History of Parliamentary Elections and Electioneering in the Old Days* (1886), p. 292; Frank O'Gorman, *Voters, Patrons, and Parties: The Unreformed Electoral System of Hanoverian England 1734–1832* (Oxford, 1991).

9 The most influential expression of this model can be found in Leonore Davidoff and Catherine Hall, *Family Fortunes: Men and Women of the English Middle Class, 1780–1850* (first publ. 1987; 1992). Its popularity has meant that it has been simplified and projected backwards, often unquestioningly. See, for example, Richard Leppert, *Music and Image: Domesticity, Ideology and Socio-Cultural Formation in Eighteenth-Century England* (Cambridge, 1988); and more recently, Betty Rizzo, *Companions Without Vows: Relationships Among Eighteenth-Century British Women* (Athens, GA, and London, 1994). Two of the most influential critiques of the model to date have been David Cannadine and Amanda Vickery. David Cannadine, 'Through the keyhole' *New York Review of Books* 19 (21 Nov. 1991), pp. 34–8; Amanda Vickery, 'Golden age to separate spheres? A review of the categories and chronology of English women's history' *HJ* 36, 2 (1993), pp. 383–414.

after the furore of the 1784 Westminster election, which is viewed as marking increasingly strict sanctions on female behaviour emanating from a large and evangelically tinged middle class.[10] Their final exclusion from public political life is generally attributed to a conservative reaction engendered by the French Revolution.[11]

A sense of women's electoral involvement can be pieced together from the patchwork of surviving sources. Whilst acknowledging that not all women took an active part in political life, and recognizing that women's inability to vote or serve in Parliament placed them under an impenetrable ceiling, this chapter will argue that gender did not automatically bar women from involvement. Instead, within these customary boundaries, women were active throughout the electoral process, from social politics (the management of people and social activities for political ends), through canvassing, to managing and directing campaigns and controlling family interests. Their electoral activities were multi-faceted and flexible, logical extensions of traditional female roles in a familial political culture; moreover, their participation was generally accepted, often expected, and sometimes demanded.

Electoral politics

Eighteenth-century electoral politics was a microcosm of the political world.[12] While general elections could raise political interest to the level of obsession among the political élite, the majority of elections were distinct, local affairs resulting from indigenous circumstances; thus, women's electoral involvement remained primarily an exercise in local politics. This is not to suggest that women who were based in the metropolis were uninvolved or apolitical. Metropolitan elections were local elections writ large. Their importance and impact was augmented by their location, the size of the electorate, the proximity and interest of the press, and by their

10 See Steinen, 'The discovery of women'; Alice Browne, *The Eighteenth-Century Feminist Mind* (Brighton, 1987).

11 The most radical statements of this thesis have been propounded in French women's history and then applied to England. See particularly Joan B. Landes, *Women and the Public Sphere in the Age of the French Revolution* (Ithaca, IL, and London, 1988). Examinations of her thesis by Deena Goodman, Daniel Gordon, David Bell and Sarah Maza are in *French Historical Studies* 17, 4 (Fall 1992).

12 For details on the electoral process and its rituals, see O'Gorman, *Voters*; and idem, 'Campaign rituals and ceremonies: the social meaning of elections in England, 1780–1860' *PP* 135 (May 1992), pp. 79–115.

tendency to reflect factional rather than familial rivalries. Candidates' personal characteristics and familial or factional connexions frequently mattered more than their ideological stances. Social events and locations were regularly used for political ends, as politicians sought to avoid contests. The ideal eighteenth-century election was uncontested, cheap and undemanding. Its demands were handled mainly by men – the candidates, their patrons or their agents. Contests or the threat of a contest, however, mobilized political families and caused women to be increasingly active. The hotter the contest, the more the women did, and the more that was expected of them: the best known examples of women's electoral involvement can be traced to the century's fiercest election battles.

Despite the best efforts of some eighteenth-century politicians, the number of contested elections rose in the second half of the eighteenth century; however, much money, energy and activity was also expended on campaigns that were never formally contested.[13] If, as Frank O'Gorman has suggested, up to three-quarters of all elections were subject to some form of contest, it becomes easier to understand the 'madness' generated by election years, even when the overall number of contests appeared to remain relatively low; moreover, even incomplete contests would dramatically increase the extent of women's political exposure and the probability of their involvement.

The extent of women's involvement depended upon the complicated interplay of a variety of factors: individual beliefs, characters, abilities and experiences; family traditions of female political involvement; and specific election circumstances. For some women, participation had less to do with an interest in politics than with a personal and emotional investment in their families or in the politicians themselves; for others, involvement stemmed from a sense of duty, or ideological or factional loyalty. Personal interest and the sheer excitement of the election game also should not be underestimated. The women who were the most active and successful in electoral politics tended to be intelligent, analytical, assertive and confident. They were interested in politics and combined a comprehensive knowledge of the political world with a thorough understanding of their regions. They also had to be sensitive to social nuance and able to work well with both sexes and all classes. Youth, beauty, wit and charm were important attributes; however, youth

13 One-quarter to one-third of all elections were formally contested between 1754 and 1790. O'Gorman, *Voters*, pp. 107–12.

and beauty could be offset by the highly developed personal and political skills of a veteran female politician.

Women's electoral involvement was most inclusive at the base level of social politics and most select at the heights of borough control. Most women took part in the politicized social activities that played such an important part in obtaining, consolidating and maintaining political control. While fewer women electioneered, formally or informally, in writing or in person, women were active in elections throughout the period; moreover, their participation was commonly taken for granted. Canvassing and campaigning were but the most political and cross-class manifestations of social politics. A select and highly political group of women were the most extensively and effectively involved in electoral politics. They acted as agents, advisors or partners in families or factions. Some took on demanding managerial roles directing campaigns, while others controlled political interests. As such, they worked with, and were often in positions of authority over, men. Their openly political involvement was accepted, not because they were viewed as honorary men, although this may have been the case occasionally, but out of respect for their political capabilities and deference for their positions within families or factions. Those women who controlled seats and family interests were predominantly widows and matriarchs. They held, at least in theory, women's most powerful political positions; like peers, however, their power was ultimately limited to directing votes in the Commons rather than voting themselves.

Between elections

In the lulls between elections, campaigning was replaced by consolidation and maintenance.[14] The importance of personality, family and reputations of service in eighteenth-century politics, and the transactional relationship between politicians and voters, encouraged political families to expend a good deal of time, effort and money on securing, strengthening or supporting their political interests. While historians often pay lip-service to the importance of these 'family interests', they are usually interpreted only in terms of male kin connexions; such a narrow definition obscures the contributions

---

14 Networks of obligations could all be turned to electoral purposes during elections. Karl von den Steinen, 'The fabric of an interest: the first Duke of Dorset and Kentish and Sussex politics, 1705–1765' (unpub. Ph.D. thesis, Los Angeles, 1969), pp. xiii, 187–90.

that women made to what were truly *family* interests.[15] Politically active families were working units and women's personal contributions were expected to complement and echo those of their menfolk. Judicious socializing, acts of charity, pardons for the unjustly accused and patronage for the deserving all contributed to a family's political credit. It was especially important for a political family to show commitment (real or assumed) to the local community, by attending or supporting local events and through personal displays of hospitality, civility and generosity. In Lady Orford's Cornish borough of Callington, even the sponsorship of local education was brought to bear, as she provided a school for the children of those voters who agreed to vote for her candidate.[16]

Women generally played an important part in activities that maintained good relations with their families' main bases of political support and emphasized their families' positions within their communities. As family representatives, or in conjunction with political men, most women took part in activities between elections that carried subliminal or blatantly political messages. Some, such as assemblies, balls, breakfasts, dinners and race meets, were unquestionably public; others, including Public Days at local great houses, special dinners for the local Corporations, or entertainments that catered for freeholders and their wives, all took place in the private setting of the home and are less easily classifiable. Even mundane or intimate socializing, such as teas, cards and visits, often had political implications.

Visibility in the community was of vital importance,[17] and between elections women were expected to attend, host or 'do the honours' at local social events. They also had to be 'mighty civil' to neighbours in the Country. Some activities were gendered – such as women's reciprocal visiting or all-male drinking parties – but others saw men and women entertaining mixed-sex groups together. This was not always easy or enjoyable work, as there were difficulties inherent in handling power relationships in social situations. The country gentry were notoriously prickly about status and quick to take offence; moreover, the need for sensitivity was multiplied when the interactions were intimate. Dinners were a political civility that could be particularly uncomfortable. Many women would have agreed with Lady Dalkeith, who felt that dining with the squire and his wife was

15 See Sir Lewis Namier, *The Structure of Politics at the Accession of George III* 2nd edn (1960).

16 A. de C. Glubb, *When Cornwall had 44 MPs* (Truro, 1934), pp. 37–8.

17 J.V. Beckett, *The Aristocracy in England, 1660–1914* (Oxford, 1989), p. 356.

a 'Tax imposed upon us all in the Country'. For her the tariff was particularly high, as a meal with the squire was always stressful and invariably left her ill:

> their excess of civility, and the number of Dish's, every one of which, prevents the desire of eating, and yet eat, you must, or the Lady begins to look red, and tells you, She is sorry there is nothing you like, when possibly She has been herself overlooking in the Kitchen the greatest part of the morning....[18]

Successful political women, especially politicians' wives, had to be able to at least give the impression of enjoying themselves. Openness, cheerfulness and naturalness were invaluable character traits. A young, vivacious and sociable woman like Lady Sarah Bunbury was the ideal partner for an aspiring county politician. She threw herself into her role with an enthusiasm that her elder sister, Lady Holland, found absolutely incomprehensible: 'she was engaged to no less than eight turtle feasts in the town of Bury last time I heard from her'.[19]

For politically active aristocratic families, weekly Public Days were a socio-political duty that accompanied residence in the country. They provided political families with an opportunity to show themselves off as families, as they were jointly hosted by husbands and wives and regularly featured children.[20] They also fulfilled a portion of the family's social and political obligations to the local community. They gathered the local élite together over food and drink, and entertained them, often with music, cards and a ball. For the astute host and hostess the Public Day was an opportunity to show off new political connections, maintain contact with well-established supporters and pay special attention to those families whose political allegiance was questionable. This latter group would be wooed assiduously and perhaps encouraged to stay the night, so as to be part of a more select crowd the following day. During the hunting season, Public Days could taper off into hunts, as local gentlemen and ladies gathered the following morning with their hounds to set off for a 'grand coursing'.[21]

18 GP PRO 30/29/4/1/52, f. 99, Lady Caroline Dalkeith to Lady Susan Stewart, Adderbury, 20 [?] 1764.

19 Lady Holland to Lady Louisa Conolly, Kingsgate, 8 Aug. 1762, *Correspondence of Emily, Duchess of Leinster (1731–1814)*, ed. Brian Fitzgerald, 3 vols (Dublin, 1949–57), I, p. 337.

20 Chats. MSS 640, Duchess of Devonshire to Lady Spencer, [Chatsworth], 19–23 Aug. 1784.

21 Ibid., 549, Duchess of Devonshire to Lady Spencer, [Chatsworth, 21 Oct. 1783].

Public Days were both costly and demanding – physically and psychically – for everyone in the host family. The quality and quantity of the entertainments and refreshments had to be high to demonstrate the family's hospitality and civility, its wealth and social standing, and the value that it placed on the locality. By augmenting the size of the family group with members of the extended family, important social or political connections and distinguished artists, musicians or writers, the host family underlined its importance in the wider world. For hostesses, Public Days involved planning and performing. They drew up guest lists, issued invitations, organized the household and servants, and planned the meals and entertainments in advance. On the Day itself, they played the part. Being 'a *great* Lady in the Country'[22] meant that elaborate attention to appearance had to be balanced by a natural and approachable manner, and an alert yet unobtrusive management of people and events – all of which had to take political considerations into account. When the Duke and Duchess of Northumberland, who had a reputation for doing things with gusto, decided to hold two Public Days a week in 1770, they were discussed with something akin to awe by contemporaries.[23]

Since socializing among groups of people who shared few interests in common was necessary for political purposes, some artificial affability was acceptable. Open rudeness, however, was unforgivable. Women who felt that mixing with the local gentry was below them and made this clear by their behaviour could materially damage their husbands' political careers or their families' political interests. If both the husband and wife were arrogant and unsociable, the result could spell political disaster, as it did for Sir Watkin Williams Wynn in Wales in the 1770s:

> Sr. Watkin has lost almost all his interest in Wales meerely by his & Ly. Williams in particular behaving rudely to their country neighbours as an example we were told of a Mr. & Mrs. Mostyn Owen people of consequence in that country that went to dine with them during the dinner Sr. Watkin & Ly W – scarcely spoke to them & after dinner went out of the Room & left them, this behaviour displeas'd them so much that he was resolved to oppose Sr. Watkin as much as possible & got Ld. Powis to set him up against him & was elected Member; they say Lady Williams makes it a rule not to speak to any of the

22 'Mrs Burgoyne to Duchess of Argyll, Kensington Palace, 7 Oct. 1773', in *Intimate Society Letters of the Eighteenth Century*, ed. Duke of Argyll, 2 vols (1910), I, p. 175.
23 'Revd Theophilus Lindsey to Huntingdon, Catterick, 4 September 1770', *HMC 78 Hastings* (1934), III, p. 150.

Country Squires; & in short Sr. Watkin who was King of Wales & whose Family has been so for a long time is now nothing very great.[24]

Maintaining good relations with the local élite required the most consistent effort from political families between elections. Occasionally, women were placed in the role of family agents and were entertained by men for political purposes. When local clubs and groups chose women to act as 'Lady patronesses' and preside over events, such as their annual feasts or banquets, the 'distinction' was often little more than a lightly veiled statement of political intent.[25] The woman who was chosen was honoured as a representative of a political family and her ceremonial services forged a connection between her family and the group. Contemporaries interpreted these appointments as indications of political inclination if not actual allegiance. When the Old Interest country gentlemen in Oxfordshire elected Miss Stapleton, the sister of a young, politically minded squire, to serve as the patroness for the annual feast of the High Borlace in 1753,[26] her appointment left little to the imagination of the practised political intelligence of the New Interest's Lady Susan Keck. Lady Susan knew that Sir Thomas Stapleton was high on the list of potential Old Interest candidates for the next election and immediately interpreted his sister's 'social' appointment as a statement of gentry support for Sir Thomas's political ambitions.[27]

While there was little need between elections to transcend class barriers and mix as extensively with the mass of the freeholders as there was during a contest, the recalcitrance of some electorates, especially some Corporations, necessitated a certain amount of regular socio-political attention. Formal calls and visits with important local women, particularly the Mayoress and the Aldermanesses, often over tea, were transactional and helped to reinforce political connexions. Just as the political élite believed that freeholders' wives could significantly influence their husbands' votes, so the freeholders recognized that the women of the political élite were prime avenues to influence and patronage.

Sometimes a gesture to a Corporation was all that was necessary. When the Corporation at Cambridge granted the Duke of Rutland

24 Badminton Muniments, FmK 1/2/7, Lady Granby to Duchess of Beaufort, Liverpool, 24 Sept. [1778?].

25 BP L.IV.7.B./30, Lady Susan Keck to Revd Thomas Bray, Great Tew, 21 Aug. 1753.

26 See R.J. Robson, *The Oxfordshire Election of 1754* (Oxford, 1949), p. 11; Bodl. Ms. D.D. Dashwood (Bucks) B.11/12/32, Sir Thomas Stapleton to Sir Francis Dashwood, Oxford [summer 1753].

27 Ibid.

the freedom of the borough at an 'overflowing meeting' in 1787, the Duchess, who was acting head of the family while the Duke was away in Ireland as Lord Lieutenant, replied by supplying the meat for the meal afterwards. A correspondent of the Duke's noted that her gesture made the right impression: 'After dinner (her Grace of Rutland having sent a buck for the Mayor's feast), the healths of yourself and family were drunk with great enthusiasm.'[28]

At other times, some judicious 'burgessing', as the Cust family called it, was necessary. This might mean little more than being hospitable to the local Aldermen by socializing comfortably but not too familiarly with them over food and drink, particularly dinners. These gatherings provided a convenient social cover for addressing current issues, monitoring the potential for opposition or the formation of disruptive new alliances, charming or placating the dissatisfied, and making plans for the future (often as a result of a shrewd evaluation of the life expectancy of the aged, the ill and the dying).[29] Developing skill in 'burgessing' took time and practice; young women often found these events stressful and only gained confidence with age. Mature, politically experienced women were the most effective, as they not only knew what was expected of them socially, but also possessed an understanding of the personalities and rivalries of the Aldermen and the politics of the Corporation. Since a woman who was skilled in these matters was a valuable member of a political family, gaining the necessary experience was part of a young woman's informal education.

In the Cust family, Lady Cust and a married daughter, Mrs Evelyn, were recognized as experts. An unmarried daughter, Lucie, was also well experienced. As Francis Cust noted to Mrs Evelyn, Lucie's expertise was called upon when their nephew's wife, Lady Brownlow, had to act as hostess for the Grantham Corporation:

> Lucie is going to assist Lady Brownlow in doing the Honrs. of the Table with the corporate Body, but as she does not pretend to shine like you in the Character of a Burgesser, I shall leave her to tell you in a Post-script how she has succeeded. You know the Business of burgessing so well, that it may be scarce News to you that Mr. Barnes died on Saturday morning.[30]

28 'John Butcher to Rutland, Cambridge, 30 September 1787' *HMC 24 Rutland* (1894), III, p. 423.

29 See, for example, BL Ms Coll Althorp Papers. Lady Spencer's residence at Holywell House near St Albans meant she was regularly more aware of Corporation politics than her son.

30 BL Ms Coll Jenkinson Loan 72, vol. 60, f. 77, Francis Cust to Mrs Evelyn, Grantham, 20 Oct. [post-1776].

Entertainments such as this were held in a variety of venues: in commercial establishments, in rooms hired specially for the purpose, or in the home itself. Sometimes only the Aldermen were invited; at other times, their wives were also included. Women usually attended as parts of family groups, although sometimes they went on their own or with other female family members. Matriarchs and women who were acting heads of families took precedence over subordinate male family members, a dominance that Corporations seem to have acknowledged. Lady Cust was the matriarch of the Cust family. She had political interest of her own at Bishop's Castle in Shropshire[31] and was also the acting head of the Cust family interest at Grantham in the stead of her eldest son, the local Member and Speaker of the House of Commons.[32] When Lady Cust invited the members of the Corporation at Grantham to celebrate the New Year in 1762, she planned a traditional all-male evening. Two of her younger sons hosted the men, but she made a point of paying them a ceremonial visit during the afternoon, when the men were still sober enough to appreciate it, with two of her daughters: 'My Mother came down to them in the afternoon with Miss Cust & Miss Lucy, & paid her comps to them in a very good natur'd way, wch they return'd intirely to her satisfaction by drinking the Speakers health with 3 Huzzaz –'[33] This allowed her to flatter the Aldermen's self-importance and provide the young women with political experience. The evening was a thorough success: 'the Corporation . . . receiv'd great satisfaction from their entertainment' and were duly sent off 'with their skins full of liquor'.[34]

Nearly thirty years later, the progress of politeness had made it possible to move beyond the bumpers-and-beer approach. When the Duchess of Rutland returned to England in 1787, she turned her political attention to the borough of Scarborough and the Rutland family's rivalry with Lord Tyrconnel. When Tyrconnel arranged to treat the Corporation to the traditional hard-drinking dinner, the Duchess upstaged him. Nearly a week before the dinner, she treated the Corporation to a play:

> Her Grace gives a play this evening to the Corporation, who are all admiration of her condescension and goodness, and I must take the liberty to acquaint your Grace that the Duchess's appearance

31 Namier, *The Structure of Politics*, pp. 247–8.
32 Ibid., p. 107.
33 'Peregrine Cust to Sir John Cust, Bt., [Belton, 9 January] 1762' *Records of the Cust Family, Series III, Sir John Cust, Third Baronet*, ed. Lionel Cust (1927), p. 217.
34 Ibid.

here, with the prudence of the Lord Bishop of Ferns, will do more good than a hundred blind spies, or the whole house of Tyrconnel combined.[35]

While her choice of entertainment coincided with her well-established personal preference for quiet, controlled socializing, even with her peers,[36] it may also have been conditioned by the impact of polite society, the rising tide of respectability among the middling sort and by a gradual redefinition of acceptable social behaviour between élite women and men of the lower orders. In 1789, when Lady Portsmouth entertained the Andover Corporation to a dinner and evening of cards in her home, the moderation that prevailed prompted one participant to note proudly that the company had spent no more than an hour at the table after Lady Portsmouth had withdrawn, before regrouping in the Library for cards: 'a very noble Entertainment indeed . . . carried on with great good humour pleasantry & chearfulness'.[37]

Perhaps the most onerous duties in the 'drudgery of pleasure',[38] as Lord Stormont termed it, were those associated with the assizes or the annual race meets. The summer social calendar in the country included the assizes, assemblies, assorted plays and concerts, but the race meets were often the most politically important and drew the largest audiences.[39] Race weeks were held in the county town or a similar centre any time from early July to September. Complaints of '*ennui*'[40] and exhaustion, from men and women, become understandable, given Lady Polwarth's description of a typical meet:

> Kelso Races begin next Tuesday, & a tolerable fatiguing time it will be: three days of public Breakfasts, Races at Noon, public Dinners & Balls at Night. So if I drop down in a Country Dance . . . you must Comfort yourself like Cato, when he says, 'My boy has done his Duty!'[41]

35 'Dr Robert Knox to Rutland, Scarborough, 20 September 1787', *HMC 24, Rutland*, p. 415.

36 See Lady Hester Stanhope's reflections on the way that the vast differences in temperaments between the Duchesses of Rutland and Gordon, the two leading political hostesses of William Pitt's first Administration, were reflected in their entertainments. Charles Meryon, *Memoirs of the Lady Hester Stanhope, as related by herself in conversations with her physician* 3 vols (1845), II, pp. 52–3.

37 ERO D/DBy C9/54, James Hayes to Howard, Holyport, 13 Sept. 1789.

38 'Lord Stormont to [Huntingdon], Wentworth, 30 August 1754', *HMC 78 Hastings*, p. 88.

39 Paul Langford, *Public Life and the Propertied Englishman, 1689–1798* (Oxford, 1991), p. 382.

40 'W. Whitehead to Harcourt, Middleton Park, 14 July 1767', in Edward William Harcourt, Esq., ed., *The Harcourt Papers* 14 vols (Oxford, 1876–1905), VII, p. 271.

41 WP L30/9/60/32, Lady Polwarth to Lady Grey, Wrest Park, 19 May 1774.

Race meets were consistently politicized. During the races, political alliances were formed and paraded; the balance among political interests was evaluated, secured or re-adjusted; and the social and political hierarchies were reinforced through family presence, ostentatious display and conscientious attention to civility and the paternalistic niceties of hospitality. Families with political aspirations took a prominent part in hosting the associated entertainments. An unexpected illness could put a family presence in jeopardy. When Lady Rockingham became ill prior to the 1770 York Races, Lord Rockingham was justifiably concerned and she made every effort to be present when it mattered most:

> I got to Wentworth only about eight or nine days before York Races,
> – and of those days – the four or five last were uncomfortable as
> Lady Rockingham's state of Health, made it continually doubtful
> whether she would be able to go to York. In the end, she was able
> – and by only staying the first two days of the Race Week at York, and
> going away for three days and returning for the Last days, she was
> able to get through the week.[42]

Young political wives approached their first race meets, and their tasks as hostesses, guests of honour or patronesses, with some trepidation, as social or political missteps were sure to be remembered and might have political ramifications. Experienced older women, mothers and mothers-in-law, often gave young women guidance. Even Lavinia, Lady Spencer, was appreciative of her mother-in-law's advice when she was facing her first race meets: 'I was frightened at first to think how I shoud go thro' all my ceremonies but I remembered your good instructions of of last year & I got over them tollerably well.'[43]

A less public and sometimes more formal way of securing or rewarding political support between elections was through patronage. After the Duchess of Rutland was widowed, she used patronage to help maintain the family interest until her son came of age. As a long-standing friend of William Pitt's, she knew how distasteful he found patronage,[44] but when the opportunity arose in 1792 to secure a man who was 'very anxious to unite his Interest to ours in Politicks', she reminded Pitt pointedly of the request's electoral implications:

42 'Rockingham to Edmund Burke, Wentworth, 5 September 1770', in T.W. Copeland *et al.*, eds, *The Correspondence of Edmund Burke* 10 vols (Cambridge, 1958–78), II, p. 151.

43 BL Ms Coll Althorp F. 29, Lavinia, 2nd Lady Spencer to Lady Spencer, Althorp, 13 Sept. 1782.

44 It made Pitt 'bilious'. John Ehrman, *The Younger Pitt. The Years of Acclaim* (1969), p. 234.

'he will be a great acquisition both to you & to us, as he is extreemly
Rich, & by that means has great Interest both in Leicestershire &
Lincolnshire –'.[45]

An impending dissolution raised the political temperature, while
an illness, death or succession precipitated an election. In either
case, candidates who were palatable to the local and national political élites had to be found, and the necessary political support
secured. Women who controlled family interests, managed boroughs
or played leading roles in contending factions had to be especially
aware of possible vacancies and contests. An aristocratic matriarch
with years of experience could be a redoubtable political force.
The Dowager Lady Howe was one of the most imperturbable.
Reputedly the illegitimate daughter of George I, she had moved in
the highest circles of the Court and the political world before and
after her marriage.[46] By 1758, when her son George, Lord Howe,
the sitting Member for Nottingham, was killed at Ticonderoga, she
had been involved in the political world as long as the Duke of
Newcastle himself: nearly 40 years. Her political skills had been
honed when, as a widow with eight children under twelve, she had
controlled the family interest on her own for ten years. Upon her
son's death she reassumed decision-making power over the family's
political interest, superseding her younger son, the new peer. She
responded to the letter of condolence and support from the Corporation[47] and then chose another son to hold the seat. She then
approached Newcastle for his endorsement, both as the leader
of the Administration and as someone with an important political interest in the county.[48] After nine days had passed without a
response to her letter, she took pre-emptive action by declaring her
son's candidacy in the local newspaper.[49] This elicited a quick and
aggrieved response from Newcastle, who had been stalling in order
to find out if John Plumptre, the son of an old friend, would have
stood a chance.[50] Despite informing Lady Howe that she could

45 PRO 30/8/174/2 ff. 251d–2, Duchess of Rutland to William Pitt, n.pl., 14 Nov.
1792.

46 As a Lady of the Bedchamber to Augusta, Princess of Wales, she was approached
with great courtesy by Newcastle. BL Add MSS 32895, ff. 197–8, Newcastle to Lady Howe,
Newcastle House, 5 Sept. 1759.

47 BL Add MSS 32883, f. 186, Lady Charlotte Howe to the Corporation of Nottingham,
30 Aug. 1758.

48 Ibid., ff. 308–9, Lady Howe to Newcastle, Battlesden, 5 Sept. 1758.

49 BL Add MSS 32883, f. 452, Lady Howe to Newcastle, London, 14 Sept. 1758; 'Horace
Walpole to Henry Seymour Conway, Arlington Street, 19 September 1758', in W.S. Lewis,
ed., *The Yale Edition of Horace Walpole's Correspondence* 48 vols (London and Oxford, 1937–
83), XXXVII, p. 571.

50 Namier, *The Structure of Politics*, pp. 92–5.

expect no further support from him, he was forced to concede defeat within the month. He pledged his support to Lt.-Col. Howe, advised Plumptre not to stand, and even persuaded him to support Howe's candidacy. Lady Howe had out-manoeuvred them both.

Women like the Duchess of Rutland and the Dowager Lady Howe are excellent examples, at opposing ends of the period, of women who had been widowed early and controlled their families' political interests for their sons until they came of age. Male mortality, even at the highest levels of society, made this kind of situation not at all uncommon. As John Cannon has shown, 70 per cent of eighteenth-century peerage families went through at least one minority, and one-third of all successions were by minors.[51] Few families suffered the four minorities of the Earls of Plymouth, but extended guardianships were not unusual. Over the course of the century, the Dukes of Bedford were minors for a total of 33.5 years, those of Beaufort for a total of 28 years, and the Hamilton family had two consecutive minorities at mid-century, for a total of 19 years. Some widows had sole control over children, estates and family interests; others shared the tasks with male guardians, usually kin connexions; even those widows who had no official control might be expected to help safeguard the family property and political interest. Lady Anne Fitzwilliam, who was widowed in 1756 when her son was twelve, worked together with Sir Matthew Lambe, her son's legal guardian, to secure the family's seat at Peterborough. On Lambe's death in 1768, she maintained the family's control over the seat by supporting the candidature of Lord Belasyse, who was elected without a contest. She then extended and consolidated the family's interest in the borough by spending £2,500 on property.[52] The Duchess of Beaufort, who was also widowed in 1756, was appointed her eight-year-old son's legal guardian; her brother served as the principal trustee of the estate. Between them, they succeeded in maintaining the family interest of five seats, as well as discovering and reducing the debt on the estate.[53] Women like the Duchess of Beaufort and her daughter, the Duchess of Rutland, who had already been politically active prior to their husbands' deaths, extended the scope of their political activities as widows; women like the Duchess of

51 John Cannon, *Aristocratic Century: The Peerage of Eighteenth-Century England* (Cambridge, 1987), p. 137.

52 E.A. Smith, *Whig Principles and Party Politics. Earl Fitzwilliam and the Whig Party 1748–1833* (Manchester, 1975), pp. 14–16. Between 1751 and the contested election of 1754, Katherine Lowther purchased 27 burgages to secure Appleby for her son, Sir James Lowther. Brian Bonsall, *Sir James Lowther and Cumberland & Westmorland Elections 1754–1775* (Manchester, 1960), pp. 15–19.

53 Cannon, *Aristocratic Century*, p. 107.

Hamilton, who had not been especially political, received a quick education by working with other guardians, trustees and political agents. A few women retired entirely from political involvement once their sons came of age, but many remained active, especially in the localities, where their personal and political experience was valuable.

Election campaigns and contests

When women's involvement in election campaigns and contests has been considered at all, attention has tended to focus on their most colourful and visible presence, mainly their participation in canvassing. While canvassing allowed women to take a direct and easily recognizable part in shaping outcomes, it was not the sum total of their participation. Women added a female dimension to electioneering and can be found in almost every aspect of the election process. Regular social events were supplemented by special election entertainments which women organized, hosted and co-hosted. They took part in processions and parades; they canvassed formally and informally; and occasionally, they entered the war of words in print or in person. During elections, homes became control centres and points of contact for political men, and the women who remained at home often acted as managers and administrators. Admittedly, some did little more than receive and dispatch information, but others co-ordinated people and events, managed correspondence networks and made decisions. As the family representatives in the local community, they dealt with local people and political concerns; a few even ran election committees. Moreover, it is worth remembering that some women were the objects of electioneering. Women in boroughs such as Maldon and Bristol, where the daughters of freemen still had the right to confer freeman status on their husbands, were canvassed in person or in print by agents and candidates.[54] Those women in control of property-based political interests were approached for electoral support in the same

54 'The Dundry Petition: Or the Countryman's humble Address to the Free-women of the City of Bristol', in *The Bristol Contest: being a collection of all the papers published by both parties, on the election, 1754* (Bristol, 1754?), pp. 54–6. My thanks to Dr Madge Dresser of the University of the West of England for bringing this address to my attention. In Maldon, John Huske solicited the women's electoral support: 'I think myself highly justified in asking you, ladies, rather than your husbands, as it is to you they owe such a privilege, and it is but justice that you should have some influence in the disposal of it'. *Chelmsford Chronicle*, 10 Dec. 1773.

way as their male counterparts, as their contemporaries recognized their political influence and their right to wield it as they saw fit.

Given the extent to which communities and social activities were politicized during campaigns, it was nearly impossible for women to remain untouched by election fever. Even those women whose families were not involved, or whose contests took place in distant boroughs, tended to be consumers of election activities in their localities. Women from politically active families were almost inevitably drawn into electioneering through their traditional participation in community and family affairs, yet not all women acted solely for family connections, out of tradition and duty; some women campaigned for friends or lovers, or for factions out of loyalty or conviction. The more doubtful the outcome, the more likely that women would be involved.

Individual family attitudes had more effect in determining the extent of women's electoral involvement than either personal preferences or ideological divisions. Women who were members of families that expected them to play a part were usually active; women who came from families without this tradition, or families that opposed it, were seldom heavily involved; similarly, ideological differences were not distinct enough on the whole to be a significant difference. The electoral activities of the Foxite women in the last quarter of the century have tended to obscure the involvement of their Pittite counterparts, an imbalance due in part to the latter receiving less press coverage at the time, but also because fewer of their papers have survived.

Whenever a dissolution was expected, the correspondence networks of the political élite buzzed, as women passed information on to political men, men wrote to political women, and political women kept each other informed. Obtaining advance warning of a dissolution could translate into success at the polls, or even prevent a poll from taking place. For someone who lived in Scotland, like Lady Galloway, being in close contact with connexions in London was vitally important:

> I trouble You My Dear Lady Gower to inquire what You hear, *or rather think*, relative to the time it is probable the Parliament may, or may not, be dissolved, such intelligence wou'd be of material Consequence, as the success of the Stewartry Election will much depend upon that epoch. . . .[55]

55 GP PRO 30/29/4/3/93, f. 451, Lady Galloway to Lady Gower, Galloway House, 27 Aug. [1780].

Once candidates were declared and campaigns were officially under way, they built up their own momentum. A close contest dominated local society; tempers frayed and political expediency supplanted politeness. Every possible opportunity was used to secure outstanding votes. Ordinary socio-political activities such as assemblies, balls and race meets were regularly split along political lines or duplicated by the opposing sides. While some election treats catered for men alone, others were mixed. Balls 'for the ladies' were hosted by candidates and their wives or a close female family member.[56] They were expected by the freeholders and were part of most eighteenth-century election campaigns.[57] When political feelings remained moderate, they could even be co-sponsored by opposing candidates. While balls could give candidates an additional opportunity to canvass,[58] they were primarily intended to entertain and impress the voters, their wives and daughters. They were also a testimony to contemporary beliefs about female influence and the need to gain women's support in order to keep the male vote.

For the women in the host families' entourages, this meant making special efforts to impress the freeholders. Dress and ornament could be used to make public statements of political affiliation. Gowns in the family or factional colours were frequently ornamented by political ribbons, sashes and cockades, all of which added to the spectacle of the ball, but also gave a visual weight to the family presence and provided an unforgettable reminder of the issue at hand. More importantly, both women and men were expected to make a show of their civility and lack of pride by crossing social barriers and dancing – especially country dances – with the local gentry and better sort of freeholders. Young political wives were repeatedly reminded to fulfil this duty. A full ten years after her marriage, Lady Spencer still chided the Duchess of Devonshire when she did not dance with enough of the Duke's voters in Derbyshire.[59] Balls made similar demands on men; even non-dancers danced. As Lady Chatham remarked of Thomas Pitt's efforts, the purpose of the activity was politics not pleasure: 'I hope the Ladies were duely

56 Even contested boroughs with less than 100 voters had parades, balls, dinners and crowds. See D. McAdams, 'Politicians and the electorate in the late eighteenth century', unpub. Ph.D. thesis (Duke, NC 1967), p. 99; O'Gorman, 'Campaign rituals', p. 86.

57 They were also an acknowledged part of Corporation politics. See BL Ms Coll Althorp F. 39, Lady Spencer to Duncannon, [Holywell?], 12 Dec. 1786.

58 Wwk RO CR1368/5/9 vol. 36, Mary [Mordaunt] to [John Mordaunt?], Wallington, 1 Aug. 1766.

59 'Lady Spencer to Duchess of Devonshire, n.pl., 26 August 1784', in Earl of Bessborough, ed., *Georgiana. Extracts from the Correspondence of Georgiana, Duchess of Devonshire* (1955), p. 92.

sensible of their obligation on the occasion, and that it will be remember'd at a proper time'.[60]

Political wives capitalized on their personal strengths when seeking voter support. Not all women were as physically active as Marcia Pitt was in 1754, when her husband was involved simultaneously in elections at Dorchester and Wareham, but as Richard Rigby's comments to the Duke of Bedford reveal, political wives were expected to make their own contributions:

> Mrs. Pitt tells me she has been a buck-hunting three days in the week at five o'clock in the morning, and drinking strong beer with the freeholders at that hour, to convince them she is an Englishwoman. She returns to-morrow to assist her worst half at the meeting of the seventh at Dorchester. I do not doubt but that upon a like occasion, where you now are, has gone off as you could wish; and desire you will inform your little candidate, that though she is not quite so robust as your Dorsetshire friend, that she must follow her example as far as she is able. I am afraid it won't be of use to draw a parallel, or else we would strike out the word hunting, and insert the word dancing. The latter though, you must insist upon. . . .[61]

Although Rigby may have exaggerated a good story to make it better, Marcia Pitt's hunting was not in itself extraordinary; moreover, her personal and familial circumstances would have encouraged her to make an extra effort. The 1754 election marked her début as a political wife, and since she was Irish by birth, it was important for her to create a good first impression and establish 'English' credentials. Her activities, however, probably owe more to the highly charged political situation in which her family found itself. While her husband's election at Dorchester was uncontested and required little more than an appearance and some effort, the election at Wareham was a classic contest that finally ended in a double return.[62] Under such conditions, every opportunity would have been taken to win over the freeholders.

Treats for the voters were another part of electioneering, either in the form of the traditional election feast or in its more polite incarnation, the election breakfast.[63] Some of these events were hosted and attended only by men, but others included women as

60 BL Add MSS 59490, ff. 10d–11, Lady Chatham to Anne Pitt, Burton Pynsent, 13 Sept. 1773.

61 'Richard Rigby to Bedford, London, 3 August 1753', in Lord John Russell, ed., *Correspondence of John, Fourth Duke of Bedford: Selected from the Originals at Woburn Abbey* 3 vols (1842), II, pp. 129–32.

62 L. Namier and J. Brooke, *The House of Commons, 1754–1790* 3 vols (1964), III, p. 284.

63 Public breakfasts appear as an election treat after 1784. McAdams, 'Politicians and the electorate', p. 187.

hostesses, guests, or both. Lady Susan Keck saw treating and feasting as central to a New Interest Whig victory in the 1754 Oxfordshire election. Her 'hail-fellow-well-met' approach and the over-indulgence that some of her treats encouraged prompted a complaint in *Jackson's Oxford Journal* in 1753:

> I am far from thinking that the Ladies are unconcern'd in our Members, or that they should sit primm'd with their hands passively before 'em, and their Mouths drawn up like the Purse of an old Usurer, whilst we are engaged in this important Business; but then neither would I have them swagger amongst the Men, and Holla, and roar, and fill out Bumpers with an Air more becoming *Colonel Bully* than *Lady Dainty*. Much less would I have Ladies of Distinction, out of an intemperate Zeal for their Country, send away from their Houses, not only Men, but even Persons of their own Sex, so disguised with Liquor as to merit the Stocks as an Example.[64]

Still, Oxfordshire women were not unique. Yorkshire women were equally avid participants, as William Tufnell discovered at a treat he sponsored for the freemen of Beverly: 'I think I never saw so many women in all my life. The voters they brought their wives along with 'em & then they introduc'd some of their acquaintances who stay till they fell off their chairs. . . .'[65] Women's enjoyment of election feasts and dinners was not always this bacchanalian. Usually, their presence aroused little more than passing comment.

By the time that Lady Bessborough was campaigning with her brother, Lord Spencer, in the family borough of St Albans before the 1796 election, a sedate respectability had triumphed:

> Conceive being dress'd out as fine as I could at eleven o'clock this morning, squeez'd into a hot assembly room at the Angel Inn, cramming fifty old Aldermen and their wives with hot rolls and butter, while John and Fred danced with the misses, playing at fourpenny Commerce and tradille, and then visiting all about the gay town of St. Albans. Can you boast of anything to surpass this?[66]

As the Spencers' actions demonstrate, women's socio-political activities during elections were not directed only at flattering voters,

64 *JOJ*, 1 June 1753.

65 'William Tufnell to Samuel Tufnell, [1754]', in Francis W. Steer, *Samuel Tufnell of Langleys, 1682–1758. The Life and Times of an Essex Squire* (Chelmsford, 1960), p. 133. See, for example, BL Add MSS 32919, f. 192, S. Shepherd to Newcastle, Bishopstone, 21 Feb. 1761; Edmund Burke to Jane Burke, [Bristol], 8 Nov. 1774, in Copeland *et al.*, eds, *Burke*, III, p. 74.

66 'Lady Bessborough to Lord Granville Leveson Gower, Holywell House, [1794–5?]', in Castalia, Countess Granville, ed., *Lord Granville Leveson Gower (First Earl Granville) Private Correspondence 1781–1821* 2 vols (1916), I, pp. 98–9.

but also at their womenfolk. The politicization of traditional female social activities – teas and visits, carriage rides and courtesies – reveals a dimension of electioneering, of women by women, that has been largely unrecognized.[67] While these activities cannot be measured directly in terms of votes, contemporary concerns emphasize their political importance and the way that the social and political arenas were understood to be interwoven. During the 1760 election, Mrs Elizabeth Montagu was decidedly smug about this aspect of her performance as a political wife. Not only had she gone to Newcastle with her husband and stayed with a local political family, but she had visited the Northumberland ladies, had the ladies of the local Corporation in to tea, and attended local plays, concerts and assemblies as necessary:

> I behave very prettily, make visits duly, and have been this evening to make my compliments to the wife of the sheriff elect; and I think if Mr. Montague had the honour to be made an alderman of Newcastle, I should become the station very well. . . .[68]

Electioneering regularly required women to mix with freeholders. This could be problematic, as the idea of élite women soliciting lowly freeholders for their votes and securing them through a combination of personal charms and persuasive abilities implied a sociosexual inversion that threatened social hierarchies and accepted modes of female behaviour. Careful mixing, with the women in safe, elevated or ceremonial positions, was always acceptable; thus, more women electioneered from their chairs, carriages and cabriolets, or rode in parades and processions, than mixed with the crowds on foot. An anecdotal, but purposefully instructive, description of electioneering in Northampton sent by Lady Spencer to her newly married daughter, the Duchess of Devonshire, during the 1774 election, reveals this deeply conservative woman's ideal of female electioneering:[69]

> that abominable Sir James Langham began canvassing North'ton on Wednesday and had so much more success than was expected that our friends took fright . . . as your Papa could not go into the town (because a Peer cannot interfere in an election after the writ is out) he wish'd I would; accordingly I set out on Thursday morning with

---

67 Paul Langford sees it as male-directed and an example of wifely obedience: 'a lady . . . could only be pitied when she was compelled to submit herself to the small-mindedness of bourgeois society'. See *Public Life*, p. 274.

68 *HMC 30 Fortescue* (1894), II, p. 144.

69 Lady Spencer's marriage had moved her into the nobility.

Mrs. Tollemache in my Cabriolet and four, . . . I no sooner got to the George than a little mob surrounded us and insisted on taking off our horses and drawing us round the town . . . in a very few minutes we had a mob of several hundd. people, screaming Spencer for ever – Tollemache and Robinson – No Langham. In this manner did they drag us about thro' every street in the town, and were so delighted with my talking to them and shewing no signs of fear at going wherever they chose, that it was with the utmost difficulty I could in the evening (for we din'd with the gentlemen at the George) prevent their drawing me quite home to Althorp. I went thro' the same ceremony again on Friday . . . it has had an extraordinary good effect in the election for it has ensur'd Mr. Tollemache a great majority. . . .[70]

Closer to the election, she became yet more actively involved. Her best friend, Mrs Howe, who was involved with her family election in Nottingham, wrote: 'I hear you harangued from the Belcony, pray tell me all how & about it.'[71] When Tollemache won, the Duchess of Devonshire congratulated her mother: 'I really think Mr. Tollemache should allow you to go sometimes to the House of Commons in his stead as you certainly have done a great deal to ensure his success'.[72]

The Duchess of Northumberland was much more secure of her rank and position than Lady Spencer and, by personality, more exuberant. During her son's contest in Westminster in 1774, she canvassed for him, took a hotel at Covent Garden, made speeches to the crowd from her window, and settled in to overlook the poll.[73] When she was criticized – by men like Horace Walpole and William Whitehead – it was for her over-familiarity with the lower orders and her supposed miserliness: 'her Grace of Northumberland goes most condescendingly out of her sphere, shakes every basketwoman by the hand, & tells them . . . that she cannot . . . give them meat & drink in abundance; for that . . . would be bribery & corruption'.[74] Her electioneering was not itself at issue.

Injudicious electioneering was at the centre of the Duchess of

---

70 'Lady Spencer to the Duchess of Devonshire, Althorp, 9 October 1774', in Bessborough, ed., *Georgiana*, pp. 15–16.

71 BL Ms Coll Althorp F. 53, Mrs Howe to Lady Spencer, Grafton Street, 14 Oct. [1774].

72 Chats. MSS 33, Duchess of Devonshire to Lady Spencer, 17 Oct. 1774.

73 GP PRO 30/29/4/2/69 f. 255d, Lady Carlisle to Lady Gower, London, 13 Oct. 1774. See also Horace Walpole's letters to Henry Seymour Conway and Sir Horace Mann, 16 and 22 Oct. 1774, in Lewis, ed., *Walpole's Correspondence* (1974; 1967), XXXIX, VII, pp. 196; 51–2.

74 See 'Walpole to Conway, Strawberry Hill, 16 October 1774', in ibid. (1974), XXXIX, p. 196; and 'W. Whitehead to Nuneham, London, 1774', in Harcourt, ed., *Harcourt Papers*, VII, p. 315.

Devonshire's notorious kisses-for-votes incident in the 1784 West-minster election.[75] The fact that she canvassed was not unusual. Unfortunately, a combination of lack of research and a superfluity of contemporary printed attacks on the Foxite Whig women in 1784 have long encouraged historians to interpret female canvassing in terms of 1784 and to see it as innovatory, temporary, and socially unacceptable;[76] so much so, that popular animosity is assumed to have driven even the irrepressible Duchess of Devonshire to with-draw from public political involvement thereafter.[77] This hypothesis is now in need of serious revision. Recent research stresses the con-tinuity of women's political experience well into the nineteenth century. Even the Duchess of Devonshire's political career is cur-rently undergoing revision, as her political participation is revealed to have been lifelong.[78]

Eighteenth-century correspondences suggest that women's involve-ment in canvassing was neither innovatory nor usually controver-sial; rather, it was an accepted and expected part of the electoral responsibilities of women whose families were involved in elections. Frequently, it aroused little discussion and became simply an item of political gossip: 'Lady Brandon is gone down to them [the Agars] about her brother Jemmy Agar's borough, which there is some viol-ent fuss about between him, Mr. Flood and Mr. Wemyss';[79] or, 'the

75 See J. Hartley, ed., *The History of the Westminster Election* (1784).

76 See O'Gorman, *Voters*, p. 93; P.J. Jupp, 'The roles of royal and aristocratic women in British politics, c. 1782–1832', in Mary O'Dowd and Sabine Wichert, eds, *Chattel, Servant or Citizen: Women's Status in Church, State and Society* (Belfast, 1995), pp. 112–13; James Vernon, *Politics and the People; A Study in English Political Culture, c.1815–1867* (Cambridge, 1993), p. 92.

77 For traditional accounts see: Brian Masters, *Georgiana, Duchess of Devonshire* (1981); John Cannon, *The Fox–North Coalition. Crisis of the Constitution, 1782–4* (Cambridge, 1969); and L.G. Mitchell, *Charles James Fox and the Disintegration of the Whig Party, 1782–1794* (Oxford, 1971). The Duchess of Devonshire's canvassing for Charles James Fox in the 1784 Westminster election is one of the few instances of female political involvement that is relatively well known. The incident in question alludes to a contemporary allegation (and one that has been referred to by historians ever since) that the Duchess exchanged kisses for votes while canvassing freeholders. For the most detailed examination of the Duchess's political activities during the election to date, see Anne Stott, ' "Female patriot-ism": Georgiana, Duchess of Devonshire, and the Westminster Election of 1784' *Eighteenth-Century Life* 17 (November 1993) 60–84. For an overview of contemporary comments in print, see Hartley, *et al.*, *The History of the Westminster Election* (1784), *passim.* Even Linda Colley's insightful but brief examination of the Duchess's political participation assumes that she was 'cowed into silence and private life'. Linda Colley, *Britons: Forging the Nation, 1707–1837* (New Haven, CT, and London, 1992), pp. 242–9.

78 See Chapter 8, 'A politician's politician: Georgiana, Duchess of Devonshire and the Whig party'.

79 'Lady Kildare to Kildare, Castletown, 23 [December 1762]', in Fitzgerald, ed., *Duch-ess of Leinster Correspondence*, I, p. 163.

Duke and Duchess of Northumberland are gone down to Andover, to canvass the town for Sir Francis Delavel.'[80]

Elections that were not particularly heated, or contests that were resolved after the initial canvass, might require women to do little more than appear in a formal canvass; however, a long battle could mean repeated canvassing, formally and informally. Election poems and songs suggest that the ideal female canvasser was young, beautiful, amiable and charming, if also politically astute and well-connected: the actuality was much more prosaic. Canvassers came in all ages, shapes and sizes, and their political experience, interest and connexions varied similarly. Lady Susan Keck's grey hair and wrinkles were more than compensated for by her temperament, acuity and experience.[81]

Lady Susan was only one of a number of women who immersed themselves in electioneering. Her involvement in the Oxfordshire election in 1754 was, if anything, more political, extensive and demanding than that of the Duchess of Devonshire in 1784. It generated similarly scurrilous publications, albeit on a smaller scale. Lady Susan's character and experience made the difference, however, as she took election-inspired criticism in her stride. Old Interest complaints that she was '*Patroness* right Antiblue' and the '*Guardian-Goddess* of the Crew' delighted her, and she signed a subsequent letter to an agent, 'Susan Antiblue'.[82] Her predilection for donning riding boots, taking a horse from her husband's stables and canvassing was deemed unladylike by the Old Interest, but chortled over by the New Interest who flaunted her participation and ability to unman the opposition.

Her letters are full of references to potential, problem or promised votes:

I have a notion that a man that keeps a shop opposit to St. Marys his name is something like Cront, is a vote, he had a part of an Estate at Radford with one Martyn, that is a minor. He is a Confectioner,

80 'Gilly Williams to George Selwyn, White's, n.d. [?1768]', in John Heneage Jesse, *George Selwyn and His Contemporaries* 4 vols (1843), II, p. 279.
81 Her birthdate is uncertain, but since her father died in 1712, she was at least 40 in 1752. See, for instance, Old Interest criticism: *Advice from Horace to Lady S—s—n* (Oxford, 1753); New Interest's approval: 'The Grey Mare the Better Horse: Or, the Oxfordshire Freeholder's Choice', in *JOJ*, 6 Oct. 1753.
82 'The Rump Worthies: or the New-Interest Supporters in their true Colours', in *Oxfordshire in an Uproar; or the Election Magazine* (Oxford, 1753), p. 34; and BP L.IV.7.B/ 49, Lady Susan Keck to Revd Bray, [?Dec. 1753].

pray enquire after him. The Confectioners name is Coast. Canvass him instantly –.[83]

She kept very close watch on political developments and took action whenever votes were in danger. When she realized that Lady Dalkeith's canvass of her mother's estate at Adderbury had been conducted ineffectually and that the Duchess of Argyll's agents might be misdirecting votes, she canvassed personally: 'I have eight in her Town, who assures me they never were askt, four of them I got so late as the Banbury entertainment . . . I have a man now informing himself of the state of that Towne, I mean Aderbury in every particulare, but in General the whole country crys out of her bad management.'[84] Her efforts at Adderbury were successful in the long run, as the New Interest candidates were returned resoundingly. Sometimes, however, even her best efforts could be frustrated when distance and a hostile wife combined. After having done all she could to secure the vote of a freeholder named Wilson, and having even obtained his word of honour, she was afraid that his wife would eventually control his vote: 'I try'd to have stroak'd her, but she is a Viper, and told me she always was of the high party –.'[85]

Poll results for the areas where Lady Susan specifically canvassed are generally favourable. The New Interest won a small victory at Heath, but trounced the Old Interest in Bodicot and Milton. The elections in Banbury and Wardington were near misses, but the results were close enough for the New Interest candidates to maintain their viability during the scrutiny and subsequent parliamentary petition.[86] Therefore, while it is impossible to quantify her influence, it cannot be discounted, as in such an extremely close contest, her efforts undoubtedly contributed to the New Interest's campaign and the candidates' eventual success.

As Lady Susan's concerns about Lady Dalkeith and the Duchess of Argyll's political interest demonstrate, women who were the acting heads of families or landholders in their own rights were also part of the canvassing ritual. They were approached and their support was solicited with little regard to gender. Women with political interests can be found throughout the period: the Dowager Lady Orford

83 BP L.IV.7.B/27, Lady Susan Keck to Revd Bray, 19 Aug. 1753.

84 BL Add MSS 61667, f. 154d, Lady Susan Keck to Marlborough, [Great Tew], 25 Jan. [1753; misdated by an archivist as 1754]; and ff. 161–2, 29 Jan. 1753.

85 BP L.IV.7.B/37, Lady Susan Keck to Revd Bray, 21 Oct. 1753.

86 *The Poll of the Freeholders of Oxfordshire, Taken at Oxford. . . .* (Oxford, 1754), pp. 17–19, 24–5, 59–60, 89.

controlled both seats at Callington and one seat at Ashburton in the 1750s and 1760s;[87] Lady Bute held one seat at Bossiney;[88] Harriot Pitt controlled one seat at Pontefract from 1756 until her death in 1763;[89] Lady Andover was the patron of one seat at Castle Rising in the 1780s;[90] and Lady Irwin inherited both seats at Horsham after her husband's death in 1778 – and fought a full-scale electoral battle to protect her interest in 1790.[91] Other women, like Lady Downing, who fought unsuccessfully but continuously for control of Dunwich in Suffolk from 1764 until her death in 1778, are less well known.[92]

In the counties and more open boroughs, women's political interests helped to make up the area's political profile. While someone like the young Countess of Sutherland, who had inherited 'almost insurmountable' influence in Sutherlandshire, was exceptional,[93] women with less sweeping political interests were also solicited assiduously. When an election in Glamorganshire took shape in 1767, Lady Charlotte Edwin's interest was sought in turn by the candidate, Lord and Lady Temple, and George and Elizabeth Grenville.[94] She resisted them all; however, they might have been too late, as the Duchess of Hamilton, her niece by marriage, was soliciting her support over a month before the Grenville onslaught began.[95]

Women's political interest was not limited only to distant or unimportant boroughs; it might even be felt in urban Westminster. The Duchess of Bedford, who controlled the Bedford family interest for her grandson, caused Charles James Fox a good deal of concern during his 1780 Westminster election: 'I wrote to the Duchess of Bedford, but have had no answer. I hope you have pressed her

---

87 See BL Add MSS 33061, ff. 206–d, 'Mr. Harris' State of the Case of the Burrough of Ashburton for Sr Wm Yonge' [1753–4]; 32995, f. 76, 'Present State of Elections for England & Wales' [1754] and 32999, f. 301, 'Cornish Boroughs and the Principal Interests' [1760–1]; Namier, *The Structure of Politics*, p. 145; and 'Horace Walpole to Sir Horace Mann, Strawberry Hill, 6 October 1774', in Lewis, ed., *Walpole's Correspondence* (1967), XXIV, pp. 46–7.

88 The extent of Lady Bute's actual involvement in the politics of the borough remains shadowy.

89 Namier, *The Structure of Politics*, p. 147.

90 Cannon, *Aristocratic Century*, p. 110.

91 WSRO Add. MSS 5190–5203.

92 See A.R. Childs, 'Politics and elections in Suffolk burroughs in the late eighteenth and early nineteenth centuries,' unpub. M.Phil. thesis (Reading, 1974), pp. 9–29.

93 She controlled 22 of the 34 votes. 'William Robertson to William Adam, Edinburgh, 15 February 1789', in Donald E. Ginter, *Whig Organization in the General Election of 1790. Selections from the Blair Adams Papers* (Berkeley and Los Angeles, 1967), pp. 46–7.

94 BL Add MSS 57804, f. 165, Temple to George Grenville, [London?], 18 Oct. 1767; and f. 167, George Grenville to Temple, Wotton, 23 Oct. 1767.

95 'Andrew Stuart to the Duchess of Hamilton, Torrance, 13 September 1767', in Argyll, ed., *Intimate Society Letters*, I, pp. 119–21.

on the subject, though I rather hope I shall have her votes even if she does not speak *for* me, provided she does not speak against me.'[96] When the Dowager Lady Rockingham married Lord Guilford, she maintained her political interest in Kent; consequently, they were approached jointly in 1763.[97] Guilford's response suggests that the couple shared political inclinations, but that she had a part in the decision-making:

> Lady Guilford who as well as my self was an approver of the Peace, & is a well wisher to an Administration in which my near Relation & Friend Ld Halifax bears a considerable part, has been so good as to say she should not like to give her interest in Kent to any person who shall declare himself to disapprove the one, or be an enemy to the [o]ther. We had no reason to suppose Sr. Brook [ha]d made any such declarations, & are extreamly well inclined towards him, ... I have desired he might be sounded on that head, & as I shall not have an answer till next post, Lady Guilford & I cannot properly make a positive declaration till we have received it.[98]

Given Lady Guilford's general distaste for writing, these may well have been her own opinions; yet more important is that both Guilford and his correspondent believed that she had a right to direct her political interest.

Since women were involved throughout campaigns, it is not surprising to find that some were also in attendance at the poll. Just by appearing in a procession, women could contribute to the spectacle and excitement of the election. Some women had a distinct dramatic flair, as Agneta Yorke noted from St Albans in 1774: 'I find Lady Melborne and Mrs Brand entered the Town in Triumph at the Head of the Melbourne Party with an open Landau filled with Musicians playing before them.'[99] Most frequently, they oversaw the hustings from the windows of neighbouring buildings or from their carriages;[100] occasionally, they were on the hustings themselves. By the time that Thomas Wenman Coke lost his seat in Norfolk in the 1784 election, for instance, his wife's persuasive powers on the hustings had already become legendary.[101]

---

96 Lord John Russell, ed., *Memorials and Correspondence of Charles James Fox* 4 vols (1853), I, p. 257.

97 Bodl. Ms. North D.9, ff. 141–d, Sir George Oxenden to Guilford, n.pl., 16 Oct. 1763.

98 Ibid., ff. 143–d, Guilford to Sir George Oxenden, Chesterton, 22 Oct. [1763].

99 WP L30/9/97/36, f. 1d, Agneta Yorke to Marchioness Grey, n.pl., 25 Oct. 1774.

100 In 1784, this provided another excuse for poetry: *On seeing Lady* BEAUCHAMP, *Lady* CARLISLE, *and Lady* DERBY, *in their Carriages, on Mr.* FOX's *Side of the Hustings*, in Hartley, ed., *History of the Westminster Election*, p. 483.

101 A.M.W. Stirling, *Coke of Norfolk and his Friends* (1912), p. 146.

After elections were finally over, the political excitement sub-
sided rapidly in most constituencies and society resumed its normal
pattern. Women played an important part in smoothing ruffled
feathers and re-establishing normal relations. Sometimes this required an ability to turn the other cheek that did not come naturally. After having Lady Salisbury nearly steal the St Albans election
from her grasp in 1784, Lady Spencer had felt that Lady Salisbury
had not been properly humbled by her loss. Lord Jersey's news
would not have pleased her: 'Ly Salisbury gave us a larger kind of
Supper on Tuesday: she endeavors to laugh off the St Albans Business, but rather ... seems to claim much honor & merit from
having made so extraordinary a Stand & so difficult a Contest.'[102]

Scrutinies and petitions to Parliament often added a postscript
to the fiercest election battles. When this happened, women might
help to locate and send witnesses to 'regularify our Votes';[103] or
they might even attend Parliament to see the proceedings in person. The Lowther–Portland petition over the Cumberland election
in 1768 drew women from both camps. Lady Mary Coke, who was
part of the Lowther camp, records attending Parliament on at least
eight occasions, as part of a group of eight or nine women.[104] Similar details are lacking for the Portland side, but it seems unlikely
that it was less well represented.

Conclusion

Political and women's historians alike have tended to view eighteenth-
century women's electoral involvement as anomalous, indirect and
increasingly unacceptable. By taking as representative the adverse
publicity that was directed at women during the 1784 Westminster
election, they have failed to identify the continuity of women's
experience or to see it in terms of its social and political contexts.
In a political world where the enthusiastic extremes of 1784 were
but one example of the 'epidemical Madness' that could emerge
whenever electoral politics came to dominate society, women's activities throughout the electoral process, and over time, were complex
and diverse, encompassing the full election process and stemming
from women's traditional female roles and their place in a fluid
and flexible socio-political world.

102 BL Ms Coll Althorp F. 109, Jersey to Lady Spencer, Grosvenor Square, [10 April
1784].
103 BP L.IV.7.C/76, Lady Parker to Revd Bray, St James's Square, 21 Dec. 1754.
104 See *The Letters and Journals of Lady Mary Coke* 4 vols (Edinburgh, 1889–96), II,
pp. 416–28.

CHAPTER EIGHT

A politician's politician: Georgiana, Duchess of · Devonshire and the Whig party

AMANDA FOREMAN

Would that I were a man, to unite my Talents, my hopes, my fortune with Charles's [Charles James Fox], to make common cause and fall or rule with him.[1]

Written by Georgiana, Duchess of Devonshire to Sir Philip Francis in November 1798, these words reveal her deep frustration. For more than twenty years she had not only presided over the most celebrated political salon of her era, but also distinguished herself as a skilled propagandist and a tireless public campaigner for the Whig party. Yet at the time of her letter to Sir Philip these triumphs seemed paltry and ephemeral to her compared to the great handicap of her sex.

In a society where élite women played a greater part in the political life of the nation than anywhere else in Europe, Georgiana's contribution was still acknowledged as remarkable. She was not simply the leading female Whig but one of the party's leading politicians. But although élite women had access to a range of important supporting roles, they were denied positions of real leadership. There is no evidence, however, that Georgiana ever considered the implications of this division of authority between the sexes until the Whig party split in 1794. The split was a personal disaster for her since between 1794 and 1801, when the government fell and the Whig party revived, Georgiana was effectively a politician without a party.

1 BL Add MSS 450763, f. 250, Georgiana Duchess of Devonshire [henceforth GD] to Philip Francis, 29 Nov. 1798.

The author wishes to thank the Trustees of the Chatsworth Settlement and the Honourable Simon Howard for permission to consult the Devonshire Papers, Chatsworth House, and the Carlisle MSS at Castle Howard.

This long stretch of enforced inactivity made her realize the fragile nature of female participation in political life and its dependence on chance and whim. Georgiana began to re-evaluate the validity of eighteenth-century society's notions of femininity. As her *cri de coeur* to Sir Philip Francis shows, the advantages she had enjoyed because of her rank and status had given her ambitions beyond the purview of her sex. Georgiana spent the last years of her life testing and pushing the limits of the political opportunities open to women.

The Duchess's career divides into two periods, 1774 to 1789 and 1801 to 1806. The first part, which includes the notorious 1784 Westminster election and the 1788–89 Regency Crisis, is well known because of the publicity that accompanied her activities. But the second, and more significant, period of her life, in which Georgiana acted as one of the chief promoters of the alliance between Charles Fox, Lord Grenville and the Prince of Wales, in what was known as the 'Union of all the Talents', remains neglected.[2] The uneven attention directed at her career has caused historians to misunderstand both the nature and scope of female participation in eighteenth-century politics, as well as Georgiana's motives for her actions.[3] In the era before the Reform Act, national politics had become a family business for the country's élite. The first part of Georgiana's career largely resembled the pattern set for the wife of a party grandee. Aristocratic women had a vital role to play in promoting their husbands' interests, and their duties spanned the gamut of political activities, from canvassing in family boroughs, to the allocation of patronage, to the safeguarding of political alliances. Georgiana was one of several political women including the Duchess of Gordon, the Duchess of Rutland and Viscountess Melbourne who enjoyed considerable political influence. But the second part of Georgiana's career, beginning in 1801, was very different from the first. Having suffered criticism for being too forward in the past, she kept her activities discreet, preferring to work away from the public eye while struggling to achieve real influence within the party. Instead

2 Leslie Mitchell, *Charles James Fox* (Oxford, 1992), p. 211. Dr Mitchell alone credits Georgiana with preventing the Prince of Wales from falling under William Pitt's influence in 1804.

3 See Karl von den Steinen, 'The discovery of women in eighteenth-century political life', in Barbara Kanner, ed., *The Women of England from Anglo-Saxon Times to the Present* (Hamden, CT, 1979), pp. 229–58; and Peter Jupp, 'The roles of royal and aristocratic women in British politics, c.1782–1832', in Mary O'Dowd and Sabine Wichert, eds, *Chattel, Servant or Citizen: Women's Status in Church, State and Society* (Belfast, 1995), pp. 103–13. Both writers accept that political activity was integrated as part of an aristocratic wife's duty, but argue that it was intermittent and of limited influence.

of merely acting as a cipher for her husband's family, Georgiana fashioned a successful role for herself as a political negotiator.

Taken as a whole, the Duchess of Devonshire's career shows her to have been a woman of acute political sense and purpose. Aided by her advantageous circumstances, Georgiana constructed her own place in the political arena. Even though few women enjoyed her wealth or status, Georgiana's political involvement should not be dismissed as unrepresentative of her peers. Georgiana's life was not an aberration but an illustration of both the hidden workings of back-room politics and the complexity of gender relations in late eighteenth-century England.

Georgiana and the Whig party, 1774–1800

Georgiana was born in 1757, and married the Duke of Devonshire when she was only seventeen, in 1774. In the eighteenth century, aristocratic marriages entailed specific social and political obligations. This was particularly true in Georgiana's case since the Duke's wealth, background and command of six seats automatically made him one of the leaders of the Whig party. The early years of her marriage were an arduous training as she learned to be a political wife *par excellence*. In the country, she was expected to represent the Duke in as many charitable activities as possible, to understand which local issues the family should support, and to act as a conduit for patronage. She also had to help campaign for her husband's interests during elections. In the 1774 general election, for example, while her mother, Lady Spencer, was canvassing for her husband in Northampton, Georgiana was canvassing for the Duke at Derby. She hosted balls and dinners and made it a point to socialize with the locals, thereby raising the Cavendish family's standing within the county: 'we were received there by a great huzza', she recorded after one such event, 'the room was very much crowded but they were so good as to split in 2 to make room for us.'[4] In town, Georgiana divided her time between patronizing the arts and her cultivation of the ton, the fashionable set, both of which tied into her chief duty which was to hostess political soirées at Devonshire House.

Although a committed Whig, the Duke was famously disinclined to exert himself, limiting his activities to bankrolling the party and voicing his opinion in private. Georgiana also became passionately

4 Chats. MSS, 32, GD to Georgiana Lady Spencer, 16 Oct. 1774.

attached to the Whig cause, and began to harbour ambitious plans for the Duke's career. 'I have also some hopes that she will turn politician too', wrote a friend in 1775, 'for she gave me an account of some of the Speeches in the House of Lords.'[5] But the Duke avoided the responsibilities of political leadership, preferring the comforts of his club, Brooks's. When he refused to become Lord Lieutenant of Ireland, Georgiana wrote: 'I did everything to persuade him. I was certain as they were that his name, his family and his extraordinary good judgement and ability would enable him to succeed.'[6]

Thwarted by her husband's lack of ambition, Georgiana sought to develop her own political role within the perimeters of her ordinary duties. Taking her cue from her ambassadorial role, Georgiana exploited every opportunity to promote not just her husband's interests but also the party's interests. Her earliest efforts occurred in 1778 during the French invasion scare, a time when the Whigs were deeply unpopular for supporting the Americans' declaration of independence. In order to prove their loyalty while maintaining a principled stand against the war, the party rushed to help with the country's defences. The Devonshires moved to the military camp at Cox-Heath, where the Duke joined his fellow Lord Lieutenants in training regiments of volunteers. But it was Georgiana who was largely responsible for increasing the party's popularity. Halfway through the summer she refined the 'military look', a riding habit converted to resemble a military uniform, to reflect the regimental uniforms in the camp. She then organized the officers' wives into an auxiliary corps to show the world that the Whigs *and* their wives were preparing to fight the French. The sight of the women parading through the camp caused a sensation, the *London Chronicle* reported:

> The Duchess of Devonshire appears everyday at the head of the beauteous Amazons at Cox-heath. who are all dressed en militaire, in the regimentals that distinguish the several corps in which their Lords etc., serve, and charm every beholder with their beauty and affability.[7]

The publicity surrounding Georgiana's imaginative display of patriotism was a propaganda *coup* for the party. Both benefited from the novelty of being connected with the other – a pretty girl and a

5 BL Althorp MSS F125, Miss Lloyd to Georgiana Lady Spencer, 30 Oct. 1775.
6 BL Althorp MSS G287, GD to Lord Althorp, April 1783.
7 *LC*, 16–18 July 1778.

political cause – and once the connection stuck, Georgiana was no longer simply representing her husband. She did not stop at military uniforms; thousands watched her christen a Royal Navy gunship, and this, along with other high-profile events, further cemented the personal tie between herself and the party.

But it was not until she became close friends with Charles James Fox, in 1778–79, that the leadership began to consider how it might harness her popularity to the Whig cause. Fox recognized her talent for propaganda – in fact, they shared a flair and enthusiasm for the public side of politics. Both understood the potency of symbols, whether it was Georgiana wearing the Prince of Wales's feathers in her hair, or Fox wearing the colours of the American army, blue and buff. Furthermore, both had an innate talent for engineering theatrical occasions. In September 1780, Fox invited Georgiana to join him on the hustings in Covent Garden to support his candidacy for the Borough of Westminster. Although the press now associated her with the Whig party, it was taken aback by her boldness. Her canvassing for a non-relative set a precedent and seemed indelicate. The response was mixed; the *Morning Post*, an anti-Whig paper, implied that Fox was Georgiana's lover:

> One day last week, her Grace the Duchess of Devonshire appeared upon the hustings at Covent Garden. She immediately saluted her favourite candidate, the Hon. Charles Fox. Unfortunately it happened not to be his shaving day; and when the candidate saluted her Grace it put one in mind of Sheridan's cunning Isaac, shaking hands with the Graces.[8]

But the wild applause Georgiana received from the crowd removed any doubt among the leadership about her presence. When Fox stood for re-election in 1782, Georgiana appeared again on the hustings wearing the Whig colours. This time the press reported the event without commenting on her appearance. 'The crowd was immense', wrote Sylas Neville, one of the many spectators at the event, in his diary, 'full of carriages and people of all ranks. The Duchess of Devonshire and another lady were on the hustings and waved their hats with the rest in compliment to Charles, who was soon after chaired under a canopy of oak leaves and myrtle amidst the acclamations of thousands.'[9] In fact there were more than two

8 *MP*, 25 Sept. 1780. It is almost certain that Georgiana had an affair with Charles Fox between 1782 and 1784/5. See Chats. MSS, 546, GD to Lady Elizabeth Foster, 18 Oct. 1783.

9 Basil Cozens-Hardy, *The Diary of Sylas Neville, 1767–1788* (Oxford, 1950), p. 291.

women on the stage. Georgiana was joined by several active female Whigs, including the two daughters of the Bishop of St Asaph, showing how the precedent set two years before had become part of electoral activity.

Georgiana's popularity with crowds was only one of several factors that strengthened her position within the party during the early 1780s. She had also developed into a fine art a wife's duty to foster her husband's social and political connections. Her talent for friendship netted her some politically powerful friends, particularly the Prince of Wales. It was not unknown for the party to lean on her to use her influence with him for political purposes. In June 1783, for example, the Fox–North coalition government feared a split in the Cabinet over the Prince of Wales's debts. Georgiana prevented a crisis by persuading the Prince to accept a lower sum for his establishment.[10]

Georgiana also combined the Cavendish family's political influence with the Duke's wealth to establish Devonshire House as the premier meeting place for the Whigs. The party celebrated there in times of victory and sought solace there in times of defeat. The Whigs met at Devonshire House after Lord North's resignation in 1782; George Selwyn recorded the occasion: 'I was at Devonshire House till 4, and then left most of the company there. All the new supposed Ministers were there except Lord Rockingham, who had probably other business and perhaps with the K.'[11] Two years later, when the king dismissed the Whigs and appointed William Pitt as prime minister, Devonshire House was again packed with party meetings.[12]

Georgiana canvassed one more time for Fox in the 1784 general election, the epic battle between George III and William Pitt, and the ousted Whigs. Her contribution to the Whig campaign is well known because she was then, and is now, generally held responsible for Fox's victory.[13] One newspaper proclaimed, 'All advertisements relative to the Westminster Election should be in the Duchess

10 GD to Prince of Wales, c. 17 June 1783, in A. Aspinall, ed., *Correspondence of George Prince of Wales, 1770–1812* 7 vols (London, 1963), I, n. 91, p. 125.

11 CH MSS, J14/1/346, George Selwyn to Lord Carlisle, 22 March 1782.

12 'There was a general meeting at Devonshire House before we went down to the House', wrote Sir Gilbert Elliot to Sir James Harris in March 1784. 'Where the question of the Short Mutiny Bill was proposed to, and several persons objected to it; and that being the case, it was the unanimous opinion that it should not be moved in the House on the ground that it could not be carried.' The Earl of Malmesbury, ed., *The Diaries and Correspondence of the First Earl Malmesbury* 4 vols (1844), II, p. 64.

13 Chats. MSS, 612, Duke of Portland to GD, 14 April 1784.

of Devonshire's name. She is the candidate to all intents and purposes.'[14] However, despite her success Georgiana's zealous canvassing
provoked national outrage and she never appeared on the hustings
again. Historians have explained the abuse Georgiana suffered by
the fact that she was campaigning for a non-relative.[15] But that would
not explain why the Duchess of Portland and Mrs Crewe, as well
as the fifteen other women who joined the Whig side, and Lady
Salisbury and Mrs Hobart, who canvassed for the government, neither suffered the same criticism nor won the same plaudits.

The pro-government press certainly took advantage of double
standards concerning female delicacy to attack Georgiana on the
grounds of impropriety. But her celebrity made her an easy target
and it was more a case of using whatever weapons came to hand
rather than specific criticism of Georgiana. Many years later, her
sister, Lady Bessborough, teased a friend about his hypocrisy:

> Your Ladies assist you in canvassing? I thought, my dear Granville,
> you were one of the people who thought my Sister and my canvass-
> ing even for our Brother, certainly for Mr Fox, so scandalous a thing
> that it could never be forgot or forgiven. How I have heard you . . .
> exclaim at the impropriety and indelicacy of both our conduct and
> the people who could suffer us to do so horrible a thing! Yet, you
> see, in Election fervour you can take up the same means you were
> so shocked at in others.[16]

Social hypocrisy allowed for Georgiana to be singled out, but her
behaviour had helped her to be victimized by the press. The reason
for the outcry against her was twofold. First, by using her personal
celebrity to impress voters, Georgiana challenged eighteenth-century
notions of femininity. Walpole reported how she 'made no scruple
of visiting the humblest of electors, dazzling and enchanting them
by the fascination of her manner, the power of her beauty and the
influence of her high rank'.[17] The way she freely moved among the
poorer sections of the city seemed like a bold assertion of autonomy.
This was problematic in a society that did not grant legal status
to married women and was in general suspicious of independent
single women. Lady Rockingham, for example, enjoyed considerable

---

14 J. Hartley, ed., *The History of the Westminster Election* (1784), p. 254.
15 See Linda Colley, *Britons: Forging the Nation, 1707–1837* (New Haven, CT, and London, 1992), p. 244.
16 Lady Bessborough to Granville Leveson-Gower, 5 March 1799, in Castalia, Countess
Granville, ed., *The Private Papers of Lord Granville Leveson-Gower* 2 vols (1916), I, p. 243.
17 Hugh Stokes, *The Devonshire House Circle* (1912), p. 201.

prestige and influence as the wife of the Whig party leader, but was censured in widowhood for expressing a continuing interest in politics.[18] Georgiana brought her own personality to the campaign in an era when the only women who had public personae were women of dubious reputation: actresses and courtesans. It showed too much freedom and independence for her contemporaries.[19] Furthermore, the direct style of her canvass challenged established patterns of social discourse. 'Assume no masculine airs', wrote the Dowager Countess of Carlisle in her book on feminine manners, 'real robustness and superior force is denied you by nature: its semblance denied you by the laws of decency.'[20] Mary Hamilton recorded in her diary that she 'met the Dss of Devonshire in her coach with a mob round her, canvassing in the Strand for Mr Fox. What a pity that any of our sex should forget what is due to female delicacy.'[21] The press responded to Georgiana's perceived masculinity by attacking her with the same force as if she were a man.

Secondly, Georgiana flouted custom by treating the lowest sections of society as equals rather than subordinates. Instead of employing *noblesse oblige* when she appealed for votes, she was seen committing *lèse-majesté* as when conveying 'common mechanics' in her coach to the hustings. Complaints about bribery and influence were mere stock-in-trade for every election. The Duchess of Northumberland used to drop trinkets from her window to the waiting crowd below, and those who returned them received a double bounty. But Georgiana surpassed all previous examples of women's canvassing by her willingness to approach voters on their own level. She spent hours chatting with them over a pint of ale or a tipple of gin. Indeed, the *Morning Post* estimated her daily alcoholic intake and wondered how she could remain standing. The French Revolution was not even on the horizon, but Georgiana's encouragement towards her inferiors seemed very dangerous to commentators. Lady

18 Lady Mary Coke wrote: 'I am surprised at what you mention relating to Lady Rockingham, it seems as if politics was her first passion and that even her great misfortune in losing Lord Rockingham is insufficient to make her forget her favourite amusement.' Scottish National Register of Archives, Edinburgh (SNRA), Douglas-Home MSS, D95/54, 17 Aug. 1782.

19 See R. Blunt, ed., *Mrs Montague* 2 vols (Edinburgh, 1923), II, p. 169.

20 Dowager Countess Carlisle, *Thoughts in the forms of Maxims to Young Ladies on their first Establishment in the World* (London, 1789), in R. Trumbach, *The Rise of the Egalitarian Family* (New York, 1978), p. 151.

21 23 April 1784, in Elizabeth and Mary Anson, eds, *Mary Hamilton, Afterwards, Mrs John Dickenson at Court and at Home, from Letters and Diaries, 1756–1816* (1925), p. 78. Also, Fanny Boscawen to Hester Pitt, 12 April 1784, in Vere Birdwood, ed., *So Dearly Beloved, So Much Admired* (1994), p. 161.

Spencer berated Georgiana for ignoring propriety. Lord Temple Nugent wrote to the Duke of Rutland that Georgiana 'had heard more plain English of the grossist sort than ever fell to the share of any lady of her rank'.[22] The anti-Whig press associated Georgiana's gift for the 'common touch' with holding herself in common with prostitutes, and William Pitt sneeringly referred to her and her companions as 'the Women of the People'.[23] Lewd cartoons depicting Georgiana kissing tradesmen or embracing Charles Fox dominated the government campaign.

Although the party defended Georgiana, its attempts to portray her canvass as a sacrifice to 'female patriotism' and wifely duty failed to stop the besmirching of her character. Georgiana had not only discredited herself but her method of canvassing. Other women, including her sister, did canvass for the Whigs in subsequent elections but never with quite such exuberance, and Georgiana was always excluded. Nevertheless, she remained at the forefront of Whig political life. In the years leading up to the Regency Crisis in 1788, she continued to organize propaganda occasions for the party, where impressive shows of political solidarity managed to hide the fact of their dwindling numbers.[24] Her efforts had a key effect on recruitment and retention. As one commentator explained, 'She really is a very good Politician. As soon as ever any young man comes from abroad he is immediately invited to Devonshire House and to Chatsworth – and by that means he is to be of the Opposition.'[25] In the 1788 Westminster election, when she was supposedly adopting a more retired part, Georgiana merely trimmed her activities to appear more discreet. A correspondent noted, 'she only writes about fifty notes, sees fifty people every day. At night the Heads of the Party meet and sup at Devonshire House, [and] are so jolly and eager that she says it is quite delightful.'[26]

The Regency Crisis marked the high point of Georgiana's career as the party's propagandist. Georgiana's diary shows how she acted as a confidante, spy, messenger and even party whip for her colleagues. But her greatest achievement lies in her organization of the public campaign that accompanied the Whigs' political campaign

22 Earl Temple Nugent to Duke of Rutland, 12 April 1784, in HMC XIV Report, Rutland MSS, I, pp. 87–8.

23 John Ehrman, *The Younger Pitt* 3 vols (London, 1969–96), I, p. 218.

24 For example, Georgiana turned Blanchard's balloon send-off into a Whig festival by cutting the ties and insisting that the colours be blue and buff. See *LC*, 30 Nov.–2 Dec. 1784.

25 SNRA Douglas-Home MSS, D95/54, 12 Sept. 1787.

26 PRO 30/29/4/7, f. 94, Miss Lloyd to Lady Stafford, 3 Aug. 1788.

in Parliament.[27] Georgiana's ideas for party uniforms as well as her skill at presenting shows of solidarity divided élite society down party lines. Public places and private houses were turned into theatres of confrontation; scenes at the opera, in the park, in drawing rooms and at balls assumed the atmosphere of a sporting contest.[28] Sir Gilbert Elliot mockingly called the women's campaign 'petticoat politics'.[29] Lord Sydney was more forthright: writing to Lord Cornwallis, he complained that 'the ladies are as usual at the head of all animosity and distinguished by caps, ribands, and other such ensigns of party'.[30] It became impossible for the two sides to mix: the Whig ladies were insulted at an assembly of Lady Buckingham's, when 'some of the Ladies on the Opposite [Pittite] side groaned and hooted at them as they came into the room'.[31] Georgiana's campaign was considered so effective by the government that Queen Charlotte stepped in to counteract its effects. She showed the royal displeasure by snubbing the Whig ladies at Court when they appeared as the only ones not wearing 'God Save the King' in their caps. Furthermore, she ordered all friends of the Court to boycott Whig assemblies, and in particular those organized by Georgiana. Georgiana's campaign was too successful in the chaos it caused to eighteenth-century high society, and she was once again criticized for overstepping propriety, while the Duchess of Gordon, who was carrying out the same function for the Pittites, largely escaped calumny.

However, public politics of the kind witnessed during the 1780s all but disappeared in the 1790s. Following the French Revolution, the Whig party was decimated by a mass of defections, including Georgiana's brother, Lord Spencer, who became First Lord of the Admiralty. Charles Fox was left with fewer than 70 supporters. His subsequent secession from Parliament in 1797 finished off the last vestiges of organized opposition. Furthermore, Georgiana's private life was in turmoil. Between 1791 and 1793 she lived abroad during a temporary separation from her husband. In addition, she suffered

27 See Georgiana's diary for this period Chats. MSS 936, passim, and her friend's diary, Lady Elizabeth Foster, which is in the British Library, BL Add MSS 41579.

28 On 9 Feb. 1789, *MP* reported, 'most of the Ladies of Fashion appeared at the Opera on Saturday in a new head dress in honour of the Prince of Wales. It consisted of three large white feathers connected by a band, on which was described . . . Ich Dien.' In retaliation, according to the *LC* on 2 April, the ladies of the Court wore their own uniform of garter blue with a gold fringe and a petticoat of white satin.

29 Sir Gilbert Elliot to Lady Elliot, 2 April 1789, in Countess of Minto, ed., *The Life and Letters of Sir Gilbert Elliot, First Earl of Minto* 3 vols (1874), I, p. 295.

30 Charles Ross, ed., *Correspondence of Charles, First Marquis Cornwallis* 3 vols (1859), I, p. 406.

31 William LeFanu, ed., *Betsy Sheridan's Journal* (Oxford, 1986), p. 153.

a severe illness in 1796 which ruined her health and left her blind in one eye. But these blows did not diminish her enthusiasm for politics or her support for Fox. In fact, some people relabelled the remaining Whigs 'The Devonshire House Party'.[32]

Georgiana realized that it was impossible for her to act on her own cognizance. She wanted to continue her political career and yet remain within the bounds of female propriety. She put her views on how far women should go very succinctly in a letter to Lady Spencer. In discussing how the French Revolution had quenched the former partisan politics of the Regency Crisis, she added: 'All Society politics are very temperate [now], an instance of which I saw at the Opera in Ld Lauderdale being a good while in the Dss of Portland's box – I think this is as it should be; and if women would only meddle as moderators they would do good instead of mischief.'[33] Fox's election celebrations in June 1796 illustrate her dilemma. The Duke went to Chiswick and left Georgiana in charge of receiving the party at Devonshire House. It was not the case, she wrote to her brother, that she had put herself forward without his consent:

> At the same time that I certainly should not have refused myself to an act of friendship to Mr Fox, I certainly feel that I ought to avoid taking any part that was separate and not under the particular guidance of the Duke of Devonshire ... for tho' you forgive me, I know, if some of my opinions are not the same as yours ... yet I could not bear that you should think I had been coming forward in a manner very unbecoming any woman.[34]

The longer the Whig party remained inactive, the greater Georgiana's frustration. When Ireland was on the verge of civil war Georgiana apologized profusely to her brother for interfering, but notwithstanding bombarded him with advice and information.

The rebirth of the Whig party, 1801–6

Pitt's resignation in 1801 split the government and not only revived the Whigs but spawned new opposition parties. Georgiana found herself in the unique position of having high-level contacts with almost all the new factions. On the Whig side, both her former

32 2 Feb. 1797, Francis Bickley, ed., *Diaries of Sylvester Douglas, Lord Glenbervie* 2 vols (1928), I, p. 124.

33 Chats. MSS 1210, GD to Lady Spencer, 1 Feb. 1794.

34 BL Althorp MSS G287, GD to George, Earl Spencer, 17 June 1796.

lovers, Fox and Charles Grey, still relied on her to be their political adjutant. She also had a direct link with the Carlton House party through her friendship with the Prince of Wales. On the other side of the political spectrum, her brother, Lord Spencer, had resigned with Pitt but was allied with William Windham and Lord Grenville, in independent opposition. Additionally, Georgiana's eldest daughter was engaged to Lord Morpeth, and through him she had regular contact with the Canningites, who remained Pitt's allies. Despite having been away from politics for nearly a decade, Georgiana's political reputation among the old and new generations of Whigs was undiminished, not least because of her extensive contacts with the French, which enabled her to pass on information about Bonaparte's regime.[35]

The extent to which she had access to inside knowledge can be seen by the frenetic activity recorded in her diary. She returned to Devonshire House on 7 February, two days after Addington had accepted office. She found the Prince of Wales waiting for her to discuss what steps Pitt's former ministers would take. As soon as he left, Lords Carlisle and Morpeth arrived for another discussion. She then visited her brother, Lord Spencer, to gather intelligence and to congratulate him on resigning his post.[36] By the end of the week, having visited or received visits from almost all the leading politicians, she wrote down her view of the current state of affairs. There were several parties, she recorded, independent of the Foxite opposition: former Pittites who remained in government and called themselves high churchmen; the Canningites, who went out on principle but were furious with Pitt for not avowing his opinion on Catholic emancipation more forcefully; and 'My brother and Lord Grenville's party who seem to think if Pitt had faced the danger he might have forced the king by the unpopularity of another administration to have yielded'.[37]

The situation was further complicated by the onset of the king's former illness, which began in the third week of February 1801 and lasted on and off for about four months. This immediately created the possibility of a regency and a new government. The Prince of Wales would have to choose between Pitt or Addington, or one of

35 Chats. MSS, 1696, Charles Fox to GD, c.1802–3, and Chats. MSS, 1686, GD to Lady Elizabeth Foster, 20 Dec. 1802. Ironically, the French misinterpreted Georgiana's willingness to act as a go-between and in 1806 attempted to bribe her with £10,000 to pass on Cabinet papers.
36 Chats. MSS, V1611C.
37 Ibid.

the parties in opposition. Georgiana feared he would choose Pitt, despite her urgings to the contrary.[38] It is a testament to her influence that he was too afraid to see her until he had made up his mind. After consultation with Pitt and Addington, he decided to invite members from all sides to form a government. Although Lord Moira actually visited the Duke of Devonshire and several others, nothing was decided before the king began to recover on 3 March. Two weeks later, Georgiana recorded that the Foxites had coalesced with some of the old Whigs, namely Lords Carlisle, Lansdowne and Fitzwilliam, and had offered their support to the Prince of Wales to lead a new opposition party. But the Prince refused their offer, and once Addington was confirmed in office, many of the Whigs, including Sheridan, were inclined to support the new ministry because of its commitment to peace. Georgiana, on the other hand, thought it would be better if they coalesced with her brother and Lord Grenville to form a new opposition. But at first she demurred against attempting to influence party opinion.

Georgiana's sister once stated to Lord Granville Leveson-Gower that 'for not withstanding all my violence in politicks and talking so much on that subject, I perfectly agree with you that no woman has any business to meddle with that or any other serious business, further than giving her opinion'.[39] Georgiana shared her sister's philosophy up to a point, although it was an exaggeration when she wrote to her brother in 1797: 'I give you my sacred word of honour that I never tried to influence any body's vote in my life except sometimes when I have very unsuccessfully attempted to soften that violence of some of my acquaintance.'[40] Georgiana knew better than anyone that it is often easier to influence policy over a hot dinner than across the crowded floor of the Commons. Furthermore, her position as confidante to a number of politicians had required her periodic intervention on specific issues, although she had always done it at the leadership's request. But it was one thing to execute orders, another to pursue an independent policy.

Georgiana did nothing until an incident in February 1802 briefly reminded her of her idea for a new coalition. Charles Grey had taken offence at an intemperate speech of Sheridan's at a Whig Club dinner, when he appeared to accuse Grey of disloyalty to the party. The attack was a thinly veiled reference to George Tierney's

38 Ibid.

39 Lady Bessborough to Granville Leveson-Gower, c. Aug. 1798, in Granville, ed., *Lord Granville Leveson-Gower*, I, p. 218.

40 BL Althorp MSS G287, GD to George, Earl Spencer, 22 March 1797.

attempt to convince Grey that he should accept office under Addington. But Grey had dismissed the idea and ended negotiations at an early stage. Sheridan's attack threatened to divide the Whigs and drive Grey into retirement. Georgiana and Fox both wrote to him to prevent this from happening. Georgiana was secretly conducting an intermittent affair with Grey, and she knew her words would carry special weight.[41] She was also one of the few people who knew the full facts behind the incident. She was certain that Sheridan had found out about the negotiations from Lady Holland and the Jerseys, who had their own reasons for exposing Grey. Georgiana also knew that Grey was innocent of the charge because her own sophisticated network of intelligence had enabled her to follow every step of the negotiations. 'I knew of the negotiation even in its infancy', she told Lady Melbourne. 'And this Mr Grey knows (this however you must tell no one for by experience you know how jealous people are).'[42] 'I have done all I can', she wrote to Lady Melbourne some time later, 'but I have found the speech, and reading it again and with an idea that did not at first strike me – I do own I think it very bad – I am furious at it.'[43] Eventually, with some difficulty, Georgiana and Fox successfully defused the row.

After the Sheridan incident, Georgiana turned away from politics for a while. In March 1802 Addington signed the Treaty of Amiens, which convinced her that there was no further need for opposition. She remained quietly at Chiswick during the general election in July, and was appalled when a newspaper reported that she was canvassing for Francis Burdett. The public side of politics now horrified her, and when she referred to her canvass in 1784 it was with an emphasis on the past; 'my former patriotism', she called it. But by autumn, Addington's triumph looked likely to be short-lived and war with France seemed imminent. Once again Georgiana's thoughts turned towards a coalition between all the parties as the best way of ensuring the continuance of peace. This time she decided to act.

41 New evidence reveals that Georgiana and Grey did not end their affair in 1794, as was previously assumed, but continued to see each other secretly until her death. A letter written by the second Mrs Sheridan in 1807 uncovers the fact that Grey conducted a simultaneous affair with both women for over ten years, always lying to each about the extent of his involvement with the other. His duplicity was exposed after Georgiana's sister, Lady Bessborough, confronted Mrs Sheridan. PRO 30/29/6/2, f. 63, Mrs Sheridan to Granville Leveson-Gower, c. Aug. 1807. After the revelation Lady Bessborough wrote, '[he] is anything but honourable among women'. Granville, ed., *Lord Granville Leveson-Gower*, II, p. 247.

42 BL Add MSS 45548, f. 18, GD to Lady Melbourne, c. Feb. 1802.

43 Ibid., f. 20.

Georgiana justified her decision on several grounds patriotism being the most important, but not the only, reason. She also felt that her long experience in politics conferred on her a special status which gave her the right to interfere. All this is clear in a statement she wrote during this time while editing her journal of the Regency Crisis. 'Having found some fragments of a journal which I wrote during the king's madness ... I am resolved to collect them tho' very imperfect ... my situation also enabled me to judge of the various little interests that agitated the party.'[44] Looking back, she could see with painful clarity the errors her party had committed, the effects of which still prevented them from playing a part in government:

> At the distance [of] 13 years I can trace that beginning of negligence and want of *ensemble* which together with the indulgence of imprudent language has destroy'd the importance of opposition and in the present circumstances of danger to the country seems to shut out the assistance of Men of the first talents and integrity.[45]

Georgiana took it upon herself to rectify the mistakes of the past by encouraging her friends to put aside their differences and to think only of the current danger with France. She was not alone in wanting a coalition: Earl Fitzwilliam's friends, erstwhile Whigs, agreed they would support Fox if he took an active line against Bonaparte. It may have been this news that prompted Georgiana to write to Fox, who was in Paris, with specific advice concerning his manner towards the First Consul.[46] She listed the reasons why he should return to rouse the Whigs into acting with the new Opposition. She was convinced, she told him, that he was the only politician who could lead an all-party government dedicated to peace. He disagreed:

> Do not be angry with me d'avance that I strongly suspect I shall not think your reasons good, and that I am more and more for complete retirement. I heartily wish I had not been overpersuaded to come into Parliament, but as I am there, and notwithstanding my system of withdrawing, I must take some opportunity of declaring my wish in favour of peace, and pray tell this to everyone to whom you can suppose at all desirous of knowing my opinion.[47]

44 Chats. MSS, V1611C.
45 Ibid.
46 Chats. MSS, 1668, Lady Elizabeth Foster to GD, 15 Nov. 1802.
47 Chats. MSS, 1661, Charles Fox to GD, 1 Nov. 1802.

In the following months the Peace of Amiens looked increasingly fragile, and talk of war dominated all discussion. Georgiana went to the House of Lords to hear the debate on whether Britain should resume hostilities with France. Although her sex barred her from attending the House of Commons, she was better informed than most men, having arranged for constant reports to be sent to her by her friend, Robert Adair. Acting on her own political intuition, and on what she heard, she pressed her brother to consider the possibility of informal links with the Prince of Wales. Fox, however, remained sceptical of her arguments and declined to cooperate with either.[48] Her friend's intransigence infuriated her since she knew that the Whigs were too few in numbers to overturn the government on their own. Unlike some members of the party, Georgiana rejected any idea of cooperating with Addington. The Whigs' opposition destabilized the ministry, but it was Pitt who benefited, not them, since by remaining unattached to any party he preserved his image of a devoted public servant. 'Pitt has not yet decided between the rival wooers', she told her mother. 'And the choice of Paris to whomever he gives the apple the others will be furious. He has however, kept away from supporting Addington which gives the Grenvilles hope of his joining them.'[49]

Georgiana scrutinized Pitt's behaviour at the beginning of the parliamentary session in 1803 for any sign that he was planning a campaign against Addington. Information from her contacts in the Pittite camp confirmed her belief that although he wanted to return to office, he was hampered by his small power base. Georgiana thought Pitt could not return without Addington. 'I cannot persuade myself that he will give up his own creation and I think he feels afraid of [illeg] in the old set of Grenville and Wyndham – If he could get my Brother and a few more I think he wd not hesitate in returning, but as it is I suspect he will keep aloof from all partys.'[50] In fact, Pitt had already lost all patience with his former friend, but Georgiana was not alone in suspecting that he might try to climb back into office using the shoulders of his erstwhile adversaries. The Whigs refused to vote for any of Pitt's motions, even if the result was to shore up Addington's tottering government. Their opposition to the ministry was therefore erratic and confusing to potential allies. In March 1803, Georgiana tried to explain to a nonplussed Prince of Wales why her friends were planning to vote with the government

48 BL Althorp MSS G287, GD to George, Earl Spencer, 21 Nov. 1802.
49 Chats. MSS, 1680.2, GD to Dowager Lady Spencer, Dec. 1802.
50 Chats. MSS, 1690.1, GD to Dowager Lady Spencer, Dec. 1802.

on the king's Address: 'Our friends will be very moderate I am sure, and if the Address is properly worded, support it, but if Pitt's friends make any motion to remove Ministers for the purpose of bringing him in for war it is impossible they can support that, having disapproved of the conduct of the last war.'[51]

The Whigs' strategy of conducting an opposition on two fronts consumed their energies without promoting their advancement. The chief issue was peace, and on this point they were prepared to back any party that supported their opposition to war. The situation resulted in a deadlock between the main parties: Pitt was acting just short of open criticism of Addington; Grenville and Spencer were opposed to both men but in favour of the war; and the Foxites were isolated. In April 1803, Addington's nerve wobbled and he offered Pitt a majority stake in his Cabinet with one or two provisos. But Pitt refused to accept any conditions and his behaviour drove the exasperated Addington into withdrawing his offer. There was talk of a coalition between the other factions, but no party was prepared to initiate negotiations. Since December, Georgiana had pursued a policy of inviting politicians from all parties to Devonshire House: 'We have every night a society in which there is often some of the cleverest and finest people of all parties – a little whist, chess, and very good music. In short it is like a large house in the country.'[52] The Grenvilles were surprised to find even the staid Addington attending one or two functions.[53] Georgiana hoped that overcoming the social barriers between the parties might enable some of the leaders to re-examine the political barriers. These informal gatherings also elicited much useful information. On 18 April Fox wrote to Charles Grey that he had heard an interesting piece of gossip from Lord Grenville concerning Pitt: 'I understood pretty distinctly from Ld G today that if P[itt] found His Majesty impracticable upon the idea of an extended administration, he [Pitt] should feel himself bound to try one by himself. These were not his words, but nearly the substance, and exactly the same idea that we hear thro' the Duchess of his having expressed to some of his friends.'[54]

The resumption of war in June broke the stalemate in Parliament. Georgiana found that the Prince of Wales now agreed with her on the necessity for a broad coalition. She wrote to her brother

51 GD to Prince of Wales, c. 5 March 1803, in Aspinall, ed., *George Prince of Wales*, IV, n. 1861, p. 553.

52 Chats. MSS, 1690.1, GD to Dowager Lady Spencer, Dec. 1802.

53 Philip Ziegler, *Addington* (1965), p. 181.

54 BL Add MSS 47565, f. 125, Charles Fox to Charles Grey, 18 April 1803.

and pleaded with him to come to London: 'I do wish you were here, as surely the moment of danger is at hand, and many people think the preparation inadequate.'[55] She was not alone in wanting some form of joint cooperation, she argued; the Prince of Wales was also keen to see him about this very subject. Georgiana wrote to Fox with a similar request from the Prince but met with a non-committal reply. He was willing to meet with the Prince, but wary of renewing old ties: 'it appears to me', he wrote to Robert Adair, who had also forwarded a request from the Prince, 'impossible that any good can come of it; it is, as the P[rince] very properly says respecting the war too soon and too late, too soon for anything like a junction of strength ... At the same time you may tell his R.H. that I am very happy to find that my general opinions are nearly the same as his.'[56] Although he had no difficulty working with Spencer, Windham and the Grenvilles, many of his friends loathed them and he did not want to provoke a futile quarrel in his own party. In his opinion, a union would have to fulfil three conditions: all coalition members would have to agree on the possibility of peace with Bonaparte; secondly, concert between the Foxites, Carlton House and the Grenvilles would only be provisional during the next session; and finally, the Prince would have to muzzle his pro-Addington supporters, such as Lord Moira.[57]

Nevertheless, on the strength of Fox's willingness to consider the proposal, Georgiana summoned Spencer to see the Prince. She wrote to him:

> Do not be alarmed, it is nothing immediate, but the prince wishes to state to you thro' me ... what has pass'd between him and several people and I want to tell you the substance of a letter of Fox's. The only use of this now is a future consideration that so far some concert may be established that nothing should arise before the next session to create new difficulties to a union of Talent and Respectability.[58]

She promised him that a meeting with the Prince would not be binding, and added that Fox had written her a candid letter expressing his respect for Spencer and Lord Grenville. The meetings were inconclusive, although Fox did seriously consider whether to take informal soundings of the various parties.[59] But he remained

---

55 BL Althorp MSS G287, GD to George, Earl Spencer, 6 June 1803.
56 BL Add MSS 47565, f. 224, Charles Fox to Robert Adair, c. 1803.
57 Ibid.
58 BL Althorp MSS G287, GD to George, Earl Spencer, 8 July 1803.
59 Charles Fox to Prince of Wales, 18 Aug. 1803, in Aspinall, ed., *George Prince of Wales*, IV, p. 402.

sceptical of the Prince's commitment to a broad coalition. He was far more concerned, he complained to Georgiana, with Sheridan who was trying to manipulate the Prince into supporting Addington.[60]

In October 1803, Georgiana changed her mind with regard to Pitt. Only the combined strength of Fox and Pitt, she thought, could dislodge Addington from power.[61] Addington's government owed its survival to the existence of a split opposition. But even though the Grenvillites were becoming disillusioned with Pitt, they were disinclined to favour Fox, nor would Canning and his friends consider acting with the opposition without Pitt's compliance. She had no choice, in her opinion, but to take charge of the situation before the Whigs lost another opportunity of building a new alliance. She justified her actions to her mother on the grounds of national expediency: 'We want strong, active enterprising abilities, we want men capable of great concentration and of firm and consistent principles. We possess such, but we do not make use of them.'[62] She was determined to halt what she saw as a decline in British politics, and began her new campaign by calling a party meeting at Devonshire House. Remarkably, instead of remaining quiet she gave her own speech on why they ought to consider a coalition. But it was an uphill struggle to drag the unwilling Fox to London. 'A summons to London. I suppose I must obey', he wrote grumpily:

> Tell me what time you expect me, for you do not even say whether morning or evening ... I dislike the thing more because I can expect no good from the P[rince], considering certain circumstances. I have not yet seen your speech, but the speeches of ladies can make no great figure now, because they can hardly ... be allowed to make use of the words Scoundrel, Bloodhound, Atheist, etc., which are the great ornaments of speeches on these occasions.[63]

Georgiana also secretly met with George Canning to explore the terms on which a coalition might be possible. Sheridan heard about it and accused Fox of contemplating a betrayal: 'Can you say upon your honour that *all those meetings between* Mr Canning and the Dss at D[evonshire] H[ouse] were not purposely to carry messages backwards or forwards between you and Pitt?'[64] Since Georgiana had

60 Charles Fox to GD, 12 Aug. 1803, in Vere Foster, ed., *The Two Duchesses* (Bath, 1975), p. 184. Also, BL Add MSS 47565, f. 96, Charles Fox to Charles Grey, 19 Oct. 1803.

61 CH MSS, J18/20/96, GD to Lady Morpeth, Dec. 1803.

62 Chats. MSS, 1742, GD to Dowager Lady Spencer, Oct. 1803.

63 Chats. MSS, 1741, Charles Fox to GD, 20 Oct. 1803.

64 Lady Bessborough to Granville Leveson-Gower, c. Oct. 1803, in Granville, ed., *Lord Granville Leveson-Gower*, I, p. 437.

deliberately kept Fox in the dark about her meetings he was genu-
inely surprised to hear about them from Sheridan. She had remained
silent about her surreptitious soundings with the Canningites until
convinced there was a genuine opportunity for talks. But once sure,
she urged Fox just to meet with Pitt and hear what he had to say:

> But Canning and my friends all think that if any one circumstance
> was to bring him into any kind of intercourse with you, he would
> fairly state his situation and opinions and would then not be able to
> retract ... As to Ld Grenville and my Brother, they are not only
> ready but anxious to join you and Tom Grenville I hear is as eager
> as he us'd to be in the days of old. After saying all this to you, pray
> dear Mr Fox do not think I am advising you to a junction with Pitt
> unless you yourself see the necessity of something being done ...
> Even if he only plans to make you the means of his return to power,
> I should not think that ought to deter you, granting that his senti-
> ments and opinions coincide with yours and that he is sincere in
> wishing for Peace and for that peace to be made by you.[65]

Georgiana excused her boldness with flattery: 'when I think the
country may be sav'd by a little exertion from the two men [Fox
and Grey] I think most highly of I should be a mauvaise amie and
mauvaise citoyenne if I did not tell you my opinion'.[66] Patriotism
was now her guide where deference to male superiority had led
before. As she put it in a letter to her daughter, 'a woman has no
business in these things unless very sure of serving La Patrie'.[67]
The recourse to patriotism cleared her of the charge of ambition
or indelicate behaviour. Yet she was careful to disguise her proactive
role in the coalition by keeping the tone of her letters meek and
submissive. She was particularly adept at using this technique with
the Prince, whose vacillating political conduct caused her much
anxiety. Employing a mixture of flattery and advice, she kept constant watch on him to ensure his loyalty.[68]

Georgiana's attempt to bring Pitt and Fox together illustrates
the subtle way she tried to direct politics without appearing to do
so. Having written to Fox, she turned her attention to the Prince,
and over dinner casually brought up the subject of cooperation

---

65 PRO 30/29/6/7, f. 5, GD to Charles Fox, marked 27th, c. 1803.
66 Ibid.
67 CH MSS, J18/20/96, GD to Lady Morpeth, c. 1803.
68 Georgiana knew how to appeal to the Prince's sense of importance: 'I am very glad
you are not in town. The whole of your line of conduct seems to me to have been as
prudent, as dignified and, I think, is likely to bring about some discussion highly to your
honour.' GD to Prince of Wales, c. Nov. 1803, in Aspinall, ed., *George Prince of Wales*, IV,
n. 1861, p. 552.

with Pitt. After a prolonged conversation he assured her he had no personal enmity towards Pitt, and agreed that 'no one party alone was strong enough to do any good, but that a union of all the great talents in the country was what he look'd to as the only measure that could be of any use'.[69] By the end of the evening, he was so struck by the idea that he authorized her to send a message to Pitt via Lord Granville.[70] Georgiana kept up the pressure when she went to Bath by reminding the Prince of his grand vision:

> I shall always think that the only place that could do good was the one you had, dearest Sir, last year, for you to have made yourself the centre of a coalition of all the talent and character of the country, for you to have assembled around you the Old Opposition, Lord Moira, the Grenvilles, Lord Fitzwilliam and Windham and have desired them to waive all old feelings and animosities. Nay, if under the principles laid down by you, Pitt and his friends had chose to join this view, so much the better.[71]

In the same letter she imparted some plain political advice: to wait until after Christmas to see how Pitt and the other parties behaved before he attempted to use his influence.

The new spirit of cooperation received a positive fillip when the Grenvilles decided to embark on a scheme of limited cooperation with the Foxites for the sole purpose of removing Addington. This small movement towards a union heartened Georgiana, who by January 1804 had begun to suspect that she was mistaken about Pitt's motives. 'Fox I know means to support Wyndham in the army business', she wrote to her daughter, 'Pitt is likewise come but I doubt his prevailing on himself to take a decided part. We shall see tomorrow.'[72] In the event, Pitt refused to attack Addington, which drove the Grenvilles closer to Fox. Georgiana was disgusted at Pitt's prevarication. Both she and Fox feared that cooperation with him would only be to his benefit. But as the king's ill health and the escalation of the war made Addington's position seem increasingly untenable, their distrust of Pitt lessened.[73]

Devonshire House bustled with visitors who came almost daily to discuss when Addington would resign. Georgiana even allowed

69 Lady Bessborough to Granville Leveson-Gower, c. 1803, in Granville, ed., *Lord Granville Leveson-Gower*, I, p. 451.

70 PRO 30/29/7/3, f. 30, memorandum by Granville Leveson-Gower.

71 GD to Prince of Wales, c. 24 Nov. 1803, in Aspinall, ed., *George Prince of Wales*, IV, n. 1861, p. 553.

72 CH MSS, J18/1/98, GD to Lady Morpeth, c. 1804.

73 Chats. MSS, 1769, GD to Dowager Lady Spencer, 25 April 1804.

herself to hope that Fox and Pitt would now assume power together: 'The part Mr Fox and Mr Pitt (whom I really believe is in concert) are trying to do is at least a noble and disinterested effort. For should they be called to act together it would answer the great and momentary purpose of restoring energy to Europe, and perhaps of giving us lasting peace.'[74] The reply to her hopes came on 29 April 1804. The Prince of Wales happened to be at the house as news filtered through of Addington's fall. 'I am writing in the greatest hurry and confusion', Georgiana wrote to her mother, 'for people are running in every moment – it is suppos'd that Ministers mean to do something today to prevent the great minority.'[75] The king asked Pitt to form a new ministry, but barred him from including Fox. Pitt unsuccessfully tried to change his mind, and then agreed to form a government on his own. Georgiana roundly condemned Pitt for his treachery: 'Should Pitt (which with my opinion of I should not wonder at) trick our friends, it is only what they expect. They have acted a most noble part', she wrote, 'in doing with their eyes open what is perhaps against their interests but certainly what they thought right.'[76]

Hampered by the lack of talent and a depleted side, Pitt pressed Addington to join his government. He also wooed first the Grenvilles and then the supporters of the Prince of Wales. But Grenville was adamant against joining without Fox. Desperate to shore up his government, Pitt concentrated on the Prince of Wales. In order to win his trust, he attempted to broker a reconciliation between the king and his estranged son with the help of three of the Prince's friends, Lord Moira, Sheridan and Tierney. Fox wrote to Georgiana in great consternation as soon as he heard of the move: 'From what I hear I suspect there will be some further attempts with respect to the Prince and that Tierney will again be at some mischief. The line is clear. The P[rince] ought to seem desirous of reconciliation but to distinguish in the most marked manner that he will not let the ministers be the channel.'[77] Since Fox remained at St Anne's Hill, Georgiana had to shoulder most of the responsibility for guarding the Prince of Wales. She wrote to her daughter:

> On Friday I was in town by chance when I received a letter from the P[rince] begging to see me at 5 . . . I was rather flurried at the idea

74 Ibid.
75 Chats. MSS, 1772, GD to Dowager Lady Spencer, 29 April 1804.
76 Chats. MSS, 1774, GD to Dowager Lady Spencer, 3 May 1804.
77 BL Add MSS 47564, f. 277, Charles Fox to GD, c. 1804.

of advising the P when luckily Mr Grenville call'd. I told him all my troubles on that account but that I should [illeg] Mr Fox's advice. Grenville very properly made me observe that it was too late, for that the message had come thro' the interference of a minister ... We agreed the best thing I could do was to send for Mr Fox. I saw the Prince that day for a moment and told him I should send for Mr Fox which he approved. He only told me that he had received an instruction that the K would see him but that he had stipulated before he would give his answer that it should have no reference to politics or be look'd upon as any concession to Ministers.[78]

Thomas Grenville remembered the meeting with Georgiana somewhat differently. According to his account, she had not asked his opinion when he arrived, but had told him that the Prince had sent for Mr Fox from Woburn.[79] The discrepancy between the two accounts illustrates how carefully Georgiana tried to conceal the true nature of her actions. Only to Grey did she admit that the decision to send for Fox had been hers. She had already written to the Prince, spelling out in clear detail why 'he should beware of shackling himself or being too much obliged to them [the ministry] for giving him power when they cannot perhaps much longer deprive him of it'.[80] Realizing how strongly Moira and Tierney were pushing for negotiation with Pitt, Georgiana countered with arguments of her own.

The outcome of the Prince's meetings with the king was beneficial for the opposition. Father and son quarrelled violently over the care of Princess Charlotte and Pitt took the king's side, thereby wrecking his standing with the Prince. On 21 November 1804, the Prince instructed Georgiana to tell her friends that all negotiations were at an end.[81] Fox was temporarily alarmed a few weeks later when it seemed as if Pitt might make another attempt. He wrote to Georgiana:

> I suppose it is not true that Ld Moira is coming again to town as the Newspapers say. When I saw the P a fortnight ago it seemed absolutely impossible that any amicable negotiation could be renewed. I should be very sorry indeed that it were, for tho' it could not succeed it would cause great scandal and of course do much mischief among our friends.[82]

78 CH MSS, J18/20/95, GD to Lady Morpeth, c. Nov. 1804.
79 BL Althorp MSS G55, Thomas Grenville to George, Earl Spencer, 14 Nov. 1804.
80 Durham University Library, Grey MSS, Box 11, GD to Charles Grey, 10 Nov. 1804.
81 BL Althorp MSS G287, GD to George, Earl Spencer, 21 Nov. 1804.
82 Chats. MSS, 1789, Charles Fox to GD, 11 Dec. 1804.

Fox continued to be uneasy about the Prince and relied on Georgiana to keep watch. With the coalition in place between the old and new opposition, he was determined to maintain a steady onslaught against Pitt. 'I am much obliged to you for your letter', he wrote to her in January 1805. 'I am afraid the Prince though much stouter than some Persons expected was not so stout as in my opinion it was in his interest to be. I hear however that in politics he is perfection . . . Pray give everybody you see notice of an active commencement of the session.'[83]

The year 1805 was to be the last of Georgiana's life. Although plagued by ill health, she exerted herself as best she could and Devonshire House continued to be known as 'le foyer de l'opposition'.[84] Her duties remained arduous, reflecting her established position within the Whig party executive. The activities she enjoyed most were those that ensured the efficient running of the party. This included acting as a conduit for the relaying of news and messages between members. She also rounded up the Whig peers to ensure they qualified to vote during each session, and notified MPs when their attendance was expected. Georgiana was even bold enough to become one of the party's chief whips. 'Pray speak to everybody you can to come down or we shall be lost on the Slave Trade', Fox ordered Georgiana in February 1805, 'Morpeth, Ossulston, Ld A.H., Ld H. Petty, all away. Pray, Pray send anybody you see.'[85] But despite their efforts the bill failed: 'The Slave Trade was lost last Night by 7', Georgiana reported sadly to Granville Leveson-Gower. 'Pitt was there, but his friends did not attend. Fox sent for Morpeth and Ld O., and I took them there and lost, by patriotism, the best scene of Young Roscius in "Frederick".'[86]

Georgiana also took great care to maintain the social side of politics by holding sumptuous dinners to fortify morale and breed an *esprit de corps* within the new coalition. The expectancy that power would soon be theirs was palpable on these occasions. After the vacillations of the previous year, the Prince of Wales gave his full support to the coalition. By chance, Pitt died in January 1806, just before the coalition could launch its major onslaught. Despite her disappointment at achieving victory by default, Georgiana had the

83 Chats. MSS, 1792, Charles Fox to GD, 7 Jan. 1805.

84 GD to Granville Leveson-Gower, 1 March 1805, in Granville, ed., *Lord Granville Leveson-Gower*, II, p. 34.

85 Durham Univ. Lib., Grey MSS, Box 11, GD to Charles Grey, 10 Nov. 1804. Also, Chats. MSS, 1820, Charles Fox to GD, c. Feb. 1805.

86 GD to Granville Leveson-Gower, 1 March 1805, in Granville, ed., *Lord Granville Leveson-Gower*, II, p. 34.

satisfaction of realizing her dream of a government composed of a 'union of all the talents'. The Prince confirmed its strength in a letter congratulating her that 'the most perfect good understanding and harmony, as well as firmness, exists between all our political friends'.[87]

Conclusion

The Duchess of Devonshire's career is a dual reminder that political activity is multi-layered and political influence multi-faceted. It reinforces the argument of the late Sir Lewis Namier and Richard Pares that eighteenth-century politics was broadly and fundamentally a social activity. Politics was as much, and sometimes more, affected by friendships, alliances, attitudes and the need to compromise as by events or principles. Eighteenth-century politics divided into some all-male areas, such as in the legislating of laws; and opened up to both sexes in others, such as in the management of borough politics. The divisions between the male and female spheres were not always distinct, and character and inclination determined involvement as much as custom. Georgiana tried to convey her own sense of the depth of political life in a short memoir:

> The intrigues and combinations of Society are more extended [than in France] thro' a vast city, and therefore are not so easily trac'd – yet many a faithful historian of the secret history of the times would have been and would be still a useful and entertaining compiler . . . I have been in the midst of action – I have seen parties rise and fall, friends be united and disunited – the ties of love give way to caprice, to interest and to vanity, and have often in private seen the repetition of scenes that wound up in consequence afterwards to its highest pitch.[88]

Fanny Burney once described Georgiana as 'the head of opposition public', the 'public' meaning politics outside Parliament. It is a title that broadly sums up the scope of opportunities available to élite women.[89] Politics was more than verbal jousting in the House of Commons; it spread through the streets and into drawing rooms, it invaded public assemblies and controlled invitation lists. People wore its symbols on their clothes and in their hair. Women partisans

87 Chats. MSS, 1802, Prince of Wales to GD, 1 May 1805.

88 Chats. MSS, 433, Anecdotes concerning HRH the Prince of Wales, Sept. 1782.

89 31 Aug. 1791, in Joyce Hemlow and Althea Douglas, eds, *The Journals and Letters of Fanny Burney (Madame D'Arblay)* 12 vols (Oxford, 1972–84), I, p. 49.

sparred with other women as well as with men. But during her 25 years in public life, Georgiana's views on women 'meddling' in politics underwent a subtle transformation. In 1784 she had justified her canvass on the grounds that she was following the Duke of Portland's orders. In 1802 she justified her striving for a coalition on the grounds that it was for the good of the country. In both 1784 and 1802, she invoked duty to a higher cause to absolve herself of the charge of that most unfeminine of attributes: personal ambition. But the difference between the two events was that in 1804 it was Georgiana who decided for herself what direction her patriotism would take. By treading a careful course, which betrayed neither her ambitions nor her conscience, Georgiana fashioned a new role for herself that took her to the highest level of eighteenth-century politics.

PART FOUR

Periodicals and the printed image

Plate 1   *Tête-à-tête* portraits of Signiora G–i and the Marquis of Granby, *Town and Country Magazine*, Jan. 1770, opp. p. 9. The Bodleian Library, University of Oxford, shelfmark Hope adds. 468–477.

CHAPTER NINE

Keeping up with the Bon Ton: the Tête-à-Tête series in the Town and Country Magazine

CINDY M^cCREERY

In January 1783 the editors of the *Town and Country Magazine* introduced their *tête-à-tête* history of the affair between Lord Hinchinbroke
and the actress Mrs Wilson in the following self-congratulatory manner: 'We have been peculiarly happy at the opening of this Literary
Campaign, in being enabled to usher to our readers two well-known
characters in the annals of gallantry, who now attract the chief
attention of the *Bon Ton*, and are the immediate subject of conversation at all the polite tea-tables about town.'[1] Three aspects of
the editors' comment are revealing: firstly, the emphasis on the
timeliness of the report, which allegedly relates to a brand-new love
affair; secondly, the deliberate invocation of both high society – the
Bon Ton – and a more middling social group, whose predilection
for exchanging gossip across the 'polite tea-tables about town' recalls
Addison's image of the readership of *The Spectator*; and thirdly, and
perhaps most importantly, the allusion to a 'Literary Campaign' to
track down and record the activities of men and women who have
caught the public's attention.[2] These three aspects of the *tête-à-tête*
– its topicality, its appeal to both fashionable and middle-class elements of society, and its place within an ongoing commentary on
gender roles and relations between the sexes – explain its remarkable success in the highly changeable world of gossip columns, and

1 'Histories of the Tête-à-Tête annexed: or Memoirs of The Generous Gallant and Mrs.
W–n', *Town and Country Magazine; or Universal repository of knowledge, instruction, and entertainment* Jan. 1783, p. 9. All references are to the *Town and Country Magazine* unless
otherwise stated. Subsequent references to *tête-à-têtes* will give the publication date and
page number only. Other sections of the *Town and Country Magazine* will be specified.
2 *The Spectator*, No. 10 [Joseph Addison], 12 March 1711, ed. with an introd. and notes
by Donald F. Bond, 5 vols (Oxford, 1965; reprinted 1987), I, p. 44.

reflect eighteenth-century society's preoccupation with comparing individuals' private lives with their public characters.

The 'Histories of the Tête-à-Tête annexed: or Memoirs of . . .' series was published in each issue of the London-based *Town and Country Magazine* between 1769 and 1792 (one per month, plus an end-of-year supplement, for a total of thirteen issues per year).[3] Each *tête-à-tête* consisted of a pair of double oval portraits of a man and a woman, accompanied by an article or 'history' of the heroine's and/or hero's romantic and sexual history. The article usually concluded with a description of the hero's current romantic relationship and often gave an estimate of its likely duration.[4] The series embodied both the literal and figurative definitions of the term '*tête-à-tête*'. The illustrations showed the man and woman literally 'head to head', and the articles described their intimate '*tête-à-tête*' meetings. Although a convenient term to describe both the physical juxtaposition and metaphorical relationship of man and woman, the term '*tête-à-tête*' was probably also chosen for its French origins. Indeed, the series is filled with foreign, and in particular French and Italian, terms, which are employed to emphasize both the artificiality and corruption of contemporary English manners.[5]

The *tête-à-têtes'* combination of graphic and written satire was unique in late eighteenth-century English publishing history. The list of individuals featured in the *tête-à-têtes* over its 24-year run resembles a 'who's who' of late eighteenth-century England, with royalty, politicians, clergymen, army and naval officers, aldermen, lawyers, actresses, singers, dancers, brewers and, in particular, male and female aristocrats, all well represented. The *tête-à-têtes* are important not just for the diversity of social ranks included, but for the variety of the pairings. While most *tête-à-têtes* described combinations of aristocratic men with middle- or lower-class women who acted, either temporarily or on a permanent basis, as paid mistresses, there were exceptions to this rule. Nor were all aristocratic male/ lower-class female combinations represented in the same way. The *tête-à-têtes* provide valuable insight into the degree to which gender and social status influenced both visual and written representations

3 There were two exceptions to this rule. The 1772 volume had two supplements for a total of fourteen issues and fourteen *tête-à-têtes;* conversely there was no supplement in the 1792 volume and thus only twelve *tête-à-têtes.* Dec. 1792 was the last issue to contain a *tête-à-tête.* The total number of *tête-à-têtes* published in the *Town and Country Magazine* in the period 1769–92 was 312.

4 See Plates 1–3 in this chapter: Jan. 1770, opp. p. 9, May 1782, opp. p. 233 and Nov. 1790, opp. p. 483.

5 See Sept. 1774, p. 457; Feb. 1776, p. 66.

in eighteenth-century England. Despite the long run of this remarkable social chronicle – 312 *tête-à-têtes* were issued in all – the high proportion of aristocratic or socially prominent figures depicted, and the relatively large circulation of the *Town and Country Magazine*, few scholars seem to have considered the *tête-à-têtes* worthy of further examination.[6]

Construction of the tête-à-têtes

The *Town and Country Magazine* was published by Archibald Hamilton junior, son of the influential editor of the *Middlesex Journal*, from its first issue in January 1769 until December 1791, and thereafter by a series of publishers until it ceased publication after the August 1795 issue. The magazine was sold by a variety of booksellers in London, Manchester, Newcastle, Dublin, Cork, Edinburgh and 'all other Booksellers in Great Britain and Ireland'.[7] As with most eighteenth-century periodicals, information about circulation figures is sketchy, and is made more complex by the contemporary practice of multiple readers perusing a single copy of the magazine. The *Town and Country Magazine* editors' boast in 1769 of monthly sales exceeding 11,000 copies and, through shared copies, a total readership of 30,000, is undoubtedly an exaggeration; a more reasonable estimate would put monthly sales at 2,000–3,000 copies, with a readership of double that figure. This would place the *Town and Country Magazine* below the market leader, the *Gentleman's Magazine*, but ahead of the more specialized and salacious periodicals such as the *Rambler's Magazine*.[8]

6 Discussion has been largely limited to a series of enquiries and responses in *Notes and Queries*. This interchange was dominated by F.G. Stephens and, in particular, Horace Bleackley, who persuasively argued for the accuracy of many of the articles and identified most of their subjects. See *Notes and Queries* 2nd series vi (1858), pp. 190, 337; 3rd series iv (1863), pp. 476, 528; x (1866), p. 187; 7th series iii (1886), pp. 287, 419; v (1888), p. 488; vi (1888), pp. 10, 136, 175; vii (1889), p. 55; 9th series iii (1899), p. 77 and esp. 10th series iv (1905), pp. 241–2, 342–4, 462–4, 522–3. See also F.G. Stephens (vols I–IV) and M.D. George (vols V–XI), *Catalogue of Political and Personal Satires Preserved in the Department of Print and Drawings in the British Museum* 11 vols (1870–1954), V, pp. xi–xxxix.

7 See the Tables of Contents pages in the *Town and Country Magazine*, 1769–95. I have found no issues of the *Town and Country Magazine* appearing after Aug. 1795, but Walter Graham, in *English Literary Periodicals* (New York, 1930), p. 180, claims that the magazine continued until Dec. 1796. See Table of Contents, Oct. 1771.

8 Supp. 1769, p. 673. For circulation estimates of magazines, see Roy Porter, *English Society in the Eighteenth Century* (1982), pp. 251–2; and James M. Kuist, *The Nichols File of* The Gentleman's Magazine: *Attributions of Authorship and Other Documentation in Editorial Papers at the Folger Library* (Madison, WI, and London, 1982), pp. 3–5.

According to convention, the *Town and Country Magazine* was 'conducted' by a Mr Beaufort, who frequented a coffee-house near St John's Gate (where the magazine was printed) and who edited the *tête-à-têtes* with an Italian Count Car[r]ac[c]ioli, but there is no concrete proof of such an arrangement.[9] In any case, the *tête-à-tête* articles seem to have often been the complete or partial work of anonymous correspondents who were also readers of the magazine, which were then revised by the editors. By contrast, the portraits were apparently the work of at least one professional engraver who seems to have often copied existing portraits or miniatures, which were either submitted by the correspondents or obtained, perhaps even commissioned, by the editors.[10]

The 'Acknowledgments to our Correspondents' page at the front of each issue of the *Town and Country Magazine* reveals a regular exchange of manuscripts submitted by hopeful correspondents to the editors. The editors' lively and witty responses to would-be contributors in the 1770s suggest that they were operating from a position of strength, and had their pick of a range of subjects. By the late 1780s and early 1790s, however, the number of contributions had apparently dwindled, as had the liveliness of the editors' responses. By 1792, the editors appear to have been far less discriminating in their judgement of manuscripts, and the quality of the articles declined, becoming less eloquent and interesting.[11]

The editors welcomed *tête-à-têtes* from abroad, and in general *tête-à-têtes* on new subjects.[12] They carefully presented the *tête-à-têtes* as the product of many readers' curiosity and knowledge, and as legitimate expressions of public interest in, and opinions of, others' behaviour. Curiosity and entertainment were probably the most common motives for submissions and requests, but revenge was another possible motive. Literary references frequently portray the *tête-à-têtes* as a vehicle for retaliation. For instance, the dissolute Lady Delacour in Maria Edgeworth's novel *Belinda* worries that her enemy, Mrs Luttridge, will avenge herself through a *tête-à-tête*.[13] Revenge does seem to have been a possible motive in the *tête-à-tête* published on Horace Walpole and the actress Catherine 'Kitty' Clive

9 See Bleackley, *Notes and Queries*, 10th series iv (1905), pp. 241–2; E.H.W. Meyerstein, *A Life of Thomas Chatterton* (1930), pp. 353, 376; and, citing a note of Revd Michael Lort (Bristol Central Library, 11457), p. 404.

10 See 'Acknowledgments to our Correspondents', Nov. 1776 and Jan. 1775.

11 See 'Acknowledgments to our Correspondents', 1769–92, esp. Feb. 1776.

12 'Acknowledgments to our Correspondents', March 1773.

13 Maria Edgeworth, *Belinda* ed. Eiléan ní Chuillean á in (1801; reprinted 1993), p. 276.

in December 1769.[14] Whether or not the article was written by the young poet, Thomas Chatterton, in response to Walpole's refusal to accept Chatterton's spurious Thomas Rowley manuscripts as genuine, the *tête-à-tête* does suggest the author's malicious intent.[15] The *tête-à-tête* professes to clear Walpole's name of a '*certain crime*' (sodomy) by citing his apparent affair with Clive as proof of the impossibility of such an accusation.[16] This rhetorical strategy merely strengthens the accusation of homosexuality, while also misrepresenting Walpole's close friendship with Clive. The fact that this 1769 *tête-à-tête* was mentioned in a 1782 letter from a friend to Walpole suggests that *tête-à-têtes* were still circulating and considered noteworthy years after publication.[17] Similarly the *tête-à-tête* on Count Haslang, which represented him as unscrupulously running up huge bills with tradesmen which he never intended to pay, was perceived as an 'atrocious calumny' on the subject by one correspondent, 'D.M.', who was probably a friend of, or possibly even, the Count himself.[18]

It is possible that the editors permitted wholly fictional *tête-à-têtes* to be inserted to maintain reader interest. Certainly many popular writers such as Richard Brinsley Sheridan claimed that the *tête-à-têtes* described fictional affairs. In the opening scene of Sheridan's 1777 comedy *The School for Scandal,* the appropriately named Snake describes how he has more than once discovered the equally well named Mrs Clackit 'causing a Tête-à-Tête in the Town and Country Magazine – when the Parties perhaps have never seen each other's Faces before in the course of their Lives'.[19] Similarly, in the first act of Hannah Cowley's 1781 comedy *The Belle's Stratagem,* Crowquil, 'the gentleman who writes the *tete-a-tetes* in the magazines', introduces himself to a young nobleman's porter. The porter replies excitedly, 'Oh, oh, what! you are the fellow that has folks nose to nose in your sixpenny cuts, that never met any where else.'[20] Although these examples demonstrate that the allegation that the *tête-à-têtes* were

14 Dec. 1769, pp. 617–20.

15 Revd William Cole to Horace Walpole, 29 June 1782, in W.S. Lewis, ed., *The Yale Edition of Horace Walpole's Correspondence,* 48 vols (London, Oxford and New Haven, CT, 1937–83), II, p. 330; see also Meyerstein, *Life of Chatterton,* p. 272.

16 Dec. 1769, p. 618.

17 'Rev'd William Cole to Horace Walpole, 29 June 1782', in Lewis, ed. *Walpole's Correspondence* II, p. 330.'

18 Oct. 1770, pp. 513–20; 'To the Printer of the Town and Country Magazine', Nov. 1770, pp. 601–2.

19 Richard Brinsley Sheridan, *The School for Scandal* (1777), I, i, lines 23–5, in Cecil Price, ed., *The Dramatic Works of Richard Brinsley Sheridan* 2 vols (Oxford, 1973), I, p. 359.

20 Hannah Cowley, *The Belle's Stratagem* (Dublin, 1781), I, ii, p. 7.

fictional was widely repeated, it was refuted by the editors. They vigorously denied Sheridan's accusation, and while they printed the letter denouncing the *tête-à-tête* on Count Haslang, they did not retract their story.[21] In Cowley's play, Crowquil rejects this charge of fabrication and points to a more plausible scenario – servants revealing information about their masters or mistresses in exchange for money. This idea of servants betraying their employers' secrets to magazines is but one example of more widespread concern about servants' loyalty to their employers. More broadly, these literary references indicate that the *tête-à-têtes* were perceived as an important and widely known form of social commentary by contemporaries.[22]

While eager to publicize affairs, the editors also seem to have been keen to maintain their self-professed reputation for accuracy – or at least to be seen trying. The editors frequently criticized submissions for being unsubstantiated, fictional or, alternatively, for concentrating on obscure individuals. Publication was frequently made contingent on alterations and substantiation; both editors and authors revised *tête-à-têtes*.[23]

Although the editors' practice of keeping their own identities and those of their correspondents secret was customary for eighteenth-century periodicals and was designed to permit a variety of correspondents, including women, to contribute on an equal footing without fear of personal criticism, it also protected the editors. While the annual editorial address frequently drew attention to the objections made against the editors, and the difficulties of their endeavour, there were few direct references to libel.[24] Perhaps the most reliable evidence of all about the limited impact of libel cases was the continued publication of the *tête-à-têtes* over 24 years: whatever the costs of libel cases, if they occurred at all, they were clearly outweighed by the profits accrued from publishing the *tête-à-têtes*. Indeed, a frontispiece to the *Town and Country Magazine* mocking a woman's anger at recognizing herself in a *tête-à-tête* suggests that the editors viewed such responses with humour rather than fear.[25]

While the editors' concern about protests and possible legal action often appears sincere, their standards of accuracy in the narratives

21 May 1777, p. 233; and 'To the Printer of the Town and Country Magazine', Nov. 1770, pp. 601–2.
22 See Paul Langford, *A Polite and Commercial People: England, 1727–1783* (Oxford, 1989), pp. 118–20.
23 'Acknowledgments to our Correspondents', Jan. 1774, Feb. 1776, Jan. 1775.
24 See 'Address of the Proprietors of the Town and Country Magazine to their Readers' (1777), pp. iii–iv; 'Acknowledgments to our Correspondents', Dec. 1773, April 1792.
25 Frontispiece (1780).

vary greatly. The *tête-à-têtes* were often only partly accurate, and occasionally completely inaccurate.[26] Yet rather than being considered as completely fictitious accounts of two people who had never met, dubious articles should perhaps rather be viewed as, for the most part, exaggerations of existing relationships; thus, the *tête-à-tête* on Horace Walpole transformed a well-documented friendship into a romance.[27] While the subjects might well bemoan these misrepresentations, such titbits were obviously appreciated by readers. It may well be that contemporaries read the *tête-à-têtes* more for the general flavour they provided of the glamorous social life of the *bon ton* than for accurate details about who was seeing whom.

Function of the tête-à-têtes

Although the editors of the *Town and Country Magazine* continually asserted the novelty of the *tête-à-tête* format, it actually drew on well-established conventions for representing men and women. The *tête-à-têtes'* pair of small oval portraits reflected contemporary enthusiasm for portraiture in general, and more specifically, for marriage portraits and miniatures. The late eighteenth century in England was, to quote a contemporary source, 'a Portrait-painting age'.[28] Men and women from the middle classes upwards frequently had their portraits painted to record key moments in their lives such as betrothal and marriage.[29] The small oval shape of the *tête-à-tête* portraits, and their position 'hanging' side by side on the magazine page, recall both the marriage portrait pairs hung in rooms (often either side of the fireplace) and the miniatures worn as jewellery or kept as mementos by both married and unmarried lovers.[30] The tender facial expressions in many of the portraits suggest that an apparently genuine love existed between the two individuals.[31] The

26 See May 1773, p. 238; Nov. 1785, p. 569; Supp. 1785, p. 681.

27 Dec. 1769, pp. 617–20, and Revd William Cole to Horace Walpole, 29 June 1782, in Lewis, ed., *Walpole's Correspondence*, II, p. 330n.

28 Anon., *A Poetical Epistle to Sir Joshua Reynolds, Knt. and President of the Royal Academy* (1777) [p. 1]; see also Marcia Pointon, *Hanging the Head: Portraiture and Social Formation in Eighteenth-Century England* (New Haven, CT, and London, 1993), p. 52.

29 For example, Sir Joshua Reynolds's portrait of the Montgomery sisters, 'Three Ladies Adorning a Term of Hymen', exhibited at the Royal Academy in 1774 and reproduced as a mezzotint in 1776, see Nicholas Penny, ed., *Reynolds* (1986), pp. 124, 262–4.

30 See Graham Reynolds, *English Portrait Miniatures* revised edn (Cambridge, 1988), pp. 142–3.

31 See Plates 1–3 in this chapter for a comparison of the juxtapositions of man and woman in the portraits. Note that while in the first pair the man looks at the woman, in

tête-à-tête portraits thus embody both the public declarations of marriage portraits and the intimate, often covert, nature of lovers' keepsakes.

The *tête-à-tête* portraits also reflect the influence of contemporary caricatures. Some of the portraits, particularly those from the mid-1780s onwards, depicted their subjects with sly, cunning, bored or complacent facial expressions.[32] Moreover, the juxtaposition of the two portraits side by side often encouraged satiric interpretations, as the sight of two different-looking and unlikely partners suggested that their relationship would not last very long.[33] Finally, the placement under the portraits of incomplete but comprehensible names recalls the practice in contemporary caricature of obscuring the subject's name to avoid prosecution for libel, or simply to increase the mysteriousness of the subject. The appearance of these names suggests, at the very least, some concern about the propriety of identifying romantic partners. Thus the portraits accompanying the *tête-à-tête* articles offered their viewers multiple ways of interpreting the relationships – as stable, loving unions, casual affairs, or even doomed encounters. Although the portraits usually suggested one interpretation, enough was left to the individual viewer's imagination to make the act of viewing the portraits an entertainment in itself.

The provision of portraits in every issue of the *Town and Country Magazine* kept readers interested and distinguished the series from the other purely text-based gossip columns, such as the 'Bon Ton Intelligence' sections of other magazines and newspapers.[34] Furthermore, the positioning of the *tête-à-têtes* at the front of the magazine, often as the first or among the first items, indicates how instrumental the *tête-à-tête* series, 'that leading feature', was considered to be in selling the magazine.[35] The placement of the portraits near the front of the magazine may well have been designed to attract readers' attention, to lure them into reading the accompanying article and, ideally, the rest of the magazine.

the second the man and woman look at each other, and in the third they look slightly away from each other. This may indicate the differing degrees of affection between the partners, or simply the preferences of the engraver. In the case of the portraits of the Marquis of Granby (Plate 1) and Sir William Hamilton (Plate 3), the original paintings may have determined the style of the engravings. See below and also George, *Catalogue*, VI, p. 715.

32 See Oct. 1785, opp. p. 513; Nov. 1785, opp. p. 569.

33 See the portraits in Supp. 1770, opp. p. 681.

34 See the 'Amorous and Bon Ton Intelligence, &c.' section of the *Rambler's Magazine* (1783–90).

35 'Address of the Proprietors of the Town and Country Magazine to their Readers' (1777), p. iv.

Moreover, including portraits of the couples described in the articles reaffirmed the connection between portraiture and biography. By seeing the individuals' faces, viewers gained a better idea of their characters than mere words could give. Some of the portraits, for example that of the Marquis of Granby, appear to have been taken from existing portraits and were good likenesses of their subjects; certainly the authors of the articles frequently claimed this.[36] One of the articles' most common claims is that the series' engraver copied the individuals' portraits, usually the woman's but sometimes both, from existing miniatures.[37] This suggests both the public nature of the individual, and possibly his or her acquiescence in appearing in the *tête-à-tête* series. Many of the portraits seem to have been intended as snapshots, like those taken of modern stars by *paparazzi*, of two people who were momentarily united, but who might soon split up. These portraits gave evidence of the couple's existence, but there was little to suggest a true union of souls.[38]

The portraits in these several guises may have interested some readers purely as visual material. Due to their expense, illustrations were uncommon in eighteenth-century magazines, with usually no more than two or three plates per issue; they were virtually nonexistent in newspapers.[39] Thus, any visual material might appeal to readers as a bonus. The fact that the *tête-à-tête* portraits followed the same format each month enabled readers to compare current issues with previous ones for aesthetic style and for updated information about headdresses and fashions. Although only depicting the head and shoulders of individuals, the *tête-à-tête* portraits did show off the latest hairstyles, necklines and ornaments of eighteenth-century fashion, particularly women's.[40] The re-publication of the *tête-à-tête* portraits and/or articles in the *Hibernian Magazine* (later known as *Walker's Hibernian Magazine*), roughly one month after their appearance in the *Town and Country Magazine,* may have been due to their provision of such topical information; moreover, the survival of

36 A comparison of the Marquis of Granby's portrait, Jan. 1770, opp. p. 9, with the engraving by François-Germain Aliamet (after a portrait by Sir Joshua Reynolds for Tobias Smollett's 1761 *Continuation*) suggests a common source. This engraving was subsequently used for a design on pottery, which indicates the popularity of Granby's image. See David Drakard, *Printed English Pottery: History and Humour in the Reign of George III, 1760–1820* (1992), pp. 151–2. See Plate 1 and also April 1770, p. 179.

37 See Oct. 1774, p. 515.

38 See Plate 3 and Feb. 1791, opp. p. 51.

39 See Jeremy Black, 'Politicisation and the press in Hanoverian England', in Robin Myers and Michael Harris, eds, *Serials and Their Readers 1620–1914* (Winchester and New Castle, DE, 1993), pp. 77–8.

40 See Plate 2.

Plate 2 *Tête-à-tête* portraits of Mrs Ellis and the Duke of Portland, *Town and Country Magazine*, May 1782, opp. p. 233. The Bodleian Library, University of Oxford, shelfmark Per. 2705e. 674.

copies of the *Town and Country Magazine* with one or both of the monthly portrait plates removed provides additional evidence that the portraits were valued in their own right.[41] In addition to being kept for information about fashion, the portraits may well have been pasted into scrapbooks or used to extra-illustrate bound volumes by collectors keeping records of famous people of the day.[42] The portraits, like the print series advertised in contemporary printsellers' catalogues, may also have been used as inexpensive room decorations.[43]

As interesting as the portraits were in themselves, clearly their primary function was to complement the articles. The articles varied in length, but were usually between two and three pages long. Even the shortest articles were longer than most of the gossip columns in contemporary newspapers and periodicals, which often allocated

41 Compare Aug. 1789, pp. 339–40, with *Walker's Hibernian Magazine: or, Compendium of entertaining knowledge*, Sept. 1789, pp. 460–1, and see George, *Catalogue*, V, p. xxx. The woman's portrait in March 1789, opp. p. 99, has been cut out of a volume of the 1789 *Town and Country Magazine* in the Bodleian Library, as have both portraits in June 1789, opp. p. 243.

42 See Pointon, *Hanging the Head*, pp. 53–78.

43 See *Robert Sayer's New and Enlarged Catalogue . . .* (1766), p. 99.

only a paragraph to an individual anecdote.[44] If the portraits were the hook that captured readers' attention, the articles contained the main substance of the *tête-à-têtes,* and often proceeded with little if any reference to the portraits.

While the portrait layout suggests that men and women were given equal attention, the articles reveal that men remained the more important subjects. The editors began the series in 1769 by noting the extraordinary 'gallantry of the present period', and expressed the hope that the *tête-à-têtes* 'will be the means of handing down to posterity a lively idea of the prevailing beauties, and their most zealous admirers, of this acra'.[45] Yet in practice it was the prevailing heroes, and only secondarily their female admirers, who were the main focus of the articles. This reflects not only contemporary interest in male biography, although this was surely part of it, but also the social distinctions between the 'beauties' and their 'admirers'. In general the women, especially mistresses, occupied a lower social rank than the men, which meant that there was likely to be both less information available about their family background, education and personality, and less reader interest in such obscure individuals. Perhaps because there was often far less biographical detail available for the women than the men, the authors of the articles frequently turned to the women's portraits to supplement their accounts of the women's characters. Thus, the author of the article on 'Lord Pyebald and Mrs M–sh' explains: 'Our engraver has given a very striking likeness of her face; it is therefore only necessary to say that she is about the middle size, much inclined to the *em-bon-point* [plump], without any thing remarkable either in her person or her conversation.'[46] Such a comment was less a criticism of the woman's blandness than an explanation that she was included in this *tête-à-tête* as a pretext to a discussion of her aristocratic lover's personal history. Many other mistresses were dismissed in the articles in like manner; without censure of their behaviour, but likewise without interest in their individual personality. Indeed, the appearance of a woman in a portrait was no guarantee that she would be discussed in the accompanying article beyond a cursory sentence. Much more often than men, women appeared in the *tête-à-têtes* as mere ornaments to their lovers, and as brief interludes in these lovers' long and varied romantic careers. Thus, Miss

44 See the 'Amorous and Bon Ton Intelligence, &c.' section of the *Rambler's Magazine* (1783–90).

45 Jan. 1769, p. 13.

46 March 1770, p. 123.

Matthews, the current mistress of the Earl of Ancram, was introduced as follows:

> To recite all the gallantries that have been ascribed to his lordship would form a list of the most celebrated demi-reps that have flourished for these last twenty years, from ducal coronets down to mop-squeezers. We shall therefore bring him acquainted with Miss M—s, who seems at present to be his only favourite.[47]

Male portraits were sometimes alluded to in the articles, as for example the Marquis of Granby's portrait mentioned above, but the articles usually spent far more time and space on the men's family background and career than on their appearance.

Men and women's differing social status was also reflected in the titles used to describe them under the portraits and in the articles. Men were usually identified by their aristocratic rank and then a fictitious, often humorous, pseudonym. Viscount Falmouth was called 'Lord Pyebald' because he apparently kept mismatched carriage-horses. Women up until the mid-1780s usually appeared with their correct, or at least their most commonly used, surnames pierced with a few dashes, ostensibly to protect their identity.[48] Thus, Lord Pyebald's partner was identified as 'Mrs M–sh', which readers would probably have deciphered as 'Mrs Marsh'.[49] Neither form effectively disguised the individuals, but they undoubtedly piqued readers' curiosity and encouraged them to read the article more carefully than if the full and correct names had been printed. This game of identifying the subject by filling in the dashes was commonly used in many periodicals, especially in gossip columns and political satire, but also in some private correspondence. Its use here suggests that the *tête-à-têtes* were both attacking the individuals cited and also protecting their identities, as well as protecting the editors from possible libel actions. The double nature of the *tête-à-têtes*, as enemy and friend, critic and apologist of the individual subjects was frequently asserted in the articles.

The *tête-à-têtes'* attitude to mistresses reflects contemporaries' uncertainty about their position in society. On the one hand the articles paid lip-service to the idea that women had more social respect to lose by sexual scandal than men, regarding the most fortunate

---

47 March 1775, p. 122.

48 Actors and actresses sometimes appeared under the name of a character they played on the stage, and occasionally other couples would be given romantic names: 'Palinurus' and 'Annabella' describe the Duke of Grafton and Nancy Parsons respectively: March 1769, p. 114.

49 March 1770, p. 121. See Plate 2, where the woman's surname is easily deciphered as 'Ellis'.

mistresses as those who were removed from London and established
in country cottages by their lovers, and the least fortunate those
who returned to London and the open market because their lovers
or protectors had spurned them or died. Young women who had
only recently begun their amorous careers were usually described
in a sympathetic way. Many were described as the impoverished
daughters or young widows of parsons, sea captains and army officers,
who had been tricked by stereotypically venal rakes or procuresses
into losing their virginity:

> Mary, for that is the Christian name of our heroine, was discovered
> in her rural retreat by an antiquated hag, who was proprietress of a
> brothel, and by the persuasion of her promises, backed with presents
> of toys and baubles, was reduced from the homely, but honest cot-
> tage of her parents, to an infamous habitation of disease and ruin in
> King's Place.[50]

Such melodramatic accounts echo contemporary conduct books in
warning women of the dangers of being led astray by their desire
for 'toys and baubles'.[51]

On the other hand the articles often dropped hints to help
readers guess the women's identity (or at least their surnames) and
treated their behaviour as mistresses as a necessary part of fashionable London society: 'a man of taste, to establish his reputation,
must have a mistress as well as a mancook'.[52] The very commonness
of these mistresses' surnames – Fisher, Green, Spencer, Watts, White
– whether accurate or not, contributed to the perception that these
women were interchangeable and, by extension, less important than
their male lovers.[53] This notion was reinforced by the language used
to describe mistresses. Mistresses were most often described by using
a relatively narrow range of adjectives and conventional phrases. In
fact, a composite woman may be formed from the clichés. She was
likely to be described as having 'coral lips', 'a row of regular ivory
teeth', 'to be inclined to the *em bon point*', and to be either 'a little
above' or 'a little below' the medium size (in height). The progress
of the relationship was likely to be marked by picnics at Windsor
and '*tête-à-têtes*' at Hampton Court, and the lucky mistress was often
reported to have been 'removed to a small house in New Building'
by her generous lover.[54] The *tête-à-têtes*' descriptions of mistresses thus

50 May 1786, p. 233.
51 Ibid.
52 July 1776, p. 345.
53 July 1769, p. 337; Aug. 1770, p. 401.
54 See March 1772, p. 122; Feb. 1776, p. 65.

varied between sympathetic reports of the dangers of an individual's career and stereotyped accounts of mistresses' physical attributes and daily routine. Such different versions were often contradictory and reflect the complexity of contemporaries' view of mistresses, combining sentiment and melodrama with curiosity, and even voyeuristic interest in the experience of women on the margin of respectable society.

More famous, established women, especially actresses and singers, aristocrats and widows, were also discussed in the *tête-à-têtes*, but less frequently than mistresses. This may have been because they were more discreet in their romantic affairs; moreover, there was less public acceptance of unchastity in women who were not professional mistresses. They were usually presented as the lovers of aristocratic men; in a handful of cases, including that of the historian Catharine Macaulay, their individual accomplishments overcame the handicap of their sex and they were treated as the primary characters in the histories.[55] In general, the tone of the articles was considerably less sympathetic to women who took the initiative in romantic affairs than to women who were led into vice through financial necessity or *naïveté*. Sexual scandal for married women was considered disastrous, although the articles often forgave wives such as Lady Sarah Bunbury who turned to adultery to escape brutal or indifferent husbands.[56] For men, the opposite was true: obscurity appeared to be a curse and publicity a boon. This double standard for the sexual conduct of men and women was openly admitted by the editors in the December 1785 *tête-à-tête*: 'We consider chastity in a man, if a virtue, as a very subordinate one.'[57] Like aristocratic men, aristocratic women were described more in terms of their family background and their behaviour than their appearance. Unlike aristocratic men, they were not permitted anywhere near the same degree of sexual freedom. It is thus not surprising that 'Lady Pyebald' (Viscountess Falmouth) was treated even more harshly than 'Lord Pyebald' (Viscount Falmouth) in her *tête-à-tête*, which appeared six years after her husband's.[58] Lady Sarah Bunbury, who left her husband and young child for a brief affair with William Gordon, was referred to

55 See Supp. 1776, pp. 675–8; March 1792, pp. 99–100.
56 June 1791, pp. 243–5.
57 Dec. 1785, p. 625.
58 March 1776, pp. 121–4. The Boscawens seem to have been a particularly decadent family, as a *tête-à-tête* seven years later (Oct. 1783, p. 513) apparently discusses the romantic adventures of George Evelyn Boscawen, fourth Viscount Falmouth, nephew and heir to Hugh Boscawen, third Viscount Falmouth and the hero of March 1770, p. 123. See Bleackley, *Notes & Queries* (1905), pp. 242, 343, 463.

as 'Messalina', the debauched wife of the Roman emperor Claudius; likewise, Lady Harrington was given the title 'The Stable-Yard Messalina' for her sexual adventures.[59]

But aristocratic adulteresses remained in the minority of women appearing in the *tête-à-têtes*. Actresses appeared more frequently: for example, Sophia Baddeley, Catherine 'Kitty' Clive, Elizabeth Hartley and Dorothy Jordan were all featured in the *tête-à-têtes*, and Mary 'Perdita' Robinson was the subject of two *tête-à-têtes*. It is difficult to measure the number of representations of women like these in the *tête-à-têtes*, however, as in addition to being the featured heroine shown in the portrait and article of one *tête-à-tête*, actresses, and indeed other women, were also listed in other *tête-à-tête* articles as being among the hero's past and present conquests. The fact that women were mentioned more frequently than men in the *tête-à-têtes*, but were discussed in much less detail, suggests that they were viewed as an interesting if secondary element of fashionable biography – rarely important enough to warrant their own long biographical accounts, but a crucial component of men's life stories.[60] Such attitudes reflected the complex balance of gender, social status and individual personality that formed contemporary women's identities.

Aristocratic vice, and in particular male aristocratic vice, was a major theme of the *tête-à-têtes* from the beginning of the series. Aristocrats could be singled out as exemplars of the general rot, or occasionally, as exceptions to the rule. Of Lord Foley, the editors noted with heavy irony: 'we do not find that he was tinctured with any of the most raging vices of nobility, which they soften with the appellations of fashionable frolics, polite pursuits, and elegant eccentricities. He neither gamed for the amusement of titled pickpockets, seduced his friends['] wives, or debauched their daughters.'[61] Although such explicit outbursts against the aristocracy or, for that matter, any particular social group were rare, attacks on individual aristocrats were often harsh. One hopeless case was described as follows: 'From such a stock, a race of heroes, senators and patriots might have been expected, but, "Oh, what a falling off!" There was indeed the procreation of the animal man, but without talents, without honour, and almost without integrity.'[62] Aristocrats were particularly criticized in the *tête-à-têtes* for behaviour that dishonoured not only

59 April 1769, p. 169; Jan. 1771, p. 9.
60 See May 1772, p. 233; Dec. 1769, p. 617; May 1776, p. 233; Dec. 1786, p. 625; May 1780, p. 233; Jan. 1781, p. 9.
61 Dec. 1784, p. 625.
62 Feb. 1791, pp. 51–3.

their own families and their rank, but the nation as a whole. The concept of *noblesse oblige*, if only used ironically, remained prominent in the *tête-à-têtes'* discussions of English society until at least the mid-1780s.

One of the central features of the *tête-à-têtes'* comments on individual aristocrats, and indeed prominent individuals in general, was the claim that 'an acquaintance with the private characters of great men throws such a light upon their conduct, as tends to explain the motives of their actions, and to clear up dubious matters in history'.[63] Beyond clearing up uncertain bits of history, an investigation of an individual's private life often revealed models of behaviour for others to copy as well as to avoid. The history of Lady Sarah Bunbury was cited as an example of both which qualities to avoid in a wife and how not to treat a wife after marriage.[64] Other individuals, such as the Duke of Rutland and his son the Marquis of Granby, were cited as true heroes to be applauded despite their romantic adventures and eccentricities.[65] Indeed, in many cases the romantic affairs of individuals were used as a foil to a discussion of their political, commercial or moral careers. Kind treatment of a mistress might alleviate a man's otherwise poor reputation, as the *tête-à-tête* on the Earl of Sandwich and his mistress Martha Ray demonstrates:

> In a word, he has made her a handsome settlement, and she so completely ingrosses his affections, and concentrates all his desires, that there are great hopes she will be able to soften some of the most disagreeable *features in the portrait* of her lover . . .[66]

Conversely, unkind or depraved romantic behaviour might reveal the hypocrisy of a seemingly moral individual. The editors repeatedly lambasted hypocrites and argued for more open discussion of individuals' private behaviour.[67] Hypocrisy was also the theme of the *tête-à-têtes* that appeared in the annual supplement issues of the *Town and Country Magazine* and focused exclusively on clergymen's romantic and sexual adventures. Although generally cynical about individual clergymen's morality, the editors used their presence to encourage others to follow those 'most elevated characters' who 'have thought proper to quit the path of dissipation, and prove to the world that they held in proper veneration the legal ties of

63 May 1773, p. 233.
64 April 1769, pp. 171–2.
65 Jan. 1770, pp. 9–11; Aug. 1771, pp. 401–5.
66 Nov. 1769, p. 564.
67 May 1774, p. 235.

matrimony'.[68] Whether the readers of the *tête-à-têtes* actually absorbed
moral lessons from these often playful anecdotes is of course open
to question, and certainly many of the details provided in the articles suggest that entertainment rather than moral instruction was
the primary objective; nevertheless, it is remarkable how frequently
the editors of the *tête-à-têtes* claimed moral instruction as a goal, and
how long readers continued to accept this justification for the discussion of ostensibly private behaviour. Morality was a convenient
theme that could be explored or ignored at will by both the authors
and readers of the articles, which could be used to express sincere
concern about the decadent state of society, to parody such concerns and, most often, to attack the hypocrisy of those social leaders
(clergymen, aristocrats) who espoused the importance of moral behaviour for others while behaving immorally themselves. Although
many individuals were forgiven their sins, others were lambasted as
poor examples for the rest of society, and their social authority
called into question.

There is little information available about how the *tête-à-têtes*
were perceived by their readers. The *tête-à-têtes* seem to have held particular appeal for London audiences. A puff for 'the Masquerade-
Subscription-ball, at Mrs Cornelys's, in Soho-Square' in London was
submitted to the editors of the *Town and Country Magazine* ostensibly because 'your curious Miscellany is so celebrated for the annals
of gallantry you constantly publish'; thus emphasizing the connection between the *tête-à-têtes*, gallantry, and London commercial
ventures such as the subscription masquerades at Mrs Cornelys's
house in Soho Square, the Pantheon in Oxford Street, the theatre,
or evening and weekend entertainments at Vauxhall and Ranelagh
gardens.[69] Although there is no concrete evidence available, it is
possible that the editors of the *tête-à-têtes* included references to
commercial London entertainments in exchange for a fee. Through
such advertisements in the *tête-à-têtes* these venues might attract new
customers, particularly those curious about the fashionable world.
On the other hand, since these commercial venues were widely
cited in the newspaper and periodical press in general, the editors
of the *tête-à-têtes* may have felt it necessary to mention these locales
in order to keep interested those readers who wished to emulate
the *bon ton*.

There are also several hints that the *tête-à-têtes* had, or were

---

68 Supp. 1772, p. 681.
69 'To the Printer of the Town and Country Magazine', May 1770, pp. 265–6.

intended to have, an audience beyond London. A letter to the *Town and Country Magazine* supposedly written by 'Astrea Brokage' evokes the image of a teenage Bristol girl eagerly deciphering the dashes in each month's *tête-à-tête* as a way of alleviating the boredom of her confinement in a boarding school.[70] The idea that the *tête-à-têtes* provided provincial women and girls with access to the social developments, fashions and ideas of the capital was repeated elsewhere, often to humorous effect. The provincial Mrs Hardcastle in Goldsmith's comedy *She Stoops to Conquer* explains how knowing 'every tête-à-tête from the Scandalous Magazine' helps her to 'enjoy London at second-hand'.[71] Literary references such as this suggest that the *tête-à-têtes* appealed in particular to women, in part due to women's love of gossip and scandal. The editors of the *Town and Country Magazine* themselves frequently repeated their gratitude to their female correspondents in the 'Acknowledgments to our Correspondents' pages, and at one point drew a direct connection between the large number of female correspondents and a large female readership.[72] A female readership was certainly considered important by the editors of the *tête-à-têtes*, and if not equal in size to the male readership, its expansion was certainly encouraged.

One of the *tête-à-têtes*' most frequent criticisms of the aristocracy as a group concerned their corruption of the lower orders. As early as February 1770, the editors complained that aristocratic West End-style vice had infiltrated other parts of London.[73] While sometimes the spectacle of London citizens imitating aristocrats was a cause for amusement, more often the *tête-à-têtes* viewed such behaviour as proof of the serious moral degeneration of middle-class London society:

> When we take a retrospective view of those citizens of London who raised that metropolis to grandeur and opulence, and compare their manners with the state of dissipation and extravagance, which, at present, almost universally prevails among their successors, who vainly attempt, by riot and profusion, to rival the nobility in the worst part of their characters, the contrast is truly ridiculous . . .[74]

Criticizing aristocratic and middle-class behaviour, even humorously, while at the same time maintaining reader support and interest

70 'To the Printer of the Town and Country Magazine', Jan. 1770, pp. 31–2.
71 Oliver Goldsmith, *She Stoops to Conquer*, II, lines 1–2, in Arthur Friedman, ed., *The Collected Works of Oliver Goldsmith* 5 vols (Oxford, 1966), V, p. 150.
72 'Acknowledgments to our Correspondents', March 1775.
73 Feb. 1770, p. 65.
74 Ibid.

was a tricky business for the editors of the *tête-à-têtes*. It may be for this reason that the articles focused disproportionately on humble stereotypical characters from the City of London. The dissolute nabob and the hapless alderman were often employed to make a point about the dangers of social emulation.[75] The cases of more genteel, middle-class West End families were largely ignored. The shift to discussing more humble individuals began in the 1770s and was in full swing by the mid-1780s. While this shift may be seen as partly due to a lack of sufficient fresh aristocratic examples to fill the space, a genuine interest in varying the subject matter and the increased publicity of adultery trials no doubt also played a part in this development. With the partial shift in subject matter, the tone of the articles underwent a significant change. Up to this point in time, the narrators of the articles had portrayed themselves as generally sympathetic to, and familiar with, their subjects, as the 1775 article on the affair between Lord Seaforth and Miss Powell indicates:

> In fine, they are, perhaps, the happiest couple out of the pale of matrimony, within the bills of mortality, and this alliance, which appears to have a very permanent basis, may be cited as one that does the least scandal to morality in the whole circle of polite gallantry.[76]

After the 1770s, however, narrators kept as much distance between themselves and their subjects as possible.[77] In place of the bright, clever narrative, a duller, more prosaic and generally negative style was substituted. The details of the adultery – for that is what these later *tête-à-têtes* tended to focus on – were related in a matter-of-fact way and there was little discussion of the individuals' characters or saving graces. The description of the end of the affair between Mr Quentin Dick and Mrs Anne Wood in 1786 is typical of the later *tête-à-têtes'* style:

> The injured husband being at last informed of his wife's conduct, and furnished with proofs of her disloyalty, determined upon a separation, and after the usual process in Doctors Commons, obtained judgment of divorce. Our hero also became disgusted, and the lady now remains a wretched sacrifice to her unchaste and loose appearance.[78]

The style of the engravings also changed in the mid-1780s.[79] The small, neat appearance of the earlier subjects was replaced

75 July 1773, p. 345; Jan. 1778, p. 9.
76 May 1775, p. 235.
77 For example, compare Feb. 1770, p. 65 with April 1791, pp. 147–9.
78 Aug. 1786, p. 402.
79 See Plate 3.

Plate 3   *Tête-à-tête* portraits of Emma Hart and Sir William Hamilton,
Town and Country Magazine, Nov. 1790, opp. p. 483. The Bodleian
Library, University of Oxford, shelfmark Per. 2705e. 674.

with a looser, larger-scale format, more conducive to physical caricature. Although more directly expressing the weaknesses of the
individuals portrayed, these engravings were discussed in the articles even less frequently than the earlier portraits had been. The
earlier link between word and image was lost. Furthermore, the practice of identifying women by their surname pierced with dashes was
abandoned. Now women as well as men were given humorous nick-
names: for example, 'The Consular Artist and the Venus de Medicis'
(Sir William Hamilton and Emma Hart); and 'The Premier Cit and
the Nonpareil of Portsoken' (William Pickett, Lord Mayor of London, and the daughter of a greengrocer).[80] This may represent a small change, but it was significant. It signalled the end of a
chivalrous tradition of treating women's innocence and vice as much
more important than men's. In the new system, female adultery,
while still considered worse than male adultery, was not deemed
worthy of particular comment or secrecy.

   With the 1791 supplement issue the portraits revert to their

---

80 Nov. 1790, pp. 483–5; April 1790, pp. 147–9. For the latter see George, *Catalogue*,
VI, p. 713.

original, less satiric style, and this persists until the *tête-à-têtes* disappear after December 1792. As M.D. George notes, these engravings were apparently made from the older plates, though the articles themselves, which mention recent events such as the provision for divorce in Revolutionary France, were undoubtedly new. It is unclear why old plates were being re-used now – it may have reflected the financial problems of the magazine or perhaps the second engraver was no longer available.[81] The articles had also become less individualistic and more generic. They no longer attempted a thorough discussion of individual characters over several pages, but merely summarized the conventional progress of an adulterous affair in a mere one-and-a-half to two pages.[82]

This lack of variety in the content of the later *tête-à-têtes*, with their repetitive focus on divorce trials, may explain their demise in 1792. The editors justified the end of the series as a response to reader boredom with the sameness of the *tête-à-tête* format, but distaste rather than boredom may also have been responsible.[83] Perhaps by 1792 the monthly discussion of what had become mainly adultery trials was seen as not just uninteresting but unsavoury; in any case, adultery trials were published elsewhere, thus tempting away the *Town and Country Magazine*'s readers. Or perhaps the deaths of the original editors had prompted the change in format. Despite the new editors' attempts to diversify their subject matter, the revamped magazine apparently failed to satisfy its readers. The *tête-à-têtes* had long been the hallmark of the *Town and Country Magazine*, and without them the magazine declined, disappearing after August 1795, less than three years after the *tête-à-têtes'* final appearance.

While the demise of the *tête-à-tête* series might suggest that by the early 1790s the public discussion of private life had fallen out of favour with the reading public, the success of the series over the previous 24 years reveals that for a long time such discussion was widely supported, or at least accepted. This success no doubt owed much to the *tête-à-têtes'* inventive format. The combinations of word and image and the focus on romantic couples rather than just individuals distinguished the *tête-à-têtes* from other purely text- or image-based forms of social commentary. But more remarkable than the format of the series was its content. The range of individuals featured was both remarkably broad and thorough for its time, and

81 George, *Catalogue*, VI, pp. xxv–xxvi; and see for example Dec. 1792, pp. 531–2. Thus Feb. 1792, opp. p. 37, uses the same portraits as July 1777, opp. p. 345.
82 May 1792, pp. 195–6.
83 'Address to the Public', *Town and Country Magazine*, Jan. 1793, pp. v–vi.

by including women as well as men the series implied that their lives were worth examining too. The *tête-à-tête* series served multiple functions and appealed to diverse tastes. It was both gossip column and moral commentary, light-hearted amusement and more thoughtful social critique, fiction and biography.

Such a range of functions indicates the multiple interests and sometimes contradictory impulses of eighteenth-century English society. The *tête-à-têtes* reveal that society's intense interest in social status, and in the way that individual romantic relationships expressed general truths about gender roles and relations between the sexes. Extra-marital affairs could be joked about and even openly admired, but contemporaries remained cynical about the role of love in such relationships. In such a competitive and observant society, romantic partners were considered to be an important part of gaining and maintaining social prestige. To some extent the *tête-à-têtes*' description of public figures' efforts to attract and keep famous romantic partners mirrored ordinary people's struggle to find appropriate husbands and wives. But such stories also appealed to middle-class readers' curiosity about an exotic sector of society very different from their own. The *tête-à-têtes* both satisfied and stimulated such curiosity, and encouraged those outside élite London society to feel that they remained in touch with its progress.

The *tête-à-têtes*' interest in aristocratic affairs reflects both outsiders' curiosity about how the most prominent members of society behaved, and increasing anxiety that aristocrats' bad example would be followed by those further down the social scale. As aristocrats were regarded as alternately the leaders and the corruptors of society, women were also viewed in different, even contradictory, ways. The *tête-à-têtes* indicate that, with a few exceptions, most women were primarily regarded in terms of their relationships with men, as mistresses or wives. Yet while gender remained the most important factor determining an individual's representation, women's social status and individual personality had enormous influence on the way their behaviour was interpreted. Aristocratic women were, in general, held to a higher moral standard than other women, while professional mistresses were initially both accepted and even admired. In the 1780s and 1790s, however, social acceptance of mistresses was replaced by criticism of their social function, and by growing concern for their individual welfare. Likewise, interest in marriage focused more on the benefits to society of happy unions than on the excitement surrounding the creation or destruction of prominent marital alliances.

Ultimately, it is this sense of connection between disparate groups and between the sexes – from aristocratic men and women to merchants and actresses – and of the relevance of their individual experiences for the rest of society, that is the *tête-à-têtes'* most telling comment on eighteenth-century English society. The eventual demise of the series should not obscure the fact that for 24 years the *tête-à-tête* series had demonstrated how much interest there was in keeping up with, and perhaps also keeping away from, the *bon ton*.

CHAPTER TEN

'A bright pattern to all her sex': representations of women in periodical and newspaper biography

STEPHEN HOWARD

... notwithstanding many women may at this day equal her in private excellencies, her literary abilities render her an honour to her sex, and give her that kind of preheminence, that is beheld with reverence and acknowledged with delight; for in proportion as the feminine character is amiable, so it ever more flies the applauding multitude, nature having pointed out the walk of obscurity as wisest, safest, best, to the generality of her fair favourites; but when we find an exception, as in the present instance, where to the domestic virtues are super-added the powers of uncommon perspicuity; we place it in the most conspicuous point of view, and unite astonishment to approbation.[1]

This brief passage, written by an anonymous author in praise of Mrs Macaulay, encapsulates the ambiguous position of the public woman in the eighteenth century: faced, on the one hand, with an expanding set of opportunities in the public realm, and, on the other, with the concern that she not be seen to abandon longer established female roles. It is largely this latter perspective that the existing historiography of the separate spheres model has chosen to emphasize, the period being depicted as a time when women were ever more confined to a private, domestic world.[2] This is not a vision, though, that contemporary newspapers and magazines necessarily reflect, particularly in the extent of their coverage of women. To take one relatively crude indicator as an example, the space London newspapers devoted to female obituaries increased

1 *LC*, 2 Aug. 1770.
2 See, for example, Marlene LeGates, 'The cult of womanhood in eighteenth-century thought' *ECS* 10 (1976); Leonore Davidoff and Catherine Hall, *Family Fortunes: Men and Women of the English Middle Class, 1780–1850* (1987).

tremendously even within the first 30 years of the century. Kathryn Shevelow reconciles this nature of disparity by arguing that the literature produced relating to women merely fostered their containment.[3] However, such a prognosis seems unduly pessimistic. This is not to deny that biographical accounts were to remain a composite, a product as much of the anxieties of their largely male authorship as of the female lives that formed their subject matter. Yet the substantial attention accorded to those women who had achieved a measure of public prominence demands acknowledgement. Furthermore, the inclination manifest in many of the accounts to focus upon women's domestic roles – itself amounting to a form of public recognition – was not necessarily the restriction it might at first appear. The purpose of this chapter will therefore be to question the validity of separate spheres theory as applied to eighteenth-century Britain, in an effort at the very least to refine some of the simplifications to which the paradigm is prone.[4]

The sources

This chapter covers a period from 1700 into the 1790s and employs a variety of sources, of which obituary is the single most substantial. Obituaries had first appeared towards the end of the previous century, and rapidly secured a significant and consistent presence in all the London newspapers. While initial examples were little more than death notices (confined to a line or two in length), the progressive growth in size of the papers soon provided scope for accounts of greater sophistication. It was the periodicals, however, that were to offer the environment most sympathetic to biographical material. The greater resources of space and preparation time at their disposal facilitated the publication of articles on historical and contemporary figures, in addition to straightforward obituaries. As early as 1701, John Dunton's innovative *Post-Angel* incorporated into each issue an entire section of biography and obituary, while, from 1738, no less a figure than Samuel Johnson penned lives for the *Gentleman's Magazine*. Later in the century, during the 1770s and 1780s, the biographical content of the periodicals enjoyed a phase

---

3 Kathryn Shevelow, *Women and Print Culture: the Construction of Femininity in the Early Periodical* (1989), ch. 1.

4 See Lawrence E. Klein, 'Gender and the public/private distinction in the eighteenth century: some questions about evidence and analytic procedure' *ECS* 29 (1995), pp. 97–105.

of further expansion, in both the existing titles and newcomers like the *Town and Country Magazine* and the *European Magazine*. Similar in many regards to the lives published in the periodicals (and sharing their concise style) were those written for the biographical diction-aries, which have also been utilized for the purposes of this study. The dictionaries ranged from pocket-sized editions to monumental multi-volume series such as the *Biographia Britannica*; and among their number were a few works of especial interest devoted exclus-ively to women.

Inevitably, the propertied classes constituted the vast majority of subjects, although the initial dominance of the aristocracy and gentry was swiftly eclipsed by the increasing numbers featured from the middling orders. In so far as obituaries were customarily the work of relatives of the deceased, authorship was similarly propertied in profile. Unfortunately, it is difficult to be precise over this mat-ter, since obituaries were almost without exception anonymous (as, indeed, were most biographical pieces in general). The correspond-ence with John Nichols, who as an editor of the *Gentleman's Maga-zine* had charge of one of the most important repositories of obituary, suggests that the majority of tributes printed to women were sub-mitted by men, commonly from within the family.[5] Alas, few contri-butions survive in their original form, making it difficult to determine how regularly women took responsibility for the obituaries of their relations; this, however, certainly did happen on occasion.[6]

Moralistic and didactic themes

If one theme could be said to dominate the biography and obituary of the eighteenth century, it would be that of moral didacticism, and the concentration upon the didactic display of virtuous ex-emplars was nowhere more intense than in the representation of women. In the majority of instances, no salacious tincture intruded. A eulogy from the *London Daily Post* in 1740 was typical, celebrating one Mrs Dyot as

> a Lady whom Providence had adorned with many good Qualities, which made her greatly respected by all who had the Pleasure to be

5 This was not always the case though: see Revd Dr Goodenough to John Nichols, 9 June 1794, Bodleian MSS Eng. lett. c. 356, f. 186.

6 See, for example, Lady Prestwich to John Nichols, 29 Sept. 1795, Bodleian MSS Eng. lett. b. 15, f. 5.

acquainted with her. She was a kind and indulgent Parent, a generous and faithful Friend; Compassionate to the Afflicted; but above all a pious and good Christian. She bore her illness with a compos'd Mind . . . The approach of Death, gave her no manner of Uneasiness, for she obey'd the Summons with a becoming Patience and Resignation to the Will of Heaven; and left the World with that Calmness and Serenity of Mind, which nothing but the Hopes that she had of entering into the Joy of her Lord could inspire her with.[7]

Similar items of praise abound: sweetness of temper, purity of heart, humanity, devoutness without superstition, piety without moroseness, and so on.[8] Although complaints against panegyrical language were widespread, women's accounts were not targeted, despite their being the most conspicuous candidates. Indeed, such protestations became assimilated into the rhetoric.[9]

The degree of wide agreement over which aspects of women's lives best merited commendation resulted in a corpus of biography and obituary that possessed relatively little individual identity. One piece was often indistinguishable from the next, a state of affairs reflected by the classification system employed in a work such as the Revd James Granger's *Biographical History of England*. Men were divided into some ten categories according to their rank or profession, while women were bundled together into one.[10] Furthermore, women's accounts typically lacked the chronological framework about which men's were generally structured. Even relatively sophisticated obituaries, for instance, often included no information of a chronological nature, but employed rather a thematic organization.[11] This seems to have been an inevitable function of the more private nature of women's lives during the period. Female obituaries, indeed, bear comparison with the Theophrastan character sketch, as they were not infrequently brief, simplistic and self-contained.[12] Clearly there was pressure encouraging the omission or (at the very least) exposition of even minor peccadilloes. An inclination on the part of Mrs Margaret Rogers to frown when expressing disapproval exercised the solicitude of her obituarist lest her character be misinterpreted: 'it was a pity it could not be concealed', wrote the anonymous author, 'for it looked like momentary ill-nature without

7 *London Daily Post, and General Advertiser*, 11 Jan. 1740.

8 For a typical example, see Mrs Hannah Waring's obituary, *GM*, Dec. 1783, p. 1065.

9 For example, John Wilford, *Memorials and Characters* (1744), p. 680.

10 Revd James Granger, *A Biographical History of England* 4 vols (1775).

11 For example, that of the Hon. Mrs Parker, *GM*, Feb. 1776, p. 75.

12 Sketches of individual character types, each embodying a particular characteristic – strictly, a failing. See J.W. Smeed, *The Theophrastan 'Character'* (Oxford, 1985), ch. 3.

being it'.[13] Dissimulation was preferable to the impression she had evidently created. Of the true nature of Mrs Rogers's character we can only conjecture; however, the remainder of her obituary offers sufficient clues to suggest a woman of self-confidence untroubled by an over-fastidious concern for the sensibilities of others.

Many biographers showed a marked proclivity to focus upon private, moralistic elements, even when dealing with women who had enjoyed lives in the public eye. A writer in the *Biographical Magazine* profiling Queen Anne concluded that she had been, in her public capacity, something of a failure: 'She was certainly deficient in that vigour of mind by which a prince ought to preserve his independence, and avoid the snares and fetters of sycophants and favourites: but, whatever her weakness in this particular might have been, the virtues of her heart were never called in question.' Her personal characteristics provided, then, adequate compensation for her deficiencies in office: 'In a word, if she was not the greatest, she was certainly one of the best and most unblemished sovereigns that ever sat on the British throne.'[14] We are left with the distinct impression that no more, in fact, was desired of her.

Circumstances were little different for women whose talents had secured them public recognition. Their biographers or obituarists would generally be enthusiastic to emphasize that they had not neglected established female roles: 'to the domestic virtues' of Mrs Macaulay, we are told, were '*superadded* the powers of uncommon perspicuity'.[15] Although the writer had already characterized her husband's career as a physician as work 'in a sphere less distinguished' than his wife's, at the end of the piece it is his public life and her private life that are extolled respectively as models for imitation. An advocate on behalf of Fanny Burney, defending the novelist against accusations that a hiatus in her publishing career indicated her previous work had been plagiarized, explained that, amid the demands of family life, it was quite natural her writing should be relegated in priority.[16]

Familial relationships were perhaps the principal means by which women's lives were defined. Admittedly, large numbers of women were simply presented in terms of their husbands (or, indeed, not themselves directly named at all), but many others were imbued with a coherence in their accounts through their portrayal as wives,

13 *GM*, Oct. 1786, p. 909.
14 *The Biographical Magazine* (1776), p. 66.
15 *LC*, 2 Aug. 1770 my emphasis. Similarly, see *EM*, Dec. 1785, p. 411.
16 Jeremiah Newman, *The Lounger's Common-Place Book* 2 vols (1796), I, pp. 89–90.

mothers and daughters – whatever roles they might have filled besides.[17] Family affectivity figured prominently in the typical roll-call of panegyric, and while accounts ordinarily opted for a certain reserve, there were on occasion displays of considerable sentimentality.[18] Indeed, recent scholarship in the field of death studies has, if anything, proposed a more ambitious time-scale for the establishment of the affective family than that originally envisaged by historians.[19] The celebration of conjugal happiness was especially pronounced.[20] Most of the sources promulgated a view in which marriage was as much dependent upon mutual feeling as prudence.[21] The *London Magazine*, to take one example, warned fathers against coercing their daughters into matches that were instead motivated by avarice.[22] The model marital relationship was a balance of affection with deference, and is well illustrated by a piece on the Countess of Orrery: 'It was a Pleasure to her to adapt herself to her *Lord's* sentiments [meaning her husband's]; and his Lordship could honour none with any Degree of his Friendship, but … [who had] Merit to recommend them to her Smiles.'[23]

The place for the celebration of female charms was, meanwhile, rather ambiguous. Reminders to the effect that not even beauty could defy the grave were by no means infrequent.[24] Nonetheless, in 1774 the *London Magazine* ran a series entitled 'Court Beauties', with each piece accompanied by a full-page engraving.[25] Obviously,

17 Cf. Cynthia S. Pomerleau, 'The emergence of women's autobiography in England', in E.C. Jelinek, ed., *Women's Autobiography* (1980), p. 38.

18 For example, Miss Charlotte Ackermann's obituary, *LC*, 1 June 1775. See also that of Mrs Eleanor Dornford, *GM*, Jan. 1790, p. 89.

19 Lawrence Stone, *The Family, Sex and Marriage in England, 1500–1800* (1977); Joshua Scodel, *The English Poetic Epitaph* (1991), p. 4; John McManners, *Death and the Enlightenment* (Oxford, 1981), p. 462: McManners argues commonsensibly that the potential for affection had always been present, and simply required an opportunity – in particular the improvement in mortality rates, hence the prospect of spending more of one's time with one's spouse and children – to release feelings of affection. Others works commenting on the affective family include: Philippe Ariès, *The Hour of Our Death* (1981), pp. 230–1, 471–2; Ralph Houlbrooke, 'Death, church, and family in England between the late fifteenth and the early eighteenth centuries', in Ralph Houlbrooke, ed., *Death, Ritual, and Bereavement* (1989), pp. 32–3; Philip Jenkins, *The Making of a Ruling Class* (Cambridge, 1983), pp. 255–63; Nigel Llewellyn, *The Art of Death* (1991), p. 121; Randolph Trumbach, *The Rise of the Egalitarian Family* (1978), p. 292.

20 See, for instance, Thomas Gibbons, *Memoirs of Eminently Pious Women* 2 vols (1777), II, pp. 455–62.

21 For example, *EM*, Jan. 1788, p. 5.

22 *LM*, Sept. 1772, p. 407.

23 Wilford, *Memorials and Characters*, p. 694.

24 For example, Francis Godolphin Waldron *et al.*, *The Biographical Mirrour* 3 vols (1795–[1810]), I, p. 29.

25 For example, *LM*, Jan. 1774, p. 3.

it was easier to celebrate this quality if demonstrably borne with propriety in the company of a range of other accomplishments. Consequently, the obituary of Lady Gerard in the *Post-Angel* assured readers of her decent attire and musical ability, as well as eulogizing her appearance.[26] Wit, though indispensable to the polite world, was handled with equivalent care. Obituaries in the *Gentleman's Magazine* began to draw notice to it only from the 1780s, alongside 'sprightly manners' and 'vivacity of spirits'. The key to approval was a 'proper' degree of self-regulation moulded by an understanding of female decorum: for instance, the case of the Countess of Yarmouth, whose wit the *London Chronicle* described as 'delicate and sprightly, but tempered with modesty, which, as it restrains her wit from any affectations of pre-eminence, so her sprightliness never degenerates into bursts of noise and laughter'.[27] Likewise, the time-consuming process of giving and receiving visits was ideally to be subject to self-imposed moderation.[28] Yet even the sternest moralist would be wary lest his message be seen to threaten conventional notions of femininity – foibles and all: one argued that women should not abandon all amusements lest 'such great abstinence from every kind of recreation might in some persons tend to sour the mind with austere and unamiable dispositions, or at least to depress the spirits to such a degree of melancholy as would unfit them for the necessary duties and offices of life'.[29] And if these hallmarks of leisured, fashionable life were subject to doubt, there was an accompanying determination to demonstrate that piety and morality were far from incompatible with wealth, status and sociability.

Outright criticism was relatively unusual in the accounts of either gender, but there was in particular a feeling that it would be 'mean ... [and] unmanly to calumniate helpless, unresisting women'.[30] Obituarists often simply opted to ignore the more dubious elements in their subjects' pasts. Generations of royal mistresses, for example, passed away without undue publicity. When revelations of misconduct did come to light, they were best forgotten. Of Lady Vane one writer observed, 'The misunderstandings, elopements, and various disgraceful situations to which she exposed herself during part of her life, are too well known to be concealed (several of them being

26 *Post-Angel*, May 1701, pp. 356–61.
27 *LC*, 10 May 1764.
28 George Ballard, *Memoirs Of Several Ladies Of Great Britain, Who Have Been Celebrated For Their Writings Or Skill In The Learned Languages Arts And Sciences* (Oxford, 1752), pp. 426–7, 449.
29 Quoted in Gibbons, *Memoirs*, II, p. 488.
30 Charles Pigott, *The Female Jockey Club* (1794), p. xi.

recorded in the Legal Reports), but may now, with no impropriety, be buried in oblivion.'[31] Other pieces were more forthright, as in the case of one unfortunate actress commemorated in the pages of the *London Chronicle*: 'It is sincerely to be wished that the truly wretched end of Mrs Baddeley . . . once well known in the vortex of inconsiderate luxury and dissipation, may make a proper and lasting impression on every female breast.'[32] Similarly, the demise of Mrs Cargill was cited as 'a melancholy proof that neither beauty nor talents, independent of prudence, can ensure reputation and felicity'.[33] Some periodicals, though, declined to adopt quite such a high moral tone. The *European Magazine* actually went so far as to declare that most fallen women were the victims of male turpitude rather than being themselves innately inclined to dissipation.[34] A piece from November 1785 in the same magazine concerned 'the once much-admired Ann Pitt, who, about 20 years ago, by the delusive promises of an Honourable Personage, forfeited virtue's dearest tribute: she soon after was discarded, and ever since has wandered about this neighbourhood, existing entirely by the casual hand of humanity'.[35] This was no doubt in part a warning, but the writer's sympathy clearly lay with the subject. Nevertheless, sternly critical pieces upon women, invoking a far gloomier assessment of female morality, were to persist.

The public position of women

To what extent was women's widespread presentation within such a narrowly domestic and largely moralistic conception a constraint? As we have seen, many biographical pieces had a tendency to concentrate upon private merit, even when documenting women with very public lives – a prioritization which could in some cases altogether obscure a subject's public character. However, in some cases outward obeisance to the standards of moral didacticism was clearly nothing more than the most meagre veneer. A collection such as *Theatrical Biography* from 1772 might have repeated ubiquitous platitudes upon female virtue, but in general displayed equanimity to

31 *GM*, May 1788, p. 461.
32 *LC*, 17 Nov. 1787.
33 *GM*, March 1784, p. 235.
34 *EM*, May 1782, p. 327.
35 Ibid., Nov. 1785, p. *396 (NB: some of the pages in this issue were numbered in duplicate; they have been distinguished by an asterisk).

the misdemeanours of the actresses whose lives it chronicled. Every cloud had its silver lining. To quote from the piece on Miss Hayward:

> Female errors are generally the inseparable harbingers of misfortune. Pursuits of this kind not only unhinge them from the affection of their friends, but introduce them to a scene of life so variously beset with alluring pleasures and dissipations, that it requires little of the art of prognostication to pronounce loss of character to be followed with loss of every thing else. Every general rule, however, has its exceptions; and the heroine of this page (however she might have been a greater ornament to morality) had, in all probability, never shared the notice of the public, had she trudged on in the humble line of her vocation.

The author makes a rather half-hearted attempt to establish for Hayward at least some moral credentials (however fragile), but takes no trouble to disguise the power with which her transgressions imbued her. 'Many *pig-tailed puppies of quality*', we are told, 'dangled in her train; – but . . . their solicitations were severally rejected. She had it now in her power to make her choice, and she was determined that choice should be totally to her mind.'[36] Hayward was certainly not the only compromised actress to have enjoyed a measure of success at the same time as avoiding condemnation. Others featured in the equally ambivalent portraits of the *Town and Country Magazine*'s *Tête-à-Tête* column, which each month provided a biographical double bill of eminent men alongside their mistresses. While the column's authors were by no means even-handed with the sexes,[37] their attitude towards the women they profiled was frequently one of humorous admiration.[38]

The very obsession with moralizing was itself attacked on occasion. Mrs Macaulay's biographer in the *European Magazine* noted that her work had recently been subject to fierce criticism:

> Perhaps there never was an instance, where the personal conduct of an author so much influenced the public opinion of their writings. We perceive no diminution of the powers she formerly displayed, and was allowed to possess, yet the ridicule which has been thrown out against her, on occasion of her marriage, has totally extinguished all curiosity about her opinions on those important subjects which she formerly discussed, with so much credit to herself, and, we think, with so much advantage to the world.[39]

36 *Theatrical Biography* 2 vols (1772), I, pp. 30–5.
37 *Town and Country Magazine*, Aug. 1770, pp. 401–2. See also Chapter 9, 'Keeping up with the *Bon Ton*: the *Tête-à-Tête* series in the *Town and Country Magazine*.'
38 *Town and Country Magazine*, Sept. 1770, p. 459; ibid., March 1770, p. 122.
39 *EM*, Nov. 1783, p. 334.

To assert that her private life was an inappropriate matter on which to judge such a talented individual was to treat her rather as a public man might have been treated: with an esteem which accepted that public achievement and private probity did not always accompany one another (though we should recall that illustrious men too could fall foul of those who insisted upon the absolute necessity of moral rectitude).[40] An essay on biography from the *Lady's Magazine* of 1787 is similarly revealing. Reading biography, the anonymous author insists, 'we . . . must, necessarily, feel some sparks of generous ambition in our breasts, and be animated to pursue those paths which lead to glory, honour, and immortality'.[41] While the piece may well have been taken from a source assuming a male readership, it was nevertheless considered suitable for inclusion in a women's magazine – and this despite the fact that it not only lacked a specifically domestic focus, but also evaded any explicit recognition of moral instruction as the fundamental purpose of biography. It is further interesting to note that an acquaintance with the lives of the great figures of history was deemed necessary for women as well as men. To quote Thomas Mortimer, editor of the *British Plutarch*, 'a competent knowledge of history in general, and that of our own country in particular, is considered a polite accomplishment; and a total ignorance of this branch of science is deemed inexcusable in the well-bred of either sex'.[42] William Mavor, editor of an equivalent work, *The British Nepos*, was able to boast of the praise his publication had attracted from the likes of the *Ladies' Annual Register* and the *Ladies' Museum.*[43]

Most authors were either quite content with, or perfectly capable of adapting themselves to, the orthodoxy on didacticism, due deference to which might comfortably be assimilated within even accounts whose primary interests lay elsewhere. The memoirs of Catherine Clive, for example, from the *European Magazine* of December 1785, united the necessary regard to an exemplary private life with a detailed assessment of the actress's stage career.[44] Nor should it be supposed that respect for the prescriptions of didacticism necessarily acted as a bar to biographers' choice of subjects: it was a matter rather of determining the means of presentation. Take, for instance, the case of Lady Augusta Campbell, applauded by the *London Magazine* as being distinguished from the 'herd of gay, dissipated

40 For instance, Lord Clive: see *GM*, April 1785, p. 200 [260].
41 *Lady's Magazine*, Aug. 1787, p. 425.
42 Thomas Mortimer, ed., *The British Plutarch* 6 vols (1776), I, p. vi.
43 William Mavor, ed., *The British Nepos* (1800), p. xvi.
44 *EM*, Dec. 1785, pp. 408–12.

women of fashion'.[45] Though touted as 'a model for imitation in these degenerate times', Campbell's primary allure was surely her position as an attractive face at court.

It has been suggested that women were actually to accrue authority from the publicization of their contributions in the private realm, especially from their role as a touchstone of morality for an otherwise mercenary world. Linda Colley has argued that women would fashion out of this rhetoric a means to assert their rights early in the following century, while Catherine Hall has used such an interpretation to elucidate the controversy that was to engulf George IV as a result of his persecution of Queen Caroline.[46] During the eighteenth century, we plainly see a colonization of the public sphere of print to celebrate the importance of female virtues – virtues which, while domestic in nature, could nonetheless cause a woman to be remembered as 'Not only a private, but a public loss'.[47] The insistent promulgation of this conception of virtuous femininity may very well have played a role in laying the foundation for a future assertion of female rights, particularly with the arrival of accounts which chose to emphasize the significance of women's morality to the public domain. In 1790 an obituarist of the Countess of Clarendon opined, 'As long as any country preserves itself pure in morals, and correct in its opinions, it will hold the domestic virtues in the highest estimation; but, if it should degenerate so far as to prefer splendid errors to the truth itself, such virtues, with every thing else most venerable, will gradually lose their honour.' The countess 'thought Religion the only source of private and public virtue', believing that 'the notion of the existence of public virtue, independent of the two former, was a dangerous error, productive of innumerable evils'.[48]

The virtuous image of women's nature could be exploited to powerful effect when placed in contrast to examples of male viciousness, as a pair of portraits in the *London Chronicle* of Lady Barrymore demonstrates. According to the first of the accounts to appear, Lady Barrymore had married her husband, the Earl, for love, and 'Doom'd . . . soon after to be the witness of his fashionable excesses', it was no wonder 'if with her *gaiete de cœur*, she for some time partook of

---

45 *LM*, June 1782, p. 259.
46 Linda Colley, *Britons: Forging the Nation, 1707–1837* (New Haven, CT, and London, 1992), pp. 273–7; Catherine Hall, 'The sweet delights of home', in Michelle Perrot, ed., *A History of Private Life* 5 vols (1990), IV, p. 49. See also G.J. Barker-Benfield, *The Culture of Sensibility: Sex and Society in Eighteenth-Century Britain* (Chicago, IL, 1992), p. xviii.
47 See, for example, Lady Delaval's obituary, *GM*, Oct. 1783, p. 894.
48 *GM*, Nov. 1790, p. 980.

them without reflection'.[49] Only subsequently did she come to repent of the wickedness into which she had been induced. A few days later, a second piece was published in answer to the first, declaring: 'Nothing can appear more strange than what the Author [of the previous article] . . . says, that she joined in all the fashionable excesses of her husband.' The character offered of Earl Barrymore in the process is unflattering to say the least. 'His lordship', we are informed, 'was an illiterate rake. . . . He very often beat his wife, and his usual amusements was to derange her dress, to tear her lace, only to have the brutish satisfaction of seeing her Ladyship in tears.'[50] Crucially, the wife is in no way compromised by her husband's degeneracy, portrayed instead as continuing to show him 'the utmost tenderness and affection'. Earlier in the century, women who felt abused by men had been handled with more ambivalence. To take an example from 1721, the misgivings of Lady Baltimore at her husband's conduct towards her are recorded, but further details were certainly not.[51] However, it would be premature to discern a distinct trend: women choosing to separate from their husbands were still prone to be regarded with incomprehension,[52] while even those clearly presented as the injured party were not always depicted as either moral paragon or helpless victim.[53]

From the variety of responses evident to the prevailing pressure to concentrate upon morality and domestic virtue, it should be clear that we ought to be wary of viewing the conservative nature of many accounts as necessarily indicative of a narrowing in women's sanctioned roles. This is all the more the case given the increasing attention devoted in the sources to women's public achievements. The progress made by women is perhaps best exemplified in changing attitudes to female scholarship and publishing, areas that generated marked controversy. Typically, the emphasis in the accounts was that education, while enhancing female virtue, otherwise left women fulfilling an unchanged position within the family and society.[54] Hence obituaries strove to demonstrate that learning did not induce a shrewish wit,[55] nor divert women from responsibilities such as charitability.[56] The possible impact on female piety

49 *LC*, 14 Sept. 1776.
50 Ibid., 19 Sept. 1776.
51 *Church-Man. Loyalist's Weekly Journal*, 28 Jan. 1721.
52 For example, Anne Viscountess Bangor, *GM*, Feb. 1789, p. 184.
53 *Theatrical Biography*, I, pp. 17–18.
54 Shevelow, *Women and Print Culture*, pp. 52–3, 174.
55 For example, Mrs Catherine Talbot's obituary, *GM*, June 1772, pp. 257–8.
56 For example, Lady Miller's obituary, *GM*, June 1781, p. 295.

also caused anxiety. When the correspondent signing himself 'W.B. Laicus' observed, 'We live in an age when religion is discountenanced among men of parts and education', it is clear that his celebration of women 'who, unattended by their husbands, are seen at church and at the altar' was contingent upon their lack of education, which had spared them the pitfalls of deism – and worse.[57] Furthermore, it was to remain prudent to guard against readers' apprehensions over the fate of bookish women. The author of Molly Leapor's memoirs recounted: 'So much indeed did she *read*, and so much did she *write*, that some of the neighbours observing her *writing passion* expressed their concern lest the girl should *overstudy herself*, and *be mopish*. But their concern was needless, for she was commonly rather a gay than of a melancholy turn.'[58]

George Ballard, author of the 1752 biographical collection, *Memoirs Of Several Ladies Of Great Britain, Who Have Been Celebrated For Their Writings Or Skill In The Learned Languages Arts And Sciences*, displayed the conventional enthusiasm that learning in women be put to the service of virtue.[59] Mrs Elizabeth Burnet, we are informed,

> was naturally inquisitive, her apprehension quick, and her judgement solid; yet she confined her enquiries to a few things: therefore when she had made some progress both in geometry and philosophy, she laid these studies aside, though she had both a genius and a relish for them . . . Her chief care was to . . . elevate her soul into an entire resignation and conformity to the holy will of God.[60]

Knowledge here, then, was not ostensibly to be a matter of empowerment. However, Ballard also insisted that learned women's contributions deserved public recognition, justifying his book on the patriotic grounds that 'England hath produced more women famous for literary accomplishments, than any other nation in Europe'.[61] His contemporaries, though, provided him with little but discouragement. One, Joseph Ames, warned: 'How you will come off with the Polite Ladies whose expectations you had raised, I don't know, for deferring the Book so long; 'tis tho[ugh]t by us men they are quick of sensation and never love to be neglected, if they are, they know how to resent.'[62] Ballard confessed in a letter to Charles Lyttelton:

57 *GM*, Feb. 1786, p. 126.
58 *Lady's Magazine*, Dec. 1779, p. 639.
59 Ballard, *Memoirs*, p. 409.
60 Ibid., p. 405.
61 Ibid., p. vi.
62 Joseph Ames to George Ballard, 25 February 1752, Bodl. MS Ballard 40, f. 240.

I have lately been mightily discouraged from proceeding in my account of the Learned & Virtuous of the fair sex by a Gentleman of distinction . . . who having ask'd me how I went on with my Learn'd Ladys, among other things told me he did not know of above one or two that deserv'd to be taken notice of. That he knew several of good Parts etc. but then they had *Modesty* enough to keep their Productions at Home; and that those who had ventur'd 'em abroad seldom met with success.

This gave Ballard some confusion, as

it came from one to whose Judgement I paid a very great deference, (& who had likewise publickly recommended useful learning to the Ladys) . . . if we have not above one or two Ladys worthy to be taken notice of, I must consequently be a very stupid Blockhead to put myself to so much Expence, & to lavish away so much Time & Pains to so little Purpose.[63]

Unfortunately, it seems that Ballard was persuaded to omit a polemical introduction berating the abuse that learned women had experienced at male hands.[64]

Male suspicion of female learning and writing was to persist alongside the evolution of more enlightened opinions. The resulting ambivalence is illustrated in the contrasting treatments afforded to Mrs Catherine Talbot, an author who died in January 1770. Her obituary from the *Public Advertiser* was comparatively lengthy, but bestowed largely upon details of her male relations. It included no hint that she was a writer.[65] An article in the *Gentleman's Magazine*, by comparison, chose to focus upon her literary attainments.[66] The author, who was designated 'a LADY',[67] noted that Talbot could, with her gifts, have wittily mocked others, but 'from principle, suppressed this power'. Eschewing this male vice, she wrote instead to investigate the workings of the human heart. Her biographer moreover declared that women in general were too sensitive about criticisms of their published work. She was particularly harsh on an unnamed individual to whom Talbot had submitted her work for

---

63 Charles Lyttelton to George Ballard, n.d., c. 1744, Bodl. MS Ballard 42, ff. 29d.–30.
64 Ruth Perry, 'George Ballard's biographies of learned ladies', in John D. Browning, ed., *Biography in the 18th Century. Publications of the McMaster University Association for 18th-Century Studies* 8 (1980), p. 93; William Parry to George Ballard, 12 Feb. 1742–3, Bodl. MS Ballard 40, ff. 158d.–9.
65 *Public Advertiser*, 12 Jan. 1770.
66 *GM*, June 1772, pp. 257–8.
67 Unfortunately this does not necessarily guarantee that the author was indeed female.

approval, whose unwarranted stringency had allegedly prevented the appearance of much that deserved to see the light of day.

Towards the end of the eighteenth century, though, some proponents of female writing were already proclaiming victory. While doubters remained, the *General Biography* of 1799 felt entitled to declare the reputation of Mary Astell (whose life had been one of the most important in Ballard's collection) utterly eclipsed by that of her literary successors. Only in 'a time when few women read, and hardly any wrote', when 'it was meritorious to suggest hints, however rude and imperfect, for the improvement of female education', was she of any significance.[68] Dissension was more commonly reported at second hand than directly raised in the biographies. Miss Seward, for example, had initially been content to acquiesce with the wishes of her mother that her literary works be suppressed, 'ready to believe those who told her, that they were much more proper employments for a young lady than scribbling verses'.[69] But, as the tone implies, this attitude was given little credence. To quote another biographical collection:

> The controversy respecting the intellectual talents of women, as compared with those of men, is nearly brought to an issue, and greatly to the credit of the fair sex. The present age has produced a most brilliant constellation of female worthies, who have not only displayed eminent powers in works of fancy, but have greatly distinguished themselves in the higher branches of literary composition.[70]

The *European Magazine* of March 1786 declared that women had augmented the country's reputation through both their scientific and literary exploits.[71] Indeed, by this time, those inclined to neglect their education were liable to ridicule, as in Charles Pigott's portrait of Viscountess Hampden. 'The whole animal system', discoursed Pigott, 'most certainly depends on the *brain*, therefore her Ladyship's excessive *imbecility* ought not to create surprize. For almost thirty years, she has pursued without interruption the same round of languor, ennui, and insipidity.'[72] Similarly, the *Town and Country Magazine* forecast that a mistress of the Duke of Clarence would not survive long, observing that: 'Youth, vivacity, and a tolerable share

68 John Aikin and Revd William Enfield, *General Biography* 8 vols (1799–1813), I, p. 433.
69 *EM*, April 1782, p. 288.
70 *The Public Characters of 1798* (Dublin, 1799), p. 308.
71 *EM*, March 1786, p. *139.
72 Pigott, *Female Jockey Club*, p. 159.

of beauty, with apparent health, form her personal accomplishments; but her mind is weak, and uncultivated.'[73]

No area of women's literary activity attracted more controversy than biography. Of peculiar interest is the debate that emerged over Samuel Johnson's treatment at the hands of two women, Anna Seward and Mrs Thrale. Seward first provoked a controversy during 1786–87, when she argued, in a set of letters to the *Gentleman's Magazine* under the signature of 'Benvolio', that biographers should not permit their esteem for Johnson's genius to obscure altogether his palpable failings.[74] She renewed her attack a few years later, in an altercation with James Boswell precipitated by what Seward alleged had been her rough usage in the biographer's supplement to his *Life of Johnson.* The matters specifically at stake – among them the circumstances surrounding the composition of one of Johnson's earlier poems – were relatively trivial; however, Seward's insistence that Johnson had been prone to falsehood, and that his version of events had therefore to be regarded with scepticism, inevitably invited disputation.[75]

Boswell testified that he had received from Seward several anec-dotes prejudicial to Johnson, which, upon further investigation, he had discovered to be false. 'As my book was to be a *real history,* and not a *novel,*' he argued, 'it was necessary to suppress all erroneous particulars, however entertaining.' Yet (at that time) he had held Seward guilty of no more than credulity, and had felt moreover the deference due a woman required him to *'let my fair antagonist down as softly as might be'.* He dismissed her allegation that Johnson had been untruthful, explaining that an instance that Seward had cited in support of her charge was merely an example of *'ardentia verba (glowing words –* I ask her pardon for quoting a Latin phrase) uttered in witty contest'.* In taking advantage of the naivety and lack of classical education presumed of women, Boswell was plainly utiliz-ing Seward's gender in order to undermine her position: but the central issue nevertheless clearly remained that any individual (man or woman) should have had the temerity to attempt 'to undermine the noble pedestal on which the public opinion has placed Dr Johnson'.[76]

73 *Town and Country Magazine,* Jan. 1790, p. 10. The mistress's social origins were, however, clearly a contributory factor to this verdict.

74 See, for example, *GM,* Feb. 1786, pp. 125–6; for an example reply, see ibid., July 1787, p. 559.

75 *GM,* Oct. 1793, p. 875.

76 *GM,* Nov. 1793, pp. 1009–11.

In response, Seward herself played the gender card, declaring that 'Mr Boswell's heroic attempts to injure a defenceless female, who has ever warmly vindicated *him*, must ultimately redound more to his dishonour than hers'.[77] This warning proved no idle threat, for Seward's plight soon attracted sympathizers incensed at Boswell's 'very unjust, and still more unmanly' behaviour[78] – including the editor of the *Gentleman's Magazine* himself, John Nichols.[79] Boswell, though, was not to be deterred, and in an unrepentant reply lamented of Seward, 'Would that she were *off*enceless! *def*enceless she is not; as she now avers that she can, at pleasure, put on the masculine attire, and lay about her as a second Drawcansir, armed *cap à pied* in the masked character of *Ben*volio.'[80] Another correspondent similarly remarked: 'I am rather surprized . . . at her calling herself a *defenceless female*, particularly after a long and elaborate letter, written in answer to Mr. Boswell's, whom she attacks with a degree of censorial authority little becoming a female.'[81] Yet her supporters (who were in the majority), even while demanding Seward be accorded greater chivalry, did not extend their condescension to the suggestion that she had encroached upon a territory unsuitable for women. They spoke of her as 'an ingenious and amiable lady' and 'a most accomplished and highly respectable female', blending an admiration for her abilities with the acknowledgement of her femininity.[82] One advocate went so far as to taunt Boswell with his opponent's literary prestige:

> as well might a little cock-boat, that sedulously follows a majestic first-rate . . . be expected to attract attention to itself by no other act than by thus *riding in the triumph, and partaking the gale*; as a conceited retailer of another's words and deeds be supposed to merit a fame superior, or even equal, to that of a celebrated lady, who is not only an excellent *judge* of poetry, but is also an admirable authoress in prose and verse.[83]

It would seem that, while it was unusual for a woman to make criticism of a public figure, existing notions of female propriety had blurred sufficiently that Seward was able to get away with it – albeit appropriating women's perceived vulnerability in the process.

77 *GM*, Dec. 1793, p. 1101.
78 *GM*, Jan. 1794, p. 7.
79 *GM*, Dec. 1793, p. 1131.
80 *GM*, Jan. 1794, p. 34.
81 *GM*, Feb. 1794, p. 121.
82 Ibid., p. 120; *GM*, Jan. 1794, p. 7.
83 *GM*, Feb. 1794, p. 121.

The information that Seward had divulged, if of a private nature, was in no sense exclusively feminine – and no doubt common knowledge in various Lichfield circles. There was, though, perhaps a fear that women were party to information of a singularly private nature that ought not to be disclosed. Both Boswell and Joseph Baretti found Mrs Thrale's contributions to Johnsoniana especially distasteful on this basis. Yet Mrs Thrale also found her defenders, and this despite the disapproval with which her second marriage had been greeted in some quarters.[84] One writer congratulated her:

> I thank her for telling us of the boiled pork, the salt buttock of beef, &c. and for *not* having suppressed those minute circumstances which give one the truest notion of the *man*. Anecdotes of *authors* are easily to be collected and heaped up into uninteresting masses; let us strip them of their prerogatives and see what sort of beings they are on our own level as *men*.[85]

Boswell, of course, was a consummate master of the anecdote: the debate was not over the device itself, but the minimum degree of privacy deemed requisite. Felicity Nussbaum has pointed out that Thrale's numerous, very private details lacked a masculine narrative authority, and thereby revealed Johnson a far more contradictory character than Boswell sought to portray.[86] However, notwithstanding the misgivings some men entertained, Thrale's biographical work drew widespread notice.

Besides publishing, public contributions made by women elsewhere were also increasingly to receive recognition by the end of the period. On one level, this is simply a matter of the obituaries recording the sheer variety of stations that women occupied: there was space for small businesswomen and shopkeepers alongside the more glamorous figures. On another, the growing exposure granted to actresses and writers as the century progressed reveals how the public arena available to women was undergoing both gradual expansion and professionalization. Readers were, of course, exceptionally inquisitive about actresses, and periodicals such as the *European Magazine* and *Lady's Magazine* capitalized upon this. The resulting accounts, though, were more interested in the public dimension of these women than the private – that is to say, in their career on stage rather than off it.[87] Another avenue by which women might

---

84 See, for example, *EM,* July 1786, p. 6.
85 *GM,* Nov. 1786, p. 920.
86 Felicity A. Nussbaum, *The Autobiographical Subject* (1989), p. 122.
87 For a more detailed account of actresses during the period, see Chapter 3, 'The public life of actresses: prostitutes or ladies?'

participate in the public realm was philanthropy, praise for female involvement in which was ubiquitous. Even politics was within the scope of a few accounts, and 'profound politics' at that, in the case of one Mrs Wright, an American who, after the War of Independence, tried to persuade her people to look towards Britain rather than France.[88] The radical Charles Pigott was also preoccupied with politics in his account of the Duchess of Devonshire. Pigott was hopeful that, in the aftermath of the French Revolution and Pitt's domestic countermeasures, the Duchess would come out on the side of liberty. He well understood that such a direct treatment of politics was unusual when discussing a woman, but insisted that he might thus address the Duchess since 'she has a soul capable of humanity, with a judgement and candour open to truth'.[89]

Conclusion

Whether in the public realm or the private, it is clear that the quantity of coverage devoted to women's activities underwent a spectacular expansion in the course of the eighteenth century. Inevitably, biographies and obituaries tended to reflect the relatively private character of women's lives during the period: but this is not necessarily to say that the inclination on the part of their authors was increasingly to concentrate upon the domestic. In fact, the continual rise in the amount of attention received by this latter area was simply a function of the growth in biographical material on women *per se.* Ironically, if the accounts of either gender shifted towards the private, it was those of men, whose private virtues and affection for wives and children were featured with ever more regularity.[90] The criticism voiced by a husband who mourned the death of his wife too intensely in the *Post-Angel* in 1701 does not find its parallel in the magazines and newspapers published at the end of the century.[91] This trend, when considered in conjunction with the ubiquity of emphasis upon women's private virtue and its significance to the public realm, would seem to add weight to the suggestion that a transition was taking place, in which the basis of civic virtue moved

88 *EM*, March 1786, p. *210.
89 Pigott, *Female Jockey Club*, p. 19.
90 Some commentators clearly no longer found the traditional martial role models satisfactory exemplars for men: see Isobel Grundy, *Samuel Johnson and the Scale of Greatness* (Leicester, 1986), p. 181.
91 *Post-Angel*, March 1701, pp. 185–6.

away from a purely male territory towards the wholesome domesticity of the family.[92] Certainly the preconditions required for such a development were present. Meanwhile, in addition to acknowledging women's importance in a domestic role, the accounts show growing appreciation of female contributions to the public domain (in particular to literature and the performing arts). This phenomenon should not be exaggerated: as we have seen, there was distinct tendency among biographers to camouflage women's public activities under a screen of private virtue. Nevertheless, by the turn of the nineteenth century, serious-minded profiles of actresses and writers had become a common feature in contemporary magazines, and had even found themselves seamlessly integrated into several of the biographical dictionaries, including works like the simply but revealingly titled *Public Characters of 1798*.[93] Together, this evidence must call into question some readings of separate sphere rhetoric as perhaps confusing polemic in the face of change for an accurate depiction of the contemporary reality.[94] The sources examined in the course of this chapter suggest that women's public role during the eighteenth century was in the ascendant.

92 Colley, *Britons*, p. 273.

93 *Public Characters of 1798*, pp. 261–2, 308–15.

94 For similar conclusions, see: Jean E. Hunter, 'The 18th-century Englishwoman: according to the *Gentleman's Magazine*', in Paul Fritz and Richard Morton, eds, *Woman in the 18th Century and Other Essays. Publications of the McMaster University Association for 18th-Century Studies* 4 (Toronto and Sarasota, 1976), p. 88; Amanda Vickery, 'Golden age to separate spheres? A review of the categories and chronology of English women's history' *HJ* 36, 2 (1993), p. 400.

Further reading

The following list of titles is designed to provide a starting place for further reading into the wide range of topics covered in this text. Primary materials have been excluded, as it would be impossible to represent the vast array of sources upon which these chapters have been based in any meaningful way. Place of publication is assumed to be London, unless otherwise stated.

General

Amussen, Susan *An Ordered Society: Gender and Class in Early Modern England* (Oxford, 1988)

Anderson, Bonnie S. and Zinsser, Judith P. *A History of their Own: Women in Europe from Prehistory to the Present* 2 vols (New York, 1988)

Colley, Linda *Britons: Forging the Nation, 1707–1837* (New Haven, CT, and London, 1992)

Davidoff, Leonore and Hall, Catherine *Family Fortunes: Men and Women of the English Middle Class, 1780–1850* (1987)

Davis, Natalie Zemon and Farge, Arlette, eds *A History of Women in the West* vol. iii *Renaissance and Enlightenment Paradoxes* (Cambridge, MA, 1993)

Fletcher, Anthony *Gender, Sex & Subordination in England, 1500–1800* (New Haven, CT, 1995)

Hufton, Olwen *The Prospect Before Her: A History of Women in Western Europe, Volume One: 1500–1800* (1995)

Langford, Paul *A Polite and Commercial People: England, 1727–1783* (Oxford, 1989)

Prior, Mary, ed. *Women in English Society, 1500–1800* (1985)

Rendall, Jane *The Origins of Modern Feminism: Women in Britain, France and the United States, 1780–1860* (Chicago, IL, 1985)

Tomaselli, Sylvana 'The enlightenment debate on women' *HWJ* 20 (1985), pp. 101–24

Weisner, Merry E. *Women and Gender in Early Modern Europe* (Cambridge, 1993)

Patriarchy

Alexander, Sally and Taylor, Barbara 'In defence of patriarchy' *New Statesman* 21 (Dec. 1979)

Bennett, Judith M. 'Feminism and history' *GH* 1 (1989)

Lerner, Gerda *The Creation of Patriarchy* (Oxford, 1986)

Rowbotham, Sheila 'The trouble with patriarchy' *New Statesman* 21 (Dec. 1979)

Separate spheres

Castiglione, Dario and Sharpe, Lesley, eds *Shifting the Boundaries: Transformations of the Language of Public and Private in the Eighteenth Century* (Exeter, 1995); see esp. John Brewer, 'This, that and the other: public, social and private in the seventeenth and eighteenth centuries', pp. 1–21

Davidoff, Leonore 'Regarding some "Old Husbands' Tales": public and private in feminist history', in *Worlds Between: Historical Perspectives on Gender and Class* (Cambridge, 1995)

Davidoff, Leonore and Hall, Catherine *Family Fortunes: Men and Women of the English Middle Class, 1780–1850* (1987)

Elshtain, Jean Bethke *Public Man, Private Woman: Women in Social and Political Thought* (Princeton, NJ, and Oxford, 1981)

Kerber, Linda K. 'Separate spheres, female worlds, woman's place: the rhetoric of women's history' *JAH* 75, 1 (1988)

Klein, Lawrence E. 'Gender, conversation and the public sphere in early eighteenth-century England', in Judith Still and Michael Worton, eds, *Textuality and Sexuality: Reading Theories and Practices* (Manchester and New York, 1993), pp. 100–15

Klein, Lawrence E. 'Gender and the public/private distinction in the eighteenth century: some questions about evidence and analytic procedure' *ECS* 29 (1995), pp. 92–109

Lewis, J. 'Separate spheres: threat or promise?' *JBS* 30, 1 (1991)

Shapiro, Ann-Louise, ed. *Feminists Revision History* (New Brunswick, NJ, 1994)

Vickery, Amanda 'Golden age to separate spheres? A review of the categories and chronology of English women's history' *HJ* 36, 2 (1993)

Gender history/women's history

Bennett, Judith M. ' "History that stands still": women's work in the European past' *FS* 14, 2 (1988)

Bennett, Judith M. 'Feminism and history' *GH* 1 (1989)

Bennett, Judith M. 'Women's history: a study in continuity and change' *WHR* 2 (1993)

Bock, Gisela *History, Women's History, Gender History,* European University Institute Working Paper No. 87/291 (Florence, 1987)

Bock, Gisela 'Women's history and gender history: aspects of an international debate' *GH* 1, 1 (Spring 1989)

Hill, Bridget 'Women's history: a study in change, continuity or standing still?' *WHR* 2, 1 (1993)

Hoff, Joan 'Gender as a postmodern category of paralysis' *WHR* 3, 2 (1994)

Kelly, Joan *Women, History, and Theory* (Chicago, IL, 1984)

Ortner, S.B. and Whitehead, H., eds *Sexual Meanings: The Cultural Construction of Gender and Sexuality* (Cambridge, 1981)

Perrot, M., ed. *Writing Women's History* (Oxford, 1992)

Riley, Denise *'Am I That Name?' Feminism and the Category of 'Women'* *in History* (Basingstoke, 1988)

Scott, Joan Wallach *Gender and the Politics of History* (New York, 1988); see esp. 'Gender: a useful category of historical analysis', pp. 28–50

Scott, Joan Wallach 'The problem of invisibility', in S. Jay Kleinberg, ed., *Retrieving Women's History* (Oxford, 1988), pp. 5–29

Shapiro, Ann-Louise, ed. *Feminists Revision History* (New Brunswick, NJ, 1994)

A gendered history of men

Amussen, Susan Dwyer ' "The part of a Christian man": the cultural politics of manhood in early modern England', in Susan Dwyer Amussen and Mark A. Kishlansky, eds, *Political Culture and Cultural Politics in Early Modern England* (Manchester, 1995)

Barker-Benfield, G.J. *The Culture of Sensibility: Sex and Society in Eighteenth-Century Britain* (Chicago, IL, 1992)

Davidoff, Leonore and Hall, Catherine *Family Fortunes: Men and Women of the English Middle Class, 1780–1850* (1987)

Fletcher, Anthony *Gender, Sex & Subordination in England, 1500–1800* (New Haven, CT, 1995)

Hitchcock, Tim 'Redefining sex in eighteenth-century England' *HWJ* 41 (1996), pp. 73–90

Klein, Lawrence E. *Shaftesbury and the Culture of Politeness. Moral Discourse and Cultural Politics in Early Eighteenth-Century England* (Cambridge, 1994)

Klein, Lawrence E. 'Gender and the public/private distinction in the eighteenth century: some questions about evidence and analytic procedure' *ECS* 29 (1995), pp. 92–109

Roper, Michael and Tosh, John, eds *Manful Assertions: Masculinities in Britain Since 1800* (1991)

Tosh, John 'What should historians do with masculinity? Reflections on nineteenth-century Britain' *HWJ* 38 (1994)

Trumbach, Randolph 'London's sodomites: homosexual behaviour and western culture in eighteenth-century Britain' *JSH* 11 (1977–8), pp. 1–33

Sexuality, reputation and the body

Boucé, P.G., ed. *Sexuality in Eighteenth-Century Britain* (Manchester, 1982)

Foucault, Michel *The History of Sexuality* trans. R. Hurley (New York, 1985)

Gallagher, C. and Laqueur, Thomas *The Making of the Modern Body* (Berkeley, CA, 1978)

Jordanova, Ludmilla *Sexual Visions: Images of Gender in Science and Medicine Between the Eighteenth and Twentieth Centuries* (Hemel Hempstead, 1989)

Laqueur, Thomas *Making Sex: Body and Gender from the Greeks to Freud* (Cambridge, MA, 1990)

Meteyard, B. 'Illegitimacy and marriage in eighteenth-century England' *Journal of Interdisciplinary History* 10, 3 (1980)

Schiebinger, Londa *The Mind Has No Sex? Women in the Origins of Modern Science* (Cambridge, MA, 1989)

Simpson, A.E. 'Vulnerability and the age of female consent: legal innovation and its effect on prosecutions for rape in eighteenth-century London', in R. Porter and G.S. Rousseau, eds, *Sexual Underworlds of the Enlightenment* (Manchester, 1987)

Trumbach, Randolph 'Sex, gender and sexual identity in modern culture: male sodomy and female prostitution in Enlightenment London' *Journal of the History of Sexuality* 2 (1991)

Trumbach, Randolph 'Sex, gender and sexual identity in modern culture: male sodomy and female prostitution in enlightenment England', in John C. Fout, ed., *Forbidden History: The State, Society and the Regulation of Sexuality in Modern Europe* (1992)

Work and poverty

Bennett, Judith M. ' "History that stands still": women's work in the European past' *FS* 14, 2 (1988)

Berg, Maxine *The Age of Manufactures, 1700–1820: Industry, innovation and work in Britain* 2nd edn (1994)

Berg, Maxine 'What difference did women's work make to the industrial revolution?' *HWJ* 35 (1993)

Clark, Alice *Working Life of Women in the Seventeenth Century* (1919)

Earle, Peter 'The female labour market in London in the late seventeenth and early eighteenth centuries' *EcHR* 2nd ser., 42, 3 (1989)

Hill, Bridget *Women, Work and Sexual Politics in Eighteenth-Century England* 2nd edn (1994)

Honeyman, Katrina and Goodman, Jordan 'Women's work, gender conflict, and labour markets in Europe, 1500–1900' *EcHR* 2nd ser., 44, 4 (1991)

Houston, R. and Snell, K. 'Proto industrialisation, cottage industry, social change and the industrial revolution' *HJ* 27, 2 (1984)

Kent, D.A. 'Ubiquitous but invisible. Female domestic servants in mid-eighteenth-century London' *HWJ* 28 (1989)

King, P. 'Customary rights and women's earnings: the importance of gleaning to the labouring poor 1750–1850' *EcHR* 44 (1991)

Pinchbeck, Ivy *Women Workers and the Industrial Revolution, 1750–1850* 2nd edn (1969; first publ. 1930)

Rendall, Jane *Women in an Industrializing Society: England, 1750–1880* (Oxford, 1990)

Sharpe, Pamela *Adapting to Capitalism: Working Women in the English Economy, 1700–1850* (Basingstoke, 1996)

Thomas, Janet 'Women and capitalism: oppression or emancipation?' *Comparative Studies in Society and History* 30 (1988)

Tilly, Louise A. and Scott, Joan W. *Women, Work and Family* 2nd edn (New York, 1987)

Valenze, Deborah *The First Industrial Woman* (Oxford, 1995)

Consumption

Brewer, John and Porter, Roy, eds *Consumption and the World of Goods* (1993); see esp. Amanda Vickery, 'Women and the world of goods: a Lancashire consumer and her possessions, 1751–81', pp. 274–301

Ellis, Joyce ' "On the Town": women in Augustan England' *HT* (Dec. 1995)

Lummis, Trevor and Marsh, Jan *The Woman's Domain: Women and the English Country House* (1993)

McKendrick, N., Brewer, J. and Plumb, J.H., eds *The Birth of a Consumer Society. The Commercialization of Eighteenth-Century England* (1982)

Crime

Beattie, J.M. 'The criminality of women in eighteenth-century England' *JSH* 8 (Summer 1975)

Ingram, Martin ' "Scolding Women Cucked or Washed": a crisis of gender relations in early modern England', in J. Kermode and G. Walker, eds, *Women, Crime and the Courts in Early Modern England* (1994)

Politics and social élites

Barker-Benfield, G.J. *The Culture of Sensibility: Sex and Society in Eighteenth-Century Britain* (Chicago, IL, 1992)

Browne, Alice *The Eighteenth-Century Feminist Mind* (Brighton, 1987)

Colley, Linda *Britons: Forging the Nation, 1707–1837* (New Haven, CT, and London, 1992)

Davis, Natalie Zemon 'Women in politics', in Natalie Zemon Davis and Arlette Farge, eds, *A History of Women in the West* vol. iii *Renaissance and Enlightenment Paradoxes* (Cambridge, MA, 1993), pp. 167–83

Harris, Francis *The Life of Sarah Duchess of Marlborough* (Oxford, 1991)

Hill, Bridget *That Republican Virago: The Life and Times of Catherine Macaulay, Historian* (Oxford, 1992)

Jupp, P.J. 'The roles of royal and aristocratic women in British politics, c. 1782–1832', in Mary O'Dowd and Sabine Wichert, eds, *Chattel, Servant or Citizen: Women's Status in Church, State and Society* (Belfast, 1995)

Langford, Paul *A Polite and Commercial People: England, 1727–1783* (Oxford, 1989)

Langford, Paul *Public Life and the Propertied Englishman, 1689–1798* (Oxford, 1991)

Lummis, Trevor and Marsh, Jan *The Woman's Domain: Women and the English Country House* (1993)

Okin, Susan Moller *Women in Western Political Thought* (Princeton, NJ, 1979)

Saxonhouse, Arlene W. *Women in the History of Political Thought: Ancient Greece to Machiavelli* Women and Politics Series, ed., Rita Mae Kelly and Ruth B. Mandel (New York, 1985)

von den Steinen, Karl 'The discovery of women in eighteenth-century English political life', in Barbara Kanner, ed., *The Women of England from Anglo-Saxon Times to the Present* (Hamden, CT, 1979), pp. 229–58

Stott, Anne ' "Female patriotism": Georgiana, Duchess of Devonshire, and the Westminster Election of 1784' *Eighteenth-Century Life* 17 (Nov. 1993), pp. 60–84

Tillyard, Stella *Aristocrats. Caroline, Emily, Louisa and Sarah Lennox 1740–1832* (1994)

Wilson, Kathleen *The Sense of the People: Politics, Culture and Imperialism in England, 1715–1785* (Cambridge, 1995)

Print culture and the arts

Ballaster, R. *et al.* 'Eighteenth-century women's magazines', in *Women's Worlds: Ideology, Femininity and the Women's Magazine* (1991)

Borsay, Peter *The English Urban Renaissance: Culture and Society in the Provincial Town, 1666–1770* (Oxford, 1989)

Donald, Diana *The Age of Caricature: Satirical Prints in the Reign of George III* (1996)

Dugaw, Diane *Warrior Women and Popular Balladry 1650–1850* (Cambridge, 1989)

George, M. Dorothy *Hogarth to Cruikshank: Social Change in Graphic Satire* (1987)

Hughes, Leo *The Drama's Patrons* (Austin, TX, 1971)

Hume, Robert *Henry Fielding and the London Theatre, 1728–1737* (Oxford, 1988)

Hume, Robert and Milhous, Judith, eds, *Vice Chamberlain Coke's Theatrical Papers 1706–1715* (Carbondale, IL, 1982)

Hunter, Jean E. 'The 18th-century Englishwoman: according to the *Gentleman's Magazine*', in Paul Fritz and Richard Morton, eds, *Woman in the 18th Century and Other Essays. Publications of the McMaster University Association for 18th-Century Studies* 4 (Toronto and Sarasota, 1976), pp. 73–88

Pearson, Jacqueline *The Prostituted Muse: Images of Women and Women Dramatists, 1642–1737* (1988)

Perry, Gill and Rossington, Michael, eds, *Femininity and Masculinity in Eighteenth-Century Art and Culture* (Manchester, 1994)

Pointon, Marcia *Hanging the Head: Portraiture and Social Formation in Eighteenth-Century England* (New Haven, CT, and London, 1993)

Pollock, G. and Parker, R. *Old Mistresses: Women, Art and Ideology* (1981)

Shevelow, Katherine *Women and Print Culture: the Construction of Femininity in the Early Periodical* (1989)

West, Shearer *The Image of the Actor* (New York, 1991)

Wilson, Kathleen 'Empire of virtue. The imperial project and Hanoverian culture, c. 1720–1785', in Lawrence Stone, ed., *An Imperial State at War: Britain, 1689–1815* (1994)

Education

Bryant, Margaret *The London Experience of Secondary Education* (1986)

Gardiner, Dorothy *English Girlhood at School: A Study of Women's Education Through Twelve Centuries* (Oxford, 1929)

Hill, Bridget *The First English Feminist: Reflections on Marriage and Other Writings by Mary Astell* (Chicago, IL, and London, 1986)

Myers, Sylvia Hardstack *The Bluestocking Circle: Women, Friendship and the Life of the Mind in Eighteenth-Century England* (Oxford, 1990)

O'Day, Rosemary *Education and Society, 1500–1800: Social Foundations of Education in Early Modern Britain* (1982)

Plumb, J.H. 'The new world of children in eighteenth-century England' *PP* 67 (1974)

Pollock, Linda A. ' "Teach her to live under obedience": the making of women in the upper ranks of early modern England' *CC* 4 (1989)

Religion

Crawford, Patricia *Women and Religion in England, 1500–1720* (1993)

Gregory, Jeremy 'Gender and the clerical profession in England, 1660–1850', in R.N. Swan, ed., *Gender and the Christian Religion* (forthcoming)

Hempton, David 'Women and evangelical religion in Ireland, 1750–1900', in idem, *The Religion of the People: Methodism and Popular Religion, c.1750–1900* (1996)

Valenze, D.M. *Prophetic Sons and Daughters: Female Preaching and Popular Religion in Industrial England* (Princeton, NJ, 1985)

Walsh, J. 'Methodism and the mob in the eighteenth century', in G.J. Cumming and D. Backer, eds, *Popular Belief and Practice: Studies in Church History* 8 (1972)

Demography

Laslett, Peter *Family Life and Illicit Love in Earlier Generations* (Cambridge, 1977)

Laslett, Peter and Wall, R., eds *Household and Family in Past Times* (Cambridge, 1972)

Wrigley, E.A. and Schofield, R.S. *The Population History of England, 1541–1871: A Reconstruction* (Cambridge, 1981)

The family

Anderson, Michael *Approaches to the History of the Western Family, 1500–1914* (Cambridge, 1980)

Ezell, Margaret *The Patriarch's Wife: Literary Evidence and the History of the Family* (Chapel Hill, NC, and London, 1987)

Goody, Jack *The Development of the Family and Marriage in Europe* (Cambridge, 1983)

Houlbrooke, Ralph A. *The English Family, 1450–1700* (London and New York, 1984)

Hunt, Margaret 'Wife beating, domesticity and women's independence in eighteenth-century London' *GH* 4 (1992)

Macfarlane, Alan *Marriage and Love in England: Modes of Reproduction, 1300–1840* (Oxford, 1986)

O'Day, Rosemary *The Family and Family Relationships, 1500–1900:*

England, France and the United States of America (Basingstoke and London, 1994)

Stone, Lawrence *The Family, Sex and Marriage in England, 1570–1640* (abridged edn, 1979)

Tadmor, Naomi 'The concept of the household-family in eighteenth-century England' *PP* 151 (1996)

Tilly, Louise A. 'Women's history and family history: fruitful collaboration or missed connection?' *JFH* 12, 1–3 (1987)

Trumbach, Randolph *The Rise of the Egalitarian Family: Aristocratic Kinship and Domestic Relations in Eighteenth-Century England* (New York, 1978)

Parents and children

Fildes, V., ed. *Women as Mothers in pre-Industrial England: Essays in Honour of Dorothy MacLaren* (1990)

Lewis, Judith Schneid *In the Family Way. Childbearing in the British Aristocracy, 1760–1860* (New Brunswick, NJ, 1986)

Pollock, Linda *Forgotten Children: Parent–Child Relations from 1500 to 1900* (Cambridge, 1983)

Schnorrenberg, Barbara 'Is childbirth any place for a woman? The decline of midwifery in eighteenth-century England' *Studies in Eighteenth-Century Culture* 10 (1981)

Schofield, R. 'Did the mothers really die? Three centuries of maternal mortality in the world we have lost', in L. Bonfield, R. Smith and K. Wrightson, eds, *The World We Have Gained: Histories of Population and Population Structure* (Oxford, 1986)

Spinsterhood, marriage, divorce and widowhood

Boulter, J. 'London widowhood revisited: the decline of female remarriage in the seventeenth and eighteenth centuries' *CC* 5 (1990)

Hufton, Olwen 'Women without men: widows and spinsters in Britain and France in the eighteenth century' *JFH* 9 (Winter 1984)

Hunt, Margaret 'Wife beating, domesticity and women's independence in eighteenth-century London' *GH* 4 (1992)

Stone, Lawrence *Uncertain Unions: Marriage in England, 1660–1753* (Oxford, 1981)

Stone, Lawrence *The Road to Divorce, England, 1530–1987* (Oxford, 1990)

Stone, Lawrence *Broken Lives: Separation and Divorce in England, 1660–1857* (Oxford, 1993)

Todd, B.A. 'The re-marrying widow: a stereotype reconsidered', in Mary Prior, ed., *Women in English Society* (1985).

Wall, R. 'Women alone in English society' *Annales de Démographie Historique* 141 (1981)

Marriage, property and the law

Bonfield, Lloyd 'Marriage, property and the "affective family"' *Law and History* 1, 2 (Fall 1983)

Brewer, John and Staves, Susan, eds *Early Modern Concepts of Property* (London and New York, 1995); see esp. Susan Staves, 'Resentment or resignation: dividing the spoils among daughters and younger sons', pp. 194–218

Erickson, Amy Louise 'Common Law versus common practice: the use of marriage settlements in early modern England' *EcHR* 43 (1990)

Erickson, Amy Louise *Women and Property in Early Modern England* (1993)

Habakkuk, H.J. *Marriage, Debt and the Estates System: English Land-ownership, 1650–1950* (Oxford, 1994)

Okin, Susan Moller 'Patriarchy and married women's property in England: questions on some current views' *ECS* 17 (1983–4)

Spring, Eileen 'The heiress-at-law: English real property law from a new point of view' *Law & History Review* 8, 2 (1990), pp. 273–96

Spring, Eileen *Law, Land, and Family: Aristocratic Inheritance in England, 1300–1800* (Chapel Hill, NC, and London, 1993)

Staves, Susan 'Pin money' *Studies in Eighteenth-Century Culture* 14 (1985)

Staves, Susan *Married Women's Separate Property in England, 1660–1833* (Oxford, 1989)

Thomas, K.V. 'The double standard' *Journal of the History of Ideas* (1959)

Index